# Dynamic Asset Allocation

Also available from
**Bloomberg Press**

Bonds:
*The Unbeaten Path to Secure Investment Growth*
by Hildy Richelson and Stan Richelson

*Guide to Economic Indicators:*
*Making Sense of Economics*
*Sixth Edition*
by *The Economist*

*Guide to Investment Strategy:*
*How to Understand Markets, Risk, Rewards, and Behaviour*
*Second Edition*
by Peter Stanyer

*Investing in REITs:*
*Real Estate Investment Trusts*
*Third Edition*
by Ralph L. Block

*Investing in Hedge Funds:*
*Revised and Updated Edition*
by Joseph G. Nicholas

*The Only Guide to Alternative Investments You'll Ever Need:*
*The Good, the Flawed, the Bad, and the Ugly*
by Larry E. Swedroe and Jared Kizer

*The Trader's Guide to Key Economic Indicators*
*Updated and Expanded Edition*
by Richard Yamarone

———————

A complete list of our titles is available at
**www/bloomberg.com/books**

# Dynamic Asset Allocation

Modern Portfolio Theory
Updated for the Smart Investor

James Picerno

BLOOMBERG PRESS
NEW YORK

BLOOMBERG, BLOOMBERG ANYWHERE, BLOOMBERG.COM, BLOOMBERG MARKET ESSENTIALS, *Bloomberg Markets*, BLOOMBERG NEWS, BLOOMBERG PRESS, BLOOMBERG PROFESSIONAL, BLOOMBERG RADIO, BLOOMBERG TELEVISION, and BLOOMBERG TRADEBOOK are trademarks and service marks of Bloomberg Finance L.P. ("BFLP"), a Delaware limited partnership, or its subsidiaries. The BLOOMBERG PROFESSIONAL service (the "BPS") is owned and distributed locally by BFLP and its subsidiaries in all jurisdictions other than Argentina, Bermuda, China, India, Japan, and Korea (the "BLP Countries"). BFLP is a wholly-owned subsidiary of Bloomberg L.P. ("BLP"). BLP provides BFLP with all global marketing and operational support and service for these products and distributes the BPS either directly or through a non-BFLP subsidiary in the BLP Countries. All rights reserved.

This publication contains the author's opinions and is designed to provide accurate and authoritative information. It is sold with the understanding that the author, publisher, and Bloomberg L.P. are not engaged in rendering legal, accounting, investment-planning, or other professional advice. The reader should seek the services of a qualified professional for such advice; the author, publisher, and Bloomberg L.P. cannot be held responsible for any loss incurred as a result of specific investments or planning decisions made by the reader.

First edition published 2010

1 3 5 7 9 10 8 6 4 2

Library of Congress Cataloging-in-Publication Data

Picerno, James.
    Dynamic asset allocation : modern portfolio theory updated for the smart investor / James Picerno.
        p. cm.
    Includes bibliographical references and index.
    Summary: "This book presents a unifying theory of long-term investing for strategic-minded investors that combines modern portfolio theory with value investing. It shows how to build a winning portfolio using dynamic asset allocation, how modern portfolio theory has changed in recent years, and how those changes affect the strategic investor and portfolio design in today's financial climate"–Provided by publisher.
    ISBN 978-1-57660-359-8 (alk. paper)
    1. Portfolio management. 2. Asset allocation. I. Title.

HG4529.5.P53 2010
332.6–dc22                                                                                           2009048905

**Mixed Sources**
Product group from well-managed forests,
controlled sources and recycled wood or fiber
www.fsc.org  Cert no. SW-COC-000952
© 1996 Forest Stewardship Council

FSC

*For Alison, Pamela, and Elizabeth—the sun, moon, and stars in my portfolio*

# Contents

# Acknowledgments

Writing a book takes a toll, mostly on one's family. But while turning out copy is a solitary affair, accumulating and interpreting the facts required the guidance and input of friends, family, colleagues, and the many professionals I've spoken with in my journalism travels. My only regret is that I can't mention everyone here, in this limited space. Nonetheless, you've all been indispensable in helping turn an idea into a book, and for that I'm forever grateful.

I begin by recognizing the intellectual and moral support of my wife Elizabeth, a scholar and author who understands the demands that come with research and writing. Without her assistance, inspiration, and patience, this book wouldn't exist. My daughters, Alison and Pamela, have remained a constant source of joy and encouragement throughout my long and at times lonely journey into publishing. And, of course, I must thank my mother and father, Eva and Joseph, who lovingly taught me the value of reading and learning. Without them, none of this would have been possible.

In the course of writing this book, I've received ideas and inspiration from a great number of people in the world of finance. Although not everyone will agree with my thesis, the countless debates and discussions through time have been highly productive, at least for me. A partial listing (in no particular order) recognizes conversations over the years with Gary Brinson, Rob Arnott, Bill Bernstein, William Sharpe, John H. Cochrane, Richard Ferri, Stan Richelson, Lakshman Achuthan, Bob Dieli, Ron Surz, Barry Ritholtz, Rodney Sullivan, Dan Strachman, Jim Sorensen, John Hussman, Burton Malkiel, Ted Aronson, Tim Argenziano, Robert "Pete" Peterson, and the late Joe Gumino. I've also benefited from ongoing discussions with a trio of extremely talented and intelligent CFAs: Jon Heller, Chris Graja, and Bill Hester, a.k.a. the "brain trust."

I also want to thank the folks at the CFA Institute for graciously sending copies of research papers at times when such works were otherwise unavailable to this writer.

In my former life as a magazine staffer, several people were instrumental in enhancing my editorial skills and capacity for critical thinking. The late Russell Roemmele was my first editor, and it was under his guidance that I learned the craft of journalism. I'm also indebted to Barry Vinocur for his support, advice, and friendly debates regarding financial journalism, finance, the world at large, and of course, REITs. Thanks as well to Bill Inman for your support early on in the new century—it made a difference; and also to Mary Ann McGuigan, a gifted editor and writer who opened the door for this book at a critical point in my career. Meanwhile, Richard Koreto and Nancy Mandell—your editorial feedback has helped in more ways than you realize.

And, thank you, James Grant, a financial writer and historian whose magical powers with the pen, although miles above my own limited capabilities, have continually amazed, informed, and motivated me to work harder and dig deeper. Finally, my admiration and respect have no bounds for the late Peter L. Bernstein, whose books enlightened and entertained by opening my eyes to the larger world of academic finance and the deeper meaning of risk.

# Introduction

WHEN HARRY MARKOWITZ'S PAPER "Portfolio Selection" appeared in *The Journal of Finance*'s March 1952 edition, it arrived in a vacuum. Investment research of one type or another may be as old as civilization, but mathematically rigorous portfolio analysis is younger than Bill Clinton.

Nearly sixty years after the publication of the founding document in what would become known as modern portfolio theory, a casual observer might wonder: have we learned anything? The heavy losses in 2008, along with a broad review of financial history, suggest that any response should err on the side of modesty. There are many victories in the pursuit of human intellect, but it's not always clear that money management is among them.

Part of the problem is that what we don't know about markets still dominates. At the same time, progress isn't unknown in finance, even if it sometimes appears otherwise. Certainly our collective intelligence in the design and management of portfolios has made great strides since Markowitz's initial foray all those years ago. But in some respects, the low-hanging fruit has been picked in the past half century. In 1952, we knew very little about asset pricing and portfolio strategy. As such, there was nowhere to go but up when Markowitz's research first hit the streets.

More than half a century later, financial economists are still a long way from "solving" the investment challenge, but no longer are we blind. Nonetheless, it's not obvious that anything even remotely resembling an absolute truth will ever grace the field of portfolio theory. Uncertainty is always lurking in finance.

No wonder, then, that the central message in portfolio theory is that investing is first and foremost a risk-management challenge. Markowitz's 1952 paper said as much, and countless studies over the years, along with real-world experience, have reaffirmed the lesson.

In other words, much of what we've learned over the decades about money management boils down to the recognition that risk is at the heart of the investment game.

Sound familiar? It should. The counsel to focus on risk management is no spring chicken, nor is the implied response: diversification. The 2,000-year-old Talmud, for example, recommends keeping one's wealth in three equally weighted forms: business, real estate, and the equivalent of what modern economists would call a risk-free asset. Financial research since 1952 more or less echoes this ancient advice, albeit with an ever-increasing amount of specificity and sophistication. But the fundamental idea that it's all about risk management remains intact. Arguing over the details is what animates much of financial economics in the twenty-first century.

If we could see the future with clarity, diversification within and across asset classes would be unnecessary. But in a world where there's always some doubt about what's coming, prudent investing is forever tethered to the belief that spreading the risk is the best solution in an otherwise poor set of choices. Much of what consumes the modern quest to understand markets and portfolio theory is figuring out *how* to spread the risk to achieve so-called optimal diversification. Markowitz laid out the basic framework for analyzing the possibilities and thinking about the challenge, although nearly six decades later we're still turning over rocks and debating what constitutes enlightened portfolio strategy.

The breadth and depth of financial economic research have exploded over the decades to the point that you can "prove" just about anything you want by cherry-picking papers that support your conclusion. The power to sway the debate by citing a particular set of research efforts also works as a negative. No concept is immune to repudiation for the simple reason that someone, somewhere has probably penned at least one study that can be referenced for casting aspersions on an idea under scrutiny.

Is there any sign of a larger truth peeking out from the massive body of investigation that's been published over the decades? Yes, as this book will argue. It's not absolutely definitive, although nothing else in finance is either. Even in the twenty-first century, no one will mistake finance for physics. But after more than fifty years of study, theory building, and endless poking and probing of the historical record, financial economists have uncovered compelling if not quite conclusive evidence that the market prices assets with a fair amount of economic logic after all. In turn, that implies that there are guiding principles for managing portfolios in a strategic context. There are still no guarantees in investing, but at least there's more confidence about how to think about portfolio design and management.

That's not always obvious to the man on the street, especially in the short run. But if we look carefully, we can see some logical texture in the expanding body of research that identifies the economic cycle as a primary driver of risk premia. Common sense suggests no less. It hardly seems plausible that returns in the capital and commodity markets are divorced from the ebb and flow of macro-economic trends, which ultimately explain everything from profits to prices.

Such ideas go back at least to the neoclassical economist Irving Fisher, whose theories from the late-nineteenth and early twentieth centuries detail such elemental concepts as the present value of future cash flow and the relationship between interest rates and inflation. In recent decades, the bond between asset pricing and economics proper has only grown closer. In the twenty-first century, the research trail is formally sympathetic to the idea that the business cycle casts a long shadow over risk and return, including the evidence that returns appear partly predictable.

On the surface, the new generation of research seems to raise questions about the validity of modern portfolio theory (MPT) as it's widely understood. In fact, MPT has evolved along with the financial research, albeit in fits and starts. The idea that MPT has evolved at all will surprise many investors, and perhaps quite a few money management professionals. Much of the classic framework for MPT was laid out in the two decades through the early 1970s and many investors still think of modern finance in terms of those early standards. If you stop there, MPT looks quite different compared with a contemporary reading of the theory.

Old habits die hard, and so MPT is still widely embraced as it was originally conceived. But it's time to update MPT's popular image, which remains stuck in the 1960s and 1970s, when the first drafts of the efficient market hypothesis (EMH), indexing, and related concepts were just beginning to attract attention from investors. But MPT has moved on, and so too should our interpretation of what modern finance advises for strategic-minded investing.

The central message in the updated MPT is that asset allocation should be dynamic, or at least partially so. That's in contrast to the conventional reading of MPT, which suggests that returns are unpredictable and therefore asset allocation should be static. But starting in the 1980s, financial researchers began casting doubt on this version of MPT, although hints of things to come had been bubbling for years previously. One of the discoveries is that the capital asset pricing model, the theoretical foundation for indexing, didn't explain returns as well as initial testing suggested. Reacting to the news, many investors and investment advisors mistakenly assumed that MPT no longer offered practical advice. But as this book will explain, MPT remains very much alive in the twenty-first century; its widely reported demise has been greatly exaggerated.

That will strike some, perhaps many, as a radical idea, if not completely misguided. But I believe that a revised interpretation of MPT offers a vibrant, relevant model for approaching the investment challenge. I say that based on 1) an expansive reading of the literature that's been published over the long arc of modern financial history and 2) a thoughtful review of market history.

MPT still draws inspiration from some of the bedrock principles identified in the first generation of this research. Risk, for instance, is still intimately linked with return. But risk is now understood as a more flexible and nuanced concept compared with the early interpretation of modern finance. Notably, the idea that a broad definition of the market portfolio's risk—so-called beta—determines everything at all times has given way to a more subtle perspective that recognizes multiple betas at work, each offering different and fluctuating payoffs through time.

Many analysts are tempted to conclude that the revisions to finance theory demonstrate that markets aren't efficient and therefore MPT, revised or otherwise, is irrelevant. But some of this debate is semantic. The research-based motivation for managing asset allocation dynamically is germane regardless of whether you see the markets as rational or not.

Nonetheless, I argue that a fair reading of the academic research doesn't invalidate the efficient market hypothesis (EMH), although the new work does refine our understanding of the theory. Indeed, efficiency and return predictability aren't contradictory notions, even if an older interpretation of MPT suggests otherwise. One common attack on EMH comes by pointing out that securities prices don't always follow a random walk, as once assumed. Quite true. But it's also true that EMH and the random walk theory aren't simply different names for a single idea, although some critics conveniently equate the pair as one. But the details matter. While one version of EMH runs through the prism of the random walk theory, that's not the only interpretation of market efficiency, nor is it the current one.

It's hardly surprising to find that an updated view of modern finance has been overlooked and misunderstood. The details are complicated, and it's hard to find anything approaching a wide-ranging review of the research for a general audience—thus the motivation for writing this book and publishing *The Beta Investment Report*, a monthly newsletter in which I expound on MPT and related matters in something closer to real time. Unless you've been willing to wade through a small library of papers that outline why and how MPT has evolved, it's all too easy to think that yesteryear's status quo still prevails. In fact, there's an alternative view to the idea that the market's irrational, even in the wake of 2008. My hope is that some of the reasoning for thinking so will unfold in the following pages as I attempt to synthesize the research into what appears, at least to me, as a larger, albeit still evolving truth.

Recognized or not, MPT's evolution has unfolded over decades, even though the changes don't make for compelling headline material in the mainstream financial media. There are no shortcuts for persuasively arguing the case in favor of rational pricing and an updated view of MPT. The associated literature is extensive, rarely intuitive for the lay reader, and it spills out over years and across a broad range of economic and financial categories that aren't obviously related. But if we're going to make sense of how modern finance has changed, and what it means for asset allocation, we need an expansive review of the research trail to appreciate the evolution and how it relates to portfolio strategy. I try to offer that review in this book, although the task is daunting, given the amount of material under consideration. Undoubtedly I've left out some key points and critical studies. Now is a good time to point out that any mistakes are clearly my own. That said, I'm optimistic that several of the major lessons embedded in the sea of financial literature will emerge from these pages. The goal is promoting a deeper, richer understanding of asset pricing and portfolio theory as it's currently understood.

For some readers, the first several chapters will be familiar, perhaps to the point of repeating the obvious. But rather than ignoring the early years of finance theory, which have been discussed extensively elsewhere, I revisit the basic history briefly if only to provide some context for assessing the evolution that follows.

One theme that arises from studying the broad arc of portfolio theory's record is that corners of finance that were once in conflict now appear more closely aligned. Consider how modern portfolio theory has inched nearer to the principles of value investing, as originally outlined in Graham and Dodd's *Security Analysis*. Over the past thirty years, the academics have slowly but persistently uncovered more nuance in how the market prices securities. One of the lessons is that we must pay closer attention to valuation on an asset class level and draw some assumptions about what this analysis implies for expected return—just as Ben Graham long ago counseled, though for individual securities.

Although modern finance now suggests that we should engage in forecasting returns for asset classes by studying fundamental data and other variables, it's important to distinguish such efforts from rank speculation. Financial economists acknowledge that assets offer investors different expected returns at different points in time. This isn't a violation of market efficiency. In order to maintain liquidity, markets must provide additional compensation at certain times, such as during periods of high economic stress that foster greater uncertainty about future cash flows. It would be inefficient if expected returns were unchanged in the face of new and bigger risks. But that's not how markets work. Expected returns vary. Deciding how and why they vary isn't entirely clear, but we know quite a bit more than when MPT was originally conceived, when the basic assumption was that returns are constant.

As a simple example, imagine a Treasury note that's priced to yield 5 percent today through maturity, ten years out. But a year later there's new information that lowers the bond's price and therefore raises the yield to maturity. It's hardly a sign of market inefficiency if investors reprice assets in the face of new information. Nor is there anything inherently irrational about adjusting the asset allocation in response to the new outlook and a change in expected return.

Not all assets are created equal, of course, and so the challenge of forecasting return varies quite a bit. Accordingly, one's degree of confidence in projecting risk premia must be factored in to the extent that we dynamically manage asset allocation and adjust the market portfolio. Some investors will be more comfortable than others with dynamically managing asset allocation, so the asset mix may fluctuate far more in some portfolios than it does in others. Meanwhile, assuming that returns are stable is a forecast too and, as it turns out, not a very reliable one, particularly in the short term. The solution is taking a more active role in managing risk by responding, if only modestly, to the expected return signals dispensed by the market.

The financial literature has come around to thinking more like Ben Graham for asset allocation. Some are persuaded that this is evidence that the market is inefficient, but an updated view of modern portfolio theory suggests different. Then again, the argument in favor of efficient markets as it relates to an updated version of modern finance isn't an easy story to tell. One critique is that prices move too much to be explained by rational pricing behavior. The market, we're told, is irrational. But this isn't as convincing as it appears.

For example, one clue that large price swings aren't necessarily a sign of inefficiency is if the price changes affect broad cross sections of securities. In that case, a common factor may be driving the volatility, which undercuts the argument for irrational market behavior. Take small-cap value stocks, which exhibit a fair amount of correlation with one another. The fact that most of these stocks rise and fall together implies that the associated risk premium is a payoff for a common factor driving return, even if we don't fully understand the process. Earning a higher return than the broad market, then, isn't a sign of efficiency so much as earning a higher payoff for assuming a particular type of risk—a risk that's different than the overall market risk.

Much of what appears to be inefficient pricing may be a case of investors discounting more granular risks in a rational way in connection with, say, the business cycle. Although the research supporting these ideas is still fairly new and evolving, the future is encouraging for thinking that we're beginning to understand the rules that govern asset pricing in a more satisfying way. That inspires the case for dynamic asset allocation. As we learn more about how securities are priced, we have more confidence in customizing the market portfolio in a way that suits our needs.

The emerging message in an updated view of MPT is that there appear to be multiple betas, each efficient within its own realm. In the aggregate, they add up to the broad market portfolio identified in the classic view of modern finance. The new MPT tells us to consider adjusting these multiple betas relative to the standard market portfolio and dynamically manage the mix to some extent through time.

But while a world of rational pricing doesn't preclude efficient markets or the possibility of return predictability, the future is still uncertain. It may be less uncertain at some points than at others, relative to what we used to think. But there are still no guarantees when dealing with prospective risk premiums. That's why they call it risk. The good news is that we're not totally clueless when it comes to estimating return and risk. Yet predicting is still hazardous, and so we must proceed cautiously. We must, at all times, think and act like risk managers.

Risk management begins by considering everyone's initial benchmark: the full market portfolio, which should be as broadly defined as is reasonable, with assets weighted by market values. Thanks to the rise of index funds and ETFs, this is now practical as well as academically correct. The broad market portfolio is the default benchmark since everyone can hold it without materially affecting prices. The old finance tells us to hold this portfolio, with some amount of cash, depending on our risk preference. The revised reading of portfolio theory counsels a more active role in redesigning the market portfolio and adjusting the asset allocation through time, based in part on the implied return estimates embedded in prices and our appetite for risk.

The old finance isn't necessarily wrong, although it looks like a blunt tool compared with what we've learned in recent decades. The new finance is more of a precision instrument that refines our understanding of asset pricing and the various payoffs for risk. But refinement brings more complication. We now know that ours is a world where multiple betas drive prices. That means that we have more choices, which potentially introduces new perils.

There's no free lunch in the new world order of portfolio theory, which suggests that we may not want to completely jettison the old finance. One of the core lessons in the original version of MPT is that the market portfolio is the optimal portfolio for the average investor over the long haul. That's still true because all investors, active as well as passive, collectively hold the market-value weighted portfolio. Some if not most investors own something different by reweighting in favor of or against certain assets at certain times. But in the aggregate, everyone holds the market portfolio.

As a result, active investors who beat the market portfolio do so exclusively because of losses borne by other active investors who stumble. Owning something other than the market portfolio is a zero sum game in terms of return. Some will win, but that must be offset by those who lose. Accordingly, the average investor must hold the market portfolio in the long run, a state of equilibrium that no one should dismiss entirely in thinking about portfolio strategy.

Indeed, the expectation that certain betas may deliver superior returns versus the market portfolio may be vulnerable if too many investors chase the associated return, in which case the broad market portfolio may dominate after all. Of course, the possibility (probability) that expected return for a given factor will rise and fall over time is also a reason why dynamic asset allocation looks compelling. The catch is that exploiting this aspect of asset pricing in the new finance requires more analytical effort and tactical finesse compared with the old finance and the single-beta model. But that's not surprising, either, since we've known all along that higher return comes only with higher risk. Beating the market portfolio, in short, will likely remain as challenging as ever, at least over the long haul.

In the meantime, the simple math of market equilibrium reminds that the average investor must hold the market portfolio over time. But we also know that there's quite a bit more nuance in asset pricing than is recognized by the single-factor model of yore. Modern finance now sanctions reassembling the market portfolio to satisfy your particular preferences for risk and return expectations. Thanks to index funds and ETFs, that's no longer an idea limited to the classroom. You can slice and dice betas as broadly or narrowly as you deem appropriate with publicly traded funds, often at low cost and with razor-sharp precision.

In the end, there's no distinction between the old and the new finance; instead, there's a continuum. In the following pages, I try to summarize this continuum by reviewing the highlights of how portfolio theory has evolved and what the evolution implies for designing and managing asset allocation. The new research doesn't replace the original work so much as it refines it, providing a more muscular, realistic view of markets and asset pricing in the process.

The revisions to portfolio theory represent a great leap forward for modern finance, although our understanding of markets still falls far short of perfection. Financial economists have uncovered lots of remarkable insights in recent years, but they're not magicians. Price continues to be a function of supply and demand, resources are finite, return remains bound up with risk, and you still can't get blood out of a stone. The good news is that we can do better in managing asset allocation, and the new finance gives us a valuable roadmap for making this strategic journey.

# In the Beginning ...

AT THE DAWN of the early twentieth century, investing was still more art than science and financial analysis wasn't quite worthy of its label. No one warned young Ben Graham of this sorry state of affairs when he secured a job on Wall Street just before World War I. As he soon learned, the financial industry of 1914 couldn't teach him what it didn't yet know.

Launching his career at Newburger, Henderson & Loeb at the tender age of twenty, the freshly minted Columbia graduate quickly discovered the most important piece of contemporary knowledge in high finance: success in the investment game, as commonly practiced at the time, had more to do with personal connections and inside information than brainpower and a talent for securities research. Determined to break with tradition, Graham intended to excel with his skills as an analyst.

His was an ambitious strategy for its day, which is to say a rarely used strategy in the matter of equity investing in the World War I era. Quantitatively driven illumination was far ahead of its time in the preregulatory age of money management, when the supply of reliable corporate information was scarce if not wholly unavailable. But the absence of relevant data opened doors. As Graham discovered, business as usual on Wall Street fostered opportunity in stock pricing—opportunity that he eventually learned to exploit.

Graham's brand of analysis was one of the first serious attempts at forging investment order out of the speculative chaos that had prevailed up to that point. There were successful speculators, of course, but investing proper was still a relatively exotic concept in the land of equities circa 1914. To the extent that the world thought otherwise in the subsequent decades was due in large part to Graham, who persuasively taught that equities were more than an excuse for gambling. He did so by promoting what would eventually become known as value investing, or identifying shares trading at prices below their perceived fundamental value. Integral to his philosophy was drawing a sharp distinction between speculation and investment.

Graham was, quite simply, the right man for the job at the right time. It was no small advantage that the investment opportunities were abundant in his formative intellectual years. A classic example of the Graham strategy comes to us from the mid-1920s, when he was intrigued by several energy pipeline companies that had previously been spun off as independent entities in the wake of the court-ordered 1911 breakup of the Standard Oil trust. Perusing documents at the Interstate Commerce Commission, he learned that Standard's corporate spinoffs held high-quality railroad bonds on their balance sheets. One of the oil trust's corporate progeny, Northern Pipeline, owned debt securities worth about $95 a share, Graham calculated. Yet the stock was trading at just $65, plus $6 of dividends payable to shareholders. The market, in other words, valued Northern Pipeline at $71—a 25 percent markdown to Graham's estimate. Seizing on what he decided was found money, he bought the shares over the course of two years and eventually earned a profit for his effort.[1]

The investment landscape was in fact rife with opportunity in those halcyon days. Denied the advantage of ubiquitous digital information and the analytic power bestowed by the integrated circuit, the ambitious investor of the 1920s was forced to uncover opportunity the old-fashioned way: by hand. But few investors were inclined to work as hard as Graham. Fewer still understood the opportunity in value investing or possessed the necessary skills. In fact, there was little motivation to even try as the 1920s unfolded. By 1928, the last full year of the great and ill-fated bull market of that magnificent and tumultuous decade, expectations of easy profits had nearly conquered the crowd's notions of what was necessary for successful investing.

Even after the dramatic collapse of stock prices in October 1929, and the subsequent bear market that ran through the early 1930s, the decline and fall of the bulls failed to spawn a mass movement of investors looking for bargains. This was more than slightly ironic, considering that bargains were abundant on a massive scale in the early thirties. But the nation was consumed with strategies for surviving the Great Depression, and so investors were easily distracted. Although few were looking, the market's bargains were extraordinary in the wake of the 80 percent decline in the stock market during the three years through the end of September 1932. The extent of the values is suggested by the magnitude of 1933's rebound, when the equity market surged by more than 50 percent that year. An even greater advance of nearly 143 percent was recorded in the niche of small-company stocks.[2]

## Buyers Beware

A witness to the nascent twentieth century's slow but steady rise of disseminated corporate information, Graham was struck by the absence of an informed strategy for analyzing the data. In his mind, the lapse was only partly a function of the intellectual innocence of the era. Wall Street, he sensed early on, harbored a dismissive view of equities. Bonds, the professionals liked to say, were both worthy of careful review and appropriate as long-term investments. Stocks, by comparison, were second-class citizens in the capital markets. In accordance with the doctrine of the times, equities were branded speculative assets and investors were warned to proceed accordingly.

On the eve of World War I, when a fair amount of the so-called smart money preferred to wade in the waters of fixed income, the explosion of financial information "was going to waste in the area of common-stock analysis," Graham recalled decades later. "The figures were not ignored, but they were studied superficially and with little interest. What counted most was inside information of various kinds—some of it relating to business operations, new orders, anticipated profits and the like, but more of it to the current activities and plans of the market manipulators—the famous 'they' who were held responsible for all the significant moves, up and down, in every important stock." Like the worldly reader of literature who looks down on pulp fiction, many investors of the early twentieth century equated stocks with gambling and treated equities as little more than a necessary evil. "To old Wall Street hands it seemed silly to pore over dry statistics [for analyzing stocks] when the determiners of price changes were thought to be an entirely different set of factors—all of them very human," Graham remembered.[3]

The dearth of careful inspection of equities made it relatively easy to be a pioneer in the field in the early 1900s. The renowned

. investor Bernard Baruch recalls the environment that confronted a new investment career in the late nineteenth and early twentieth centuries. "When I entered Wall Street a man had to be his own analyst. Nor was there a Securities and Exchange Commission to require the disclosure of the information that was needed to measure the value of securities. In those days secrecy was the prevailing rule. Many stories were told of how uncommunicative the titans of finance were. The head of one corporation defined his company's business as 'addition, division and silence.'"[4]

The railroad companies, the hot investment of the day, were prime examples of the wall of secrecy that awaited investors intent on studying a firm's earnings and balance sheet. In the late 1800s, the rail industry dominated the stock market, attracting much of the nation's investment capital and setting a standard for public company disclosure, or a lack thereof. As late as 1898, railroad shares comprised roughly 60 percent of the stocks on the New York Stock Exchange (NYSE).[5] The supremacy of the industry in the capital markets was beyond question. Yet when it came to investors seeking information, the industry was notoriously tight-lipped.

An early sampling of the dismissive attitude is documented from 1866, when the New York Stock Exchange requested financial information from the Big Board–listed Delaware, Lackawanna & Western Railroad. The company's president replied that the railroad "made no reports, publishes no statements, and...[has] not done anything of the kind for the last five years." Another example: during the 1870s and 1880s, the New York Central Railroad issued no annual reports for shareholders.[6]

Careless disregard for shareholders would long pass for standard operating procedure in the field of investor relations. For some in the business community, secrecy and obfuscation were a publicly touted point of pride. Consider the 1899 testimony of Henry O. Havemeyer, president of the American Sugar Refining Company, in response to questions from Thomas Phillips of the U.S. Industrial Commission:

> Phillips: You think, then, that when a corporation is chartered by the State, offers stock to the public, and is one in which the public is interested, that the public has no right to know what its earning power is or to subject them to any inspection whatever, that the people may not buy this stock blindly?

Havemeyer: Yes, that is my theory. Let the buyer beware; that covers the whole business. You cannot wet-nurse people from the time they are born until the time they die. They have got to wade in and get stuck, and that is the way men are educated and cultivated.[7]

Even when companies dispensed reports in the preregulated age of Wall Street, it wasn't always clear that a release constituted improvement over silence. Accuracy, it seems, was a recurring victim. The *Railroad Gazette* in 1893 was sufficiently distressed to offer this warning: "The annual report of a railroad is often a very blind document and the average shareholder taking one of these reports generally gives up before he begins."[8]

But the concerted efforts of the captains of industry to deter and confuse shareholders were only a temporary impediment in the flow of information. Progress in advancing the state of corporate reporting, though sluggish, was persistent, largely due to the rise of the accounting profession and its associated rules of conduct and tools of analysis. The American Association of Public Accountants was established in 1886; a decade later the independent certified public accountant became a legally recognized designation when New York State conferred legitimacy on the title in 1896.

The evolution of the accounting profession was driven by the broader evolution underway in finance in the late 1800s. The rise of financial capitalism was an essential prerequisite for the creation of modern accounting, explains *A History of Accounting in America*.[9] As companies grew larger and more complex, management became separated from ownership, which inspired the growing ranks of investors, creditors, and accountants to demand reliable and detailed corporate information. By one account, there were already 1.25 million shareholders in the U.S. in 1893, or about 2 percent of the national population.[10] The growing ownership of stock encouraged calls for an independent profession to decipher and scrutinize corporate finances, which gave rise to the modern accounting industry.

Henry Clews, who enjoyed a long and prosperous career on Wall Street in the latter half of the 1800s, was calling for more transparency on the corporate landscape by the early twentieth century. In a 1906 address to the Wharton School of Finance at the University of Pennsylvania, the veteran trader argued that New York and other states should "respond to the popular agitation for publicity by passing laws requiring all corporations ... to make at least semi-annual reports of their condition, certified to by registered public accountants ... Only the insolvent and the crooked would have anything to fear from this wholesome publicity." He added that skilled accountants could deliver the transparency to the public "because the certified results of their examinations would be accepted as conclusive of the actual conditions being as they state or described." To produce creditable professionals in sufficient numbers to carry out the task, "every college and university should have a department for the special training of accountants, who on graduating should receive a diploma or degree, as in the medical or legal profession."[11]

Despite the rising chorus of calls for improved accounting standards, the lack of clarity regarding the rules was more or less rectified only after the excesses of the 1920s, which culminated in the 1929 stock market crash and the economic depression of the 1930s. From the ashes of financial and economic debacles came the political will for comprehensive modernization and regulation of the securities industry. Such were the seeds from which the Securities and Exchange Commission grew. The depths of the Great Depression and the associated loss of capital across the economic spectrum finally gave Washington the political resolve to set a higher standard of conduct on Wall Street and the business of selling and trading securities. The modern era of finance, in sum, traces it roots to the economic upheaval of the 1930s.

The introduction of tougher reporting rules and standards of conduct for financial institutions provided investors with a new motivation for developing more sophisticated research tools that went beyond merely second-guessing corporate insiders and professional traders. It's no accident that in the years following the financial reforms of the 1930s, the modern era of quantitative-oriented securities research was forged. The necessary first step of legally requiring routine and reliable financial reports created the opportunity for a new profession of investing based on analyzing the numbers. But the opportunity initially demanded an investment theory worthy of the name.

## Securities Analysis, in Name and Substance

In the wake of the reforms of the 1930s, rules of thumb and decisions based on gut instinct and inside information would no longer suffice. Federal regulation didn't magically create a new paradigm for securities and market research overnight. Nor did sophisticated tools drop out of the sky the moment Washington got serious about enforcing financial integrity. But the financial reforms of the 1930s marked an essential and unprecedented first step in rousing the creative forces of modern investment analytics.

It was during this period of upheaval that the so-called bible of fundamental stock picking made a timely arrival: *Security Analysis*, the classic 1934 treatise on the subject by Ben Graham and David Dodd.[12] It's no small irony that in the depths of capitalism's darkest days emerged one of stock investing's most enduring champions. The public's appetite for stocks at the time had all but vanished, leaving shares trading at extraordinarily low valuations. Therein lay some of the inspiration for a book that explained the finer points of identifying companies trading at what appear to be bargain prices.

If there was a singular moment when investment strategy came of age; when accounting-inspired research became a viable alternative to speculation in the equity market; when income statements and balance sheets provided the raw materials for true investors; when the idea that stocks had an intrinsic value if only an enterprising investor would search for it; the publication of *Security Analysis* symbolizes the moment. Embedded in the book's logic is the belief that informed analysis enhances the odds of success when venturing into the capital markets. Higher returns over time, the book preaches, spring from a rigorous, objective analysis of the numbers.

To be fair, the notion of investment theory didn't suddenly appear with the arrival of Graham and Dodd's book. Any number of contributors, before and after the publication of *Security Analysis*, can rightly lay a claim to advancing the evolution of financial analysis. Edgar Lawrence Smith in 1924, for instance, penned *Common Stocks as Long Term Investments*, a work that was decades ahead of its time in conceptualizing investment strategy. But whereas Smith's book was light on technique, *Security Analysis* was detailed while remaining accessible to the lay reader. *Security Analysis*, in fact, set a new standard for practical yet robust elegance in the task of identifying equities with alluring expected returns from those with lesser prospects.

Graham and Dodd, in short, gave the study of stocks a legitimacy formerly unknown in investing. In the book's wake, stock picking was no longer just a game of hunches and inside pool. It was no longer simply studying price charts and speculating on the trend. Equity analysis had become a profession, a business, a science, as *Security Analysis* announced to world.

But for all its insight and reasoned approach to equities analysis, the book was flawed. The defect was focusing on the trees, one at a time, while ignoring the forest. Graham and Dodd's great gift to finance was also its limitation in that the value strategy saw the capital markets only as a pool of individual securities—securities that sometimes harbored opportunity. The book advised that by carefully scrutinizing the potential candidates, one company, one balance sheet, one income statement at a time, through an accountant's lens, the truth would out and opportunity would be revealed, or not. What was missing was seeing the investment portfolio as a whole, as something more than a collection of individual decisions.

Then again, the investment business needed clarifying by the 1930s, and the quantitative focus in *Security Analysis* delivered it. The book was timely, sensible, and far and away the most enlightened investment treatise up to that point. But it was only the start of an intellectual revolution in finance—a revolution that elevated reasoned judgment over raw speculation and guesswork. Graham and Dodd's contribution was a crucial step in this journey, but it left to others to tackle the broader effort of formalizing the theory of portfolio investing.

## Chapter Notes

1. Phalon (2001), p. 13.
2. *Ibbotson* (2009), p. 31.
3. Graham (1996), pp. 142–143.
4. Baruch (1957), p. 261.
5. Previts and Merino (1979), p. 72.
6. Sobel (1965), p. 85.
7. Sylla and Smith (1995), p. 195.
8. Previts and Merino (1979), p. 81.
9. Ibid., p. 129.
10. Ibid., p. 78.

11. Clews (1915), pp. 808–809.

12. Graham and Dodd (1934). Even with the arrival of tougher federal securities laws, the distinction between speculation and investment, a thinly veiled reference to stocks and bonds, respectively, was still up in the air when *Security Analysis* was published in 1934. Courtesy of the Great Depression and the 1929 stock market crash, any progress in moving the public's perception of equities toward something deserving of long-term investment was halted. But in the bull market of the 1920s, observers of the financial scene could be forgiven for expecting a more favorable perspective on stocks over time. On the eve of the economic turmoil of the 1930s, the doctrine of stocks for the long run briefly found traction, a byproduct of the sharp rise in prices during the 1920s. But the concept quickly fell into decline in the following decade, Graham and Dodd observed in their book's introduction. Nonetheless, by the tome's close, the authors laid out a methodology for finding undervalued companies, firmly establishing the notion of stocks as something more than a gambler's toy.

## Chapter 2

# Inventing Portfolio Theory

THE IDEA OF diversifying assets to control and manage risk is probably as old as civilization. For as long as people have collected and stored objects of value, preserving and protecting wealth has been part of the human experience. But in the quest to conserve if not grow today's assets for use in tomorrow's consumption, a question arises: what's the best strategy?

Nearly 2,000 years ago, the Talmud counseled: A man should always keep his wealth in three forms; one-third in real estate, another in merchandise, and the rest in liquid assets. Another famous endorsement of diversification made an appearance quite a bit later, in the theatrical voice of the late sixteenth century, when Shakespeare's Antonio affirms the case for diversifying wealth and commercial activities in *The Merchant of Venice* by reasoning:

> My ventures are not in one bottom trusted,
> Nor to one place; nor is my whole estate
> Upon the fortune of this present year:
> Therefore my merchandise makes me not sad.[1]

As a formal inquiry, the strategy of putting one's proverbial eggs in multiple baskets earned a new level of respect when, in 1738, Daniel Bernoulli analyzed risk in his legendary article on the St. Petersburg Paradox. Among the lessons in this mathematical treatise: "It is advisable," he wrote, "to divide goods which are exposed to some small danger into several portions rather than to risk them all together."[2]

In practical application, diversification's appeal has grown more conspicuous in finance over the centuries. An early example of pooling assets for managing risk comes to us from Holland in 1774, when Adriaan van Ketwich sold subscriptions to *Eendragt Maakt Magt* (Unity Creates Strength), an investment trust comprised of bonds floated by several European governments. Nearly a century later, in 1868, the forerunner to the modern closed-end fund was listed in London. By 1924, when the first U.S. mutual fund was launched, their listed equivalent—investment trusts, which featured varying degrees of diversification—had been changing hands for decades on stock exchanges on both sides of the Atlantic.[3]

Observing that diversification in the early twentieth century was well established as a general strategy in money management is to state the obvious. The growing business in investment trusts, mutual funds, and other portfolio-minded efforts demonstrated the practical value and basic appeal of owning multiple securities in one account. In 1945, *Trusts and Estates* published "Diversification of Investments," an article by D. H. Leavens, who reports on the related literature up to that point: "An examination of some fifty books and articles on investment that have appeared during the last quarter of a century shows that most of them refer to the desirability of diversification," he writes. But there was something missing, added Leavens: "The majority [of authors], however, discuss it in general terms and do not clearly indicate why it is desirable."[4]

A more precise explanation of the desirability arrived a few years later with the publication of "Portfolio Selection" in *Journal of Finance*'s March 1952 issue.[5] Author Harry Markowitz, then a 25-year-old graduate student, offers a proper theory of diversification that quantitatively describes the strategy, including why it works and how it achieves something close to its ideal. It wasn't obvious at the time, but the world of finance would be forever changed by Markowitz's fourteen-page article. Diversification as an idea had been around for thousands of years, but only in 1952 did it enter the realm of financial economics proper.[6]

Author Peter Bernstein, in *Capital Ideas* (his grand history of the evolution of modern portfolio theory) writes that Markowitz's paper constitutes "the most famous insight in the history of modern finance and investment ...."[7] The essence of the insight is the paper's mathematical explanation of the relationship between return and risk, showing that a security's true worth can be measured only within the context of its expected contribution to the overall portfolio.

The not-so-subtle implication of Markowitz's paper: the value of securities analysis lies in focusing on the whole rather than the parts. In other words, the primary appeal in analyzing securities comes from projecting how they will change a portfolio's risk/reward profile. Security analysis in isolation of the larger portfolio is irrelevant if not misleading, "Portfolio Selection" suggests. A stock or bond that looks unattractive on its own merits may in fact be quite valuable when analyzed in context with an existing portfolio. The opposite may be true as well: a security that warrants a "buy" recommendation in its own right may be of lesser and perhaps negative value when considered as part of broader portfolio.

Context, in short, is everything. "Portfolio Selection" emphasizes the message by way of a mathematical recipe for building portfolios with the highest expected return at the lowest risk. The key is finding enough securities that move independently to some degree. The lower the correlation—a measure of the relationship between price changes—the higher the implied diversification benefit, everything else being equal.

A portfolio's overall risk is driven by the extent to which the components exhibit price changes that are independent of one another. But here's the best part: building a portfolio informed by Markowitz's research raises the possibility of lowering a portfolio's risk without lowering expected return. Arguably, this is the closest thing to a free lunch in the investment universe.

Mathematically speaking, the free lunch begins by recognizing that the expected return of a portfolio is the weighted average of the expected returns for each security. On the other hand, volatility risk (standard deviation) sums to less than its weighted average if—and this is critical—the correlation between securities is less than absolute. This, then, is Markowitz's main lesson: intelligently mixing securities can produce either a higher expected return at a given level of risk, or a lower risk at a given level of return compared to a naïve portfolio design. If you develop reasonably accurate estimates for correlation, return, and volatility, you can build portfolios that maximize risk-adjusted results in your favor.

It's important to emphasize that Markowitz is referring to a specific and relatively uncommon form of diversification that's required for extracting the maximum benefit from a given portfolio. Some if not most of the portfolios that could be formed from a pool of security choices are less than efficient because the portfolio's expected return is lower, or the expected risk is higher than it could be. Maximizing the expected return and minimizing the risk is the goal. Portfolios that meet these criteria sit on what's known as the efficient frontier, as per **FIGURE 2.1.**

It's hard to exaggerate the historical import of "Portfolio Selection," which many consider to be among the single greatest intellectual advances in investment finance. Looking back, it's clear that a revolution in financial theory arrived in the spring of 1952, a view duly recognized in 1990, when Markowitz shared a Nobel Prize for "pioneering work in the theory of financial economics."[8]

Bernstein (1992) explains that "Portfolio Selection".

> ... transformed the practice of investment management beyond recognition. [The paper] put some sense and some system into the haphazard manner in which most investors were assembling portfolios. Moreover, [the paper] formed the foundation for all subsequent theories on how financial markets work, how risk can be quantified, and even how corporations should finance themselves.[9]

One could say that Markowitz gave to portfolio theory what Graham and Dodd delivered to the analysis of individual securities. He provided respectability via a quantitative application that

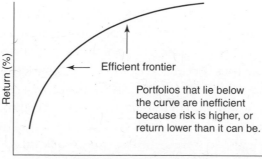

Figure 2.1    The Efficient Frontier

dispensed with rules of thumb and instinct in favor of hard numbers and exacting theory for enhancing a strategy previously grounded largely in common sense and intuition.

It all seems obvious from the vantage of the twenty-first century, but naïve assumptions about diversification still prevailed in 1952. Even so, Markowitz didn't work in a vacuum; as he recalls: "The basic principles of portfolio theory came to me one day while I was reading John Burr Williams, *The Theory of Investment Value.*"[10]

Williams argues in his 1938 book that individual securities have intrinsic value and it is this value that determines stock prices. The underlying theory is based on the concept of discounted cash flows. Projecting a stock's future cash flows and discounting those flows to the present with a suitable risk-free interest rate determines a share's fundamental value. A security, in short, is worth the sum of its discounted future cash flows. A security's "investment value," Williams explains, is "defined as the present worth of future dividends, or of future coupons and principal," and is of "practical importance to every investor because it is the *critical* value above which he cannot go in buying or holding, without added risk."[11]

The dividend discount model (DDM) that Williams details in 1938 was groundbreaking, although it evolves from earlier works, including Irving Fisher's *Theory of Interest*, published in 1930. Williams, too, acknowledges that his theory wasn't born in a vacuum. In the book's preface, he gives credit to several preceding efforts that represented "a pioneer step in the measurement of intrinsic value." Whatever debts DDM owes to its forebears, Williams' model ultimately distinguishes itself as the first significant quantitative tool for stock valuation.

Williams' reliance on algebraic formula in the DDM was both innovative and controversial. He apologizes in the book's preface for the mathematics, noting that "the mathematical method is a new tool of great power, whose use promises to lead to notable advances in Investment Analysis. Always it has been the rule in the history of science that the invention of new tools and new methods is the key to new discoveries, and we may expect the same rule to hold true in this branch of Economics as well."[12]

But Williams' DDM, like *Security Analysis* before it, offers no guidance on the investment portfolio per se. As one finance professor observes of Williams' approach to investment analysis, "[he] had very little to say about the effects of risk on valuation, because he believed that all risk could be diversified away." Williams and others were "seduced by Jacob Bernoulli's law of large numbers," writes Professor Mark Rubinstein of the University of California, Berkeley in a fifty-year retrospective of Markowitz's paper. Williams admits as much in his 1938 tome: "Given adequate diversification, gains ... will offset losses .... Thus, the *net risk* turns out to be nil."[13]

Defining "adequate" was left to the imagination in the pre-Markowitz era. Like Graham and Dodd, Williams gives diversification little thought because he is looking at securities individually. These authors aren't blind to diversification, of course. But risk management for stock pickers, even enlightened ones, is primarily a task to be managed by improving the stock selection process and owning a variety of the best picks. Diversification itself isn't analyzed. The real action is in picking companies.

Graham and Dodd's principal risk management tool is one of buying a portfolio of stocks and bonds at prices that offer a substantial "margin of safety." The definition is detailed in *Security Analysis,* but the basic premise is buying shares at prices below the company's fundamental net worth. The bigger the discount, the higher the margin of safety. The embedded assumption: purchasing stocks in this manner will deliver a portfolio of companies with relatively high expected returns and relatively low risk.

But if each security is independently chosen, portfolio strategy will be determined by stock selection, and so diversification proper may suffer. A savvy investor might choose to vary the selection among different industries, for instance, but fundamental analysis of securities via Graham and Dodd is, at its heart, about building a portfolio by one independent decision at a time. Diversification, in short, is of secondary importance in the world of Graham and Dodd and the DDM of Williams.

Markowitz looks at investing from a completely different perspective. Whereas investing is a bottom-up exercise for Williams and Graham and Dodd, Markowitz attacks the problem from the top down, transforming the investing challenge into a strategic problem in need of a strategic solution. In contrast to the stock picker who focuses on the pieces, Markowitz favors optimizing the whole with the goal of building the efficient portfolio. The individual securities that deliver the statistical nirvana are of secondary importance.

"Portfolio Selection" represents a revolution in thinking about the investment process for at least two reasons. First, it considers the portfolio as an end unto itself rather than a byproduct of picking individual securities. Second, Markowitz places strategic risk management on an equal if not higher footing with the pursuit of return. Investment performance is inextricably linked with risk, the paper proclaims. Higher return invariably comes packaged with higher risk. Theory had finally caught up with what many investors intuitively understood for years.

## Diversification and Beyond

Markowitz (1952) and the more-detailed Markowitz (1959) lay the foundation for what would become known as modern portfolio theory, or MPT, but it was only the first revelation of many that followed. A critical advance in portfolio theory was detailed in a 1958 paper by James Tobin, an economics professor at Yale.[14]

Tobin streamlines the task of choosing an efficient portfolio. Building on Markowitz's 1952 paper, Tobin recognizes the existence of multiple efficient portfolios on the efficient frontier, as depicted in Figure 2.1. Each efficient portfolio offers varying degrees of expected return and risk. In theory, investors would choose the specific efficient portfolio that suited them. Conservative investors would favor an efficient portfolio with relatively low risk; an aggressive investor would pick one with higher risk. But choosing one from many efficient portfolios had no place in Tobin's model, which asserted that one efficient portfolio alone excels over all others.

The so-called super efficient portfolio is always the superior choice, so it's the portfolio that's appropriate for all investors. Both conservative and aggressive investors—and everyone in between— should own the super efficient portfolio.

On its face, Tobin's conclusion looks naïve if not reckless. Investors come in all shapes and sizes, as do their risk and return needs. Some are trying to grow assets over decades; others are concerned with conserving wealth. Some are young workers building nest eggs for retirement; others are retirees trying to live on a fixed income. In a world with a rainbow of investment needs and risk tolerances, how could anyone sensibly promote the idea that everyone should own the same investment portfolio?

The reasoning is quite persuasive, actually. Tobin (1958) argues that everyone should hold the super efficient portfolio along with a risk-free asset, such as Treasury bills. By adjusting the ratio of the two components—a risk portfolio and cash—an investor can customize portfolio to match his particular financial needs and risk tolerance.

Tobin's 1958 research marks the dawn of the modern age of asset allocation, albeit a simplified version by twenty-first century standards. In Tobin's world, there are just two asset classes: the risk portfolio and a risk-free asset. The first step in designing the asset allocation plan is finding the super efficient portfolio via Markowitz. The next question: what percentage of an investor's assets should be invested in the super efficient portfolio and what percentage should go to the risk-free asset?

A conservative investor might allocate 60 percent of portfolio to risk and 40 percent to the risk-free component. An aggressive investor might choose a 90 percent allocation to risk and just 10 percent in risk-free T-bills. What if 100 percent didn't satisfy an investor's appetite for risk? The investor can borrow money and engineer a leveraged portfolio with an effective 110 percent, 120 percent, or higher exposure to risk. Leverage, after all, magnifies return and risk.

The Tobin model, in sum, offered a range of risk allocations, from zero to 100 percent and beyond. In practice, investors had been doing as much throughout history. The Talmud's ancient advice is one example, although its asset allocation advice is little more than a guess—and a generic one at that. Markowitz's and Tobin's main achievements amount to minimizing the guesswork in portfolio design by introducing a quantitative framework for portfolio design. It was a huge step forward, but it was only the beginning.

## Mr. Market's Portfolio

Markowitz's and Tobin's research marked a revolution for thinking about investing, but the associated strategies are hardly user friendly.

It's one thing to say that investors should own the super efficient portfolio; it's quite another issue when it comes to building portfolios informed by the research.

The computational nuisance of identifying efficient portfolios ensured that Markowitz's and Tobin's insight was virtually worthless as a practical matter when the papers were first published. Neither the requisite computing power nor the databases were generally available in the 1950s for analyzing securities on a level that could easily identify the super efficient portfolio. As Bernstein (1992) observes, the practical hurdles for turning Markowitz's portfolio theory into reality were enormous well into the 1960s, a decade that was only just beginning to experiment with computer-based analysis.

Impractical or not, Markowitz's efficient frontier idea slowly attracted attention and inspired additional research by academics as the 1960s rolled on. That includes work by William Sharpe, a young economist who delivers a key theoretical advance in the nascent world of portfolio theory with his 1964 paper "Capital Asset Prices: A Theory of Market Equilibrium Under Conditions of Risk."[15] The research is a milestone for several reasons, starting with its simplification of Markowitz's methodology for identifying efficient portfolios.

Sharpe lays out the basics of what would become known as the capital asset pricing model, or CAPM.[16] Among the model's core lessons: "the market" portfolio is in fact Tobin's super efficient portfolio, an assertion that effectively dispensed with the tedious work of calculating expected returns, volatilities, and covariances of individual securities in search of the ideal efficient portfolio as per Markowitz. Owning "the market" is a shortcut to owning the portfolio with the highest expected return at a given level of expected risk, the paper effectively advises.

In a CAPM world, "the market" is all the world's assets: stocks, bonds, commodities, real estate, art, human capital, and more—every asset. CAPM weights each asset according to its market value. For stocks, market value is determined by shares outstanding multiplied by price—market capitalization. Weighting by market cap is necessary to satisfy CAPM's assumption that everyone holds the market portfolio. The only way to comply with the condition is if investors hold shares in proportion to their market cap, in which case the stock market is in equilibrium, meaning that demand matches supply.

Other key CAPM assumptions:

- All investors have identical return expectations and investment horizons.
- There are no transactions costs or taxes.
- All investors can trade all securities and have access to unlimited borrowing and lending opportunities at the risk-free interest rates.
- All investors seek to maximize return and minimize risk as per Markowitz.
- The market pricing mechanism is perfectly efficient so that all known information is reflected in market prices.
- Asset returns are normally distributed.

These are stylized assumptions that are impractical, of course. But that's the nature of economic models: they make grand assumptions about how the world works in search of fundamental, if limited truths with practical resonance. On that score, CAPM was—and remains—an enormous point of progress for thinking about the behavior of markets and what it means for portfolio design. Despite CAPM's simplifying assumptions, it's still a bedrock in finance theory. It's not perfect, by any means, but neither is it irrelevant.

Sharpe's paper elevates Markowitz's and Tobin's ideas from complex academic notions to something fairly simple, practical, and therefore highly relevant in the real world of money management. It does this by first asserting that the market's influence—systematic risk—is present in every security in varying degrees. The remaining influence is labeled unsystematic risk. The critical revelation is that systematic risk can't be avoided. As such, the market factor, dubbed beta, ultimately dominates a portfolio of securities. What's more, beta risk is unavoidable because it's present in every security to some degree. As a result, beta risk tends to prevail in a diversified portfolio.

Beta risk explains why some securities deliver higher or lower returns than others, according to CAPM. This leads to the central point that higher return only comes through higher risk—beta risk.

But beta's not alone; there's a second risk factor, Sharpe finds. Unsystematic risk influences securities prices too. The second factor, which is known as alpha, is everything other than beta. Each security harbors some mix of beta and alpha. But in contrast to beta, alpha risk can be avoided. CAPM counsels that alpha should be marginalized because investors aren't sufficiently rewarded for assuming unsystematic risk. Alpha can be dispatched easily with adequate diversification. The various alpha risks that inhabit individual securities tend to cancel each other out in a diversified portfolio. What's left is beta, the primary determinant of a portfolio's risk and return profile.

All of this boils down to what is essentially a simple framework for thinking about investing: own the market. In addition to being the superior portfolio, it's also a portfolio that requires no analysis. The basic lesson: attempts at second guessing the market portfolio by owning certain securities and avoiding others will result in an inferior—inefficient, in the parlance of Markowitz—portfolio. Diversification by way of owning the market portfolio "enables the investor to escape all but the risk resulting from swings in economic activity—this type of risk remains even in efficient combinations," Sharpe concludes. "And, since all other types [of risk, i.e., alpha risk] can be avoided by diversification, only the responsiveness of an asset's rate of return to the level of economic activity is relevant in assessing its risk."[17] Meanwhile, assets that are unmoved by economic activity—assets with zero beta—will generate the return of the "pure interest rate," which is to say cash and its equivalents.

This was radical stuff for 1964, when the cult of the money manager was in full swing. The decade of the sixties was the age of the so-called go-go years, when mutual fund managers like Gerry Tsai were flying high and defining state-of-the-art investing strategies. Chasing alpha, to put it in CAPM terms, was all the rage.[18]

Treated like movie stars, hot mutual fund managers caught the public's imagination. Tsai and his contemporaries were celebrated as proof that active management works—an idea that was the antithesis of the counsel embedded in CAPM. Sharpe's paper asserts the exact opposite to Tsai's approach, albeit in the oblique language of financial economics. Attempts at beating the market are misguided, CAPM explains, so the enlightened investor should instead latch on to the performance wave powered by the market portfolio.

Almost no one was prepared to embrace such a rebellious idea in 1964. Even if the spirit was willing, Sharpe's idea was virtually impossible to implement. CAPM was only a theory in 1964, and it looked destined to remain so indefinitely. There were no index funds when the paper was published, nor would there be until the early 1970s. Even then, the first efforts at indexing were quiet affairs, run exclusively for a handful of institutional investors. It wasn't until 1976 that the first index mutual fund for retail investors was launched.

Buying the stock market in the years immediately following Sharpe's 1964 paper required purchasing all the securities piecemeal and passively holding them. Yet embracing CAPM's prescription, even if such a strategy was practical, was doomed in those days because of the associated trading costs. Before commissions were deregulated in 1975, buying securities meant paying hefty commissions, so the idea of running an index fund and buying hundreds if not thousands of securities looked like a sure flop.

Nonetheless, several of the intellectual building blocks of modern portfolio theory were in place by 1964, even if they were widely uncelebrated and impractical. Markowitz showed that the investing problem could effectively be resolved to a degree with the efficient portfolio. Tobin extended Markowitz's strategy by marrying the super efficient portfolio with varying degrees of cash in search of an investment strategy that matched each investor's appetite for risk. Sharpe rounded out the theory by explaining that the market portfolio was in fact the optimal portfolio.

There was one additional line of research that would join with Markowitz, Tobin, and Sharpe to collectively form the classic foundation of what would become known as modern portfolio theory. As it happened, the fourth leg of MPT was at once old and new—blossoming in the 1960s but also drawing strength from an obscure research paper published six decades earlier.

## Random Discoveries

The academic introduction to what eventually evolved into the efficient markets hypothesis (EMH) was initially greeted with a shrug, and it quickly went downhill from there. Louis Bachelier delivered his dissertation in 1900 to the Faculty of Sciences at the Academy of Paris for the degree of doctor of mathematical sciences.

The paper was, to put it diplomatically, unappreciated at the time, a surprising oversight considering that the paper marks "the birth date of mathematical finance."[19] History eventually corrected the insult and "Théorie de la Spéculation,"[20] earned recognition as the first serious econometric study of the forces determining securities prices.[21]

Analyzing the French stock and options markets, Bachelier found no observable pattern in the fluctuations of prices. Instead, he discovered that the influences on price changes are "innumerable" and that "past, present, and even discounted future events are reflected in market price, but often show no apparent relation to price changes." He explains, "The determination of these fluctuations depends on an infinite number of factors; it is, therefore, impossible to aspire to mathematical prediction of it. Contradictory opinions concerning these changes diverge so much that at the same instant buyers believe in a price increase and sellers in a price decrease." Moreover, he advises, "The calculus of probabilities, doubtless, could never be applied to fluctuations in security quotations, and the dynamics of the Exchange will never be an exact science."[22]

Bachelier, in essence, sees securities prices following a random walk, which means that price changes are independent and are dispersed in what's called a normal distribution, or a bell curve, as it's more commonly known. Accordingly, the greatest frequency of price changes will be relatively small, up or down. The incidence of larger price changes, by comparison, are fairly rare. Bachelier's central lesson is that the price movements in the securities market, in the short term at least, are random and therefore unpredictable. The expected return in such a market, therefore, is zero.

Peter Bernstein, in *Capital Ideas*, observed that Bachelier's paper

... laid the groundwork on which later mathematicians constructed a full-fledged theory of probability. He derived a formula that anticipated Einstein's research into the behavior of particles subject to random shocks in space. And he developed the now universally used concept of stochastic processes, the analysis of random movements among statistical variables. Moreover, he made the first theoretical attempt to value such financial instruments as options and futures, which had active markets even in 1900. And he did all this in an effort to explain why prices in capital markets are impossible to predict![23]

Quite an accomplishment for 1900. Yet history provides little insight for why one man could be so far ahead of conventional thinking in matters of finance theory. Perhaps nothing more can be said other than to chalk it up to genius. If so, it was a genius that nearly vanished into the mists of the academic abyss.

Bachelier's paper, for all its innovation and anticipation of academic theory to come, still managed to slip into oblivion for decades, at least as financial economics was concerned.[24] But while his work was overlooked, or at least underappreciated from an investment perspective, research on what would become known as the random walk theory rolled on. For instance, Holbrook Working, an agricultural economist with Stanford University's Food Research Institute, is the author of a 1934 paper that offered additional support for Bachelier's conclusion that historical prices offered no forecasting value.[25]

A year earlier, economist Alfred Cowles III published the results of an ambitious five-year project in search of evidence that stock market predictions are reliable.[26] Poring over forecasts from various sources published over the years, this 1933 effort meticulously reconstructed market data (no mean feat in the pre-computer age) in search of answers. Despite the heroic chore, the data showed that prediction skill was virtually nonexistent.

Cowles didn't rush to judgment. He studied a broad pool of market prophecies, including 7,500 recommendations of individual stocks issued by sixteen financial services for the four years through 1932. He also pored over investment advice from twenty-five insurance companies for the three years through 1931, and he reviewed stock forecasts published in twenty-four financial publications that covered more than four years through 1932. Cowles even re-created twenty-six years worth of forecasts by William Peter Hamilton, editor of *The Wall Street Journal*. In some of his columns, Hamilton lays out the basics for a trading system that came to be known as the Dow Theory, a stock market forecasting system named for its inventor, Charles Dow, one of the founders of Dow Jones & Co., the *Journal's* original publisher.

The astonishing result is that despite all the attempts at divining the market's future, Cowles found no evidence that analysts can predict prices with any consistency. And just to be sure, he updated his research in 1944 by looking at even longer time periods.[27] But the conclusion was unchanged. If skilled market prognosticators exist, Cowles wasn't able to find the evidence in the data.

The quest for evidence that past prices could be used to see the future continued in the 1950s. Maurice Kendall, in his 1953 study of British equity and commodity prices, searched for clues about future economic cycles but only offers more evidence that prices moved randomly. "In a series of prices which are observed at fairly close intervals the random changes from one term to the next are so large as to swamp any systematic effect which may be present," Kendall concludes. "The data behave almost like wandering series."[28] And in 1959, M. F. M. Osborne equated the movement of stocks with Brownian motion, a reference to the random movement of particles in nature as first identified by biologist Robert Brown in the early nineteenth century.[29]

In the early 1960s, a new era of empirical studies began as the computer was harnessed for stock market analysis on a grand scale for the first time in a groundbreaking project conducted at University of Chicago's Center for Research in Security Prices (CRSP). Supported with financing from Merrill Lynch & Co. and others, the CRSP computer database of stock prices was established in 1960. This unprecedented quantitative resource delivered a treasure trove of research opportunities for James Lorie, CRSP's director, and Lawrence Fisher, a finance professor and associate director of CRSP. The two researchers published a paper in 1964 that summarizes their analysis, including the astonishing conclusion at the time that the average annual rate of return for all stocks on the New York Stock Exchange was 9 percent a year from 1926 through 1960, assuming all dividends were reinvested and no income taxes paid.[30] The news that the unmanaged equity market had generated such a high return shocked readers in the mid-1960s. Indeed, 9 percent a year was about double the yield on investment-grade corporate bonds at the time.

The idea that stocks offered a return premium over bonds wasn't new. Edgar Lawrence Smith advocates as much in his 1924 book *Common Stocks as Long Term Investments*. Analyzing prices for U.S. stocks and corporate bonds for 1866–1923, Smith reports that equities generally delivered a sizable performance edge over debt. Forty years later, Lorie and Fisher's paper confirmed Smith's verdict, and with the added bonus of introducing the world to computer-based quantitative analysis in finance.

## Efficiency Rules

Bachelier's paper was enjoying a revival as the 1960s unfolded. Rediscovered by economists in the decade before, the 1900 study's recovery from obscurity inspired new efforts at examining the presumed randomness in securities pricing. The next generation of analysis includes a 1965 paper by MIT economics professor Paul Samuelson, "Proof That Properly Anticipated Prices Fluctuate Randomly," which presents the first formal economic argument for the efficient market hypothesis. Along the way, the paper suggests that studying historical prices as a strategy for making forecasts is "doomed to failure." The market "has already ... discounted all knowable future information ...."[31] This leads to the conclusion that if there was a reason for expecting a stock's price to rise or fall, it would have already done so.

In a market of free-flowing information and zero-transaction costs, price changes tomorrow will be determined by new information, Samuelson's theory posits. No one knows what tomorrow's news will be, and on that basis no one can predict price changes. What's more, news is unpredictable, and therefore random. Such is the nature of history as it unfolds in real time. Accordingly, tomorrow's price changes are random relative to today's, the paper explains. This means simply that prices fluctuate randomly in an efficient market, so market prices are the best estimates of intrinsic value.

That doesn't mean that market prices are always correct. In fact, sometimes they're wrong. But "wrong" means that market prices at any moment in time may not accurately anticipate a security's future returns, although that's an outcome that's unknowable in the here and now. By that definition, "wrong" doesn't violate the tenets of EMH because no one can see the future, not even the market. The future is full of surprises. At the same time, not all estimates are created equal. Some predictions are better than others. Or perhaps it's more accurate to say that some predictions are less prone to error than others. Samuelson offers a theory that shows that the market's estimates of future value are superior as a general rule. Indeed, Samuelson's paper is careful to note that it's a proof of "properly anticipated prices," which aren't to be confused with the actual prices. The distinction reminds that an economically sound forecast of prices doesn't always coincide with the actual prices that arrive.

The future is unknowable. The question, then, becomes: how best to deal with the future? EMH suggests an answer. The essence of EMH is that the only reason to buy or sell is because new information has arrived—information that wasn't factored into the previous market price. Meantime, all known information is reflected in prices in an efficient market. Short of new information, the market price stands as the best estimate of fair value.

Bachelier's paper effectively comes to a similar conclusion in 1900. Even then, the idea wasn't entirely new but had been bumping around for centuries, albeit in varying states of formality. In 1889, George Gibson, in *The Stock Markets of London, Paris and New York*, opines that when "shares become publicly known in an open market, the value which they acquire may be regarded as the judgment of the best intelligence concerning them."[32] Three centuries earlier, in the mid-1500s, Italian mathematician Girolamo Cardano wrote that the sum of a gambler's winnings in a fair game today is the best forecast for tomorrow's total winnings.[33]

The concept of a fair game, or "martingale," as gamblers have come to call it, is formalized in Samuelson (1965). The same year witnessed another seminal paper advancing EMH's case by studying the empirical evidence. Eugene Fama's "The Behavior of Stock-Market Prices," published in the *Journal of Business*, is the author's PhD thesis, which combines original research with a survey of the existing literature up to that point.[34] Fama, like Samuelson, asserts that stock prices generally follow a random walk. But while Samuelson focuses on building a theory, Fama tests the idea by analyzing stock market data. Along the way, Fama coined the term "efficient" market, defining it in his 1965 paper as "a market where, given the available information, actual prices at every point in time represent very good estimates of intrinsic values."[35]

Fama's paper takes direct aim at so-called technical analysis, or the study of historical price charts in the belief that past trends impart information about what's coming. Like Cowles, he finds no confirmation that analyzing historical prices is useful for predicting prices. Bachelier, it seems, got it right back in 1900, or so the academics in 1965 advised.[36]

If chart reading and other strategies that focus on historical prices for predicting the future are of limited if any value, what of fundamental analysis à la Graham and Dodd's *Security Analysis?* The father of fundamental investing, Ben Graham, preached that above-average investment gains can be tapped by exploiting mispriced securities through the study of earnings, dividends, book value, and other fundamental data. He wrote as much and, perhaps more persuasively, his investment record seconds the motion with the message that an informed investor can use such information to estimate a company's true value and thereby profit from the knowledge when the market misprices the security. To the extent a firm's stock trades above (below) the company's intrinsic value, the shares are overpriced (underpriced), which in turn implies below-average (above-average) future returns.

Fama recognized the existence of "intrinsic values" and explains that their existence "is not inconsistent with the random walk hypothesis." His paper also distinguishes between fundamental analysis and chart reading. He even considers the possibility that skilled security analysts may uncover mispricings and profit from the revelation. But such efforts ultimately promote market efficiency. As Fama (1965a) explains, "If there are enough superior analysts, their existence will be sufficient to insure that actual market prices are, on the basis of all *available* information, best estimates of intrinsic values." The end result, he concludes, is that as more analysts study securities, and the harder they look for mispricings, the more the opportunities fade, the more prices fluctuate randomly and the closer the market moves to a state described by EMH. "In this way, of course, the superior analysts make intrinsic value analysis a useless tool for both the average analyst and the average investor."[37]

Predictably, the arrival of EMH has unleashed waves of criticism. The fact that the market's estimate of fair value isn't 100 percent accurate all of the time, relative to what to the future ultimately reveals, suggests to some that EMH is wrong. Another complaint turns EMH against itself by claiming that the randomness in securities prices is evidence that the stock market is little more than a giant casino, so its pricing shouldn't be taken seriously. Others charge that the failure to find anything more than a random walk in prices suggests that new statistical techniques are needed to uncover meaning in the apparent chaos of equity pricing.

Yet the fact that very few professional investors beat the market, or their relevant index over time, suggests that the market is efficient in some sense. Certainly if the market is totally inefficient, there would be gads of money managers posting excess returns over the market's performance on a regular basis, a state of affairs that most certainly doesn't exist. Then again, different markets exhibit different levels of efficiency. No one should confuse the U.S. stock market with trading in, say, high-yield bonds.

What does all this mean? If the world behaves according to EMH, which is to say that market prices reflect good estimates of fundamental value, the implication is that "the primary concern of the average investor should be *portfolio analysis*." In that case, Fama (1965a) recommends, investors should: 1) decide on an acceptable balance of risk and expected return; 2) rank securities according to their risk; and 3) establish how securities interact to form portfolios in risk-adjusted terms. "If actual prices at any point in time are good estimates of intrinsic values," investors "need not be concerned with whether individual securities are over- or under-priced."[38]

That's just another way of reaffirming the ideas of Markowitz (1952), Tobin (1958), and Sharpe (1964). But as we'll learn in the chapters ahead, investing isn't quite as simple as the early literature on portfolio theory suggests.

## Chapter Notes

1. Markowitz (1999) quotes this passage in reference to diversification.

2. Bernoulli (1738), p. 30.

3. Rouwenhorst (2004).

4. Leavens (1945).

5. Markowitz (1952).

6. In fact, a 1940 paper ("The Problem of Full-Risk Insurances") by Italian mathematician Bruno de Finetti anticipated the general concepts that Markowitz wrote about in 1952. Because de Finetti's research was focused on actuarial topics, the paper was largely unknown in the literature of finance and economics. The oversight was finally rectified in Rubinstein (2006). In another strange twist of history, Markowitz devised his theory

as a similar methodology was being developed independently in Roy (1952). Both papers were published in 1952, although Markowitz's made it to print ahead of Roy's by four months. It's debatable why Markowitz's paper received greater acclaim. Bernstein writes, "I am at a loss to explain why Roy's paper failed to cut the swath that Markowitz's paper did … And yet he comes to essentially the same conclusions as Markowitz does." (Bernstein [1992], p. 55).

7. Bernstein (1992), p. 41.

8. http://nobelprize.org/nobel_prizes/economics/laureates/1990/

9. Bernstein (1992), p. 43.

10. Markowitz (1991), p. 470.

11. Williams (1956, 1938), pp. vii–viii.

12. Ibid., p. ix.

13. Rubinstein (2002), p. 1042.

14. Tobin (1958).

15. Sharpe (1964).

16. Sharpe wasn't alone in developing CAPM, but he's arguably the first among equals in the model's design. For a more comprehensive history of CAPM that profiles its multiple contributors, see Chapter 10 in Bernstein (1992).

17. Sharpe (1964), pp. 441–442

18. See, for instance, Brooks (1999, 1973) for a profile of the personalities and trends of Wall Street in the 1960s.

19. Courtault et al. (2000), p. 341.

20. Bachelier (1900).

21. Bachelier's paper is actually the first academic study to find that prices follow a random walk, which is often equated with the efficient market hypothesis. In fact, the two are related but distinctive, with the random walk being one of several versions of the efficient markets theory, as detailed below.

22. Bachelier (1900), p. 18.

23. Bernstein (1992), p. 18.

24. In contrast to his obscurity in economics, Bachelier earned a degree of recognition in his own lifetime in the field of mathematics, according to Courtault et al. (2000).

25. Working (1934).

26. Cowles (1933).

27. Cowles (1944).

28. Kendall (1953), p. 11.

29. Osborne (1959).

30. Fisher and Lorie (1964), p. 9.

31. Samuelson (1965), pp. 47–48.

32. Shiller (2000), p. 172.

33. Tapiero (1998), pp. 81–81, and David (1998, 1962), Chapter 6.

34. Fama (1965a).

35. Ibid., p. 90.

36. In fact, declaring that prices follow a random walk was premature, as we'll discuss in more detail in later chapters. Meanwhile, it's important to distinguish between the random walk theory and the efficient market hypothesis. Although the two are sometimes confused as equivalent, the random walk theory is just one interpretation of the efficient market hypothesis as well as one that has fallen from grace in the wake of ongoing research over the recent years. As a result, dismissing the random walk theory doesn't require rejecting the efficient market hypothesis.

37. Fama (1965a), p. 40.

38. Ibid., p. 40.

## Chapter 3

# Other Betas

PORTFOLIO THEORY WORTHY of the name in 1951 was conspicuous by its absence. Over the next fourteen years, a bold attempt at filling the void by explaining how markets work unfolded in a series of published academic papers. Collectively, this research lays out the theoretical basis for the modern age of portfolio management and delivers context for thinking about the design and management of asset allocation. Among the highlights:

- Markowitz's portfolio optimization theory quantifies the investment instinct for maximizing return and minimizing risk.
- Tobin's separation theorem formalizes the concept of asset allocation.
- Sharpe and company explain that the market portfolio is the optimal portfolio.
- Research on the efficient market hypothesis counsels that it is difficult, if not impossible to outguess the market over time and that market prices are likely to be a robust estimate of asset value as a general rule.

As financial revolutions go, the 1952–1965 burst of inquiry and analysis arrived with lightening speed, which is all the more impressive if you consider the dramatic changes in the study and practice of managing money that was unleashed by these papers. Investing isn't close to being "solved" by these theoretical innovations, nor do these papers have a monopoly on the reordering of finance that unfolded in the second half of the twentieth century. But as a group, the ideas in these papers have been front and center in reinventing the framework for analyzing and executing portfolio strategy.

Even after more than fifty years, the concepts still reverberate, inspiring innovation and debate and driving progress in the quest to understand the strategic investment challenge.

Perhaps the greatest legacy of these papers—the core elements of so-called modern portfolio theory (MPT)—is orienting investing around risk management. Risk has always been at the heart of investing, of course, even if return tends to steal the spotlight. The difference is that MPT elevates risk as the primary focus and provides a quantitative, theoretical lens for seeing risk and return as two halves of the whole. The main lesson: risk and return must be analyzed together, in the context of portfolio design. Why? Because return and risk are inseparable, and each is inextricably linked with the other.

The market price of risk, as we'll discuss in later chapters, becomes central for thinking about portfolio management. All assets carry risk; the question is, what's the price? The answer determines if we should expect to earn a premium, or not, over the return from cash, or more generally, the risk-free rate of return.

A healthy dose of what's been researched, practiced, and disputed in the world of strategic-minded investing in the decades since the publication of MPT's founding papers connects back to one or more of these concepts, or their intellectual heirs. The principles of MPT, while addressing some rather ancient but eternally crucial questions, continue to inspire for analyzing the forces that determine success and failure in the money game.

The basic line of inquiry sparked by Markowitz's first paper is still blossoming in the twenty-first century, with no end in sight. But even after a sea of research spawned by the 1952 paper and its heirs, the investigation has only scratched the surface. The good news is that we now have structure for examining, debating, and thinking about the laws that govern investing. The true answers are still elusive, and the arguments over what's relevant and what's not are as fierce as ever. But at least we know how to frame the questions, focus the studies, and organize the discussion as we continue to unravel the mysteries of finance. That's a direct legacy of Markowitz's opening bid on analyzing portfolio strategy and the resulting rise of MPT.

Formally solving the question of what constitutes the ideal portfolio, however, is all but impossible for several reasons. One is that what's optimal for one investor is likely to be less so for another. There's also the complication of finance itself. Full and complete answers in matters of investing are eternally obscure because absolute knowledge of how the human mind works and how assets will interact with one another in the future is beyond comprehension. Fifty years of financial economic study give us some confidence for making general assumptions—confidence that was sorely lacking previously. But the hunt for knowledge is still in its infancy, and much of the low-hanging fruit has already been picked. There are some basic laws that govern pricing and determine risk, and we've learned a thing or two over the decades. Studying MPT principles, testing the implications, and considering the alternatives is productive. Yet the idea that the laws of investing are now fully transparent remains the stuff of dreams.

In contrast with physics, mathematics, and other hard sciences, finance depends on the decisions of *homo economicus*. The future is unknowable in finance largely because it's never fully clear what investors will do in a world of fluctuating financial variables, particularly in the short term. That doesn't preclude the possibility of a deeper, richer understanding of portfolio design and the nature of markets. But an investment solution in any sense of the word will remain forever unspecified. We can and have moved closer to that ideal over the decades, but that's largely because when we started on this journey fifty years ago, we knew comparatively little about the nature of strategic-minded investing.

Today, by comparison, we have some clues to consider and principles to interpret. By studying investing through the prism of risk, financial economists have deduced some of the fundamental rules of thumb for managing money. MPT's focus on identifying and illuminating these fundamental laws is part of what makes the theory's core concepts so enduring. Yes, there's a wide variety of agreement—and disagreement—over MPT's assumptions and conclusions, including the debate about how and if investors should depart from the portfolio structure that MPT implies. But the associated ideas have proven durable as a benchmark for designing portfolio strategies because MPT identifies truisms regarding risk management, starting with the theory's prime message: higher return only comes with higher risk.

The power of MPT as a suite of ideas is evident even among those who disagree with it in the sense that so-called damning evidence is often presented as refutations of its basic principles, such as indexing and the efficient market hypothesis. Pointing out MPT's limitations, flaws, and blemishes, which is inevitable as well as productive, is regarded as something of a coup for those who take issue with some or all the ideas laid out by Markowitz, Sharpe, et al. MPT continues to define the investment framework, even for those who reject its lessons.

In a process that resembles the financial equivalent of the Hegelian dialectic, new theories and fresh empirical findings are thrown back and forth in a war of mustering corroborating and conflicting evidence. The river never runs dry on research confirming and rejecting MPT. The debate, it seems, will run on forever.

Perhaps the greatest challenge in surveying the ongoing research is maintaining perspective and separating the digressions from the principal ideas that advance the cause of informed portfolio design. It's easy to get sidetracked, if not confused, amid the tidal wave of analysis that routinely flows from academia and investment managers. But for investors who look carefully, there's a narrative in the literature that imparts wisdom about strategic-minded investing. The basic lesson: we're all risk managers now. As such, the primary challenge is identifying the sources of risk.

## The Illusion of Perfection

Like all economic theories, MPT indulges in simplifying assumptions, and those assumptions are vulnerable to testing in the real world. The question, then, is deciding if the empirical results support or invalidate MPT or merely remind us that there are no absolutes in finance and so we must search for what works reasonably well.

Perhaps the first order of business is managing our expectations. On the one hand we need a model, a system, a stylized view of the investment process as a guide for designing and managing the portfolio. At the same time, we must recognize that every model will fall short of reality. The true set of laws that govern risk and return is beyond the powers of human understanding. That leaves us with the next best alternative: identifying the fundamental lessons that capture some of the essential forces in the market.

The problem is that the search for these lessons requires us to make assumptions—simplifying assumptions about how the world works. We must trade a bit of reality for modeling the wickedly complex process that we call investing.

Money management suffers numerous complications in practice that aren't always recognized in theory—taxes, trading costs, and so on. No wonder, then, that critics can always identify deviations in actual market results relative to a model's predictions. That's unsurprising, since the economic forces driving capital markets are infinitely more nuanced than any one financial model can capture.

Simplifying infinitely complex systems, such as national economies and the laws that govern investing, is a necessary evil in the cause of advancing knowledge. That assures that building theories intent on deciphering the nature of profit and loss is an eternal struggle for balancing truth with pragmatism. Definitive answers are forever elusive in the money game, but after five decades of turning over rocks, we're not nearly as clueless as when Markowitz launched this endless strategic inquiry.

Compromise is simply the cost of doing business in the quest to find investment perspective. Ideally the resulting model captures most of the relevant variables that are the building blocks for generating satisfying results. But as a general proposition, every model, by definition, is incomplete, so the opportunity for improvement, and criticism, is eternal.

Consider the debate over the capital asset pricing model (CAPM), a key pillar of MPT. Owning a passive, equilibrium-based version of "the market" and thereby minimizing short-term trades are among the embedded lessons that spring from the theory. Are these reasonable lessons for summarizing the rules of investing? One reason for answering "yes" comes from looking at the competitive returns of index funds that hold securities in accordance with their market values, as CAPM instructs. On balance, the performance of these funds offers compelling evidence for thinking that CAPM works. But there's also room for doubt, which is fueled by reviewing the voluminous literature that details how CAPM falls short of reality.

More papers have probably been written about CAPM, pro and con, than any other concept in finance. The caveats and conditions that surround CAPM are at once enlightening and debilitating. The related literature, after decades of analysis, is so extensive and so deeply entrenched in the financial debate that it's now virtually impossible to objectively accept or reject the world's most famous pricing model.

As a portal for assessing risk, CAPM is a blunt tool, to be sure. Yet it still provides valuable insight about how the market works, which is to say that investors could do a lot worse than using CAPM as a guiding philosophy in the business of investing. Certainly CAPM's simple elegance makes it popular among supporters. The attribute also marks it as easy prey for critics. But in the course of rethinking CAPM's lessons, after years of probing its conclusions and questioning its value in the real world, has come a deeper understanding of the capital markets and portfolio design.

As Sharpe's 1964 paper recognizes, CAPM doesn't explain all risks, nor does it try. Instead, it assigns risk to two buckets: market risk, or beta, and everything else, which is dubbed alpha. That makes life easier for thinking about investing and the forces that define investing results. Yet CAPM's binary view also raises a question: is a finer reading of the whole truth about risk necessary for success in money management?

Several prominent studies in the early 1970s offered support for the theory, albeit with caveats. Nonetheless, the early research provided intellectual cover for embracing CAPM. It's no coincidence that the first index funds were launched in the first half of the decade, when the academic endorsement of CAPM was at its apex.

Among the more influential studies of the period is Black et al. (1972), which examines prices of New York Stock Exchange–listed shares from 1926 through 1966 and documents that something approaching a linear relationship exists between the beta of CAPM and equity returns. Fama and MacBeth (1973) also look at NYSE data, this time for 1926 through 1968, and reach a similar conclusion: CAPM does a pretty good, if not perfect job of explaining the connection between risk and return.

But even the supporters of CAPM recognized some glitches. Low beta stocks appear to earn higher returns than the beta predicts while high beta stocks deliver returns that are lower than the model's expectations. That has remained true in subsequent studies over the years, including Fama and French (2004), as shown in **FIGURE 3.1.**

Is this limitation of CAPM a smoking gun that dooms the theory to irrelevance? Not necessarily. Black (1972) argues that a less-than-perfect fit between CAPM's forecast and what the market delivers isn't an automatic death sentence for the model's

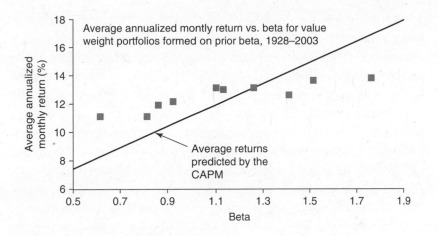

**Figure 3.1    Theory Versus Results**

Source: "The Capital Asset Pricing Model: Theory and Evidence," by Eugene F. Fama and Kenneth R. French, *Journal of Economic Perspectives*, 2004 (Vol. 18, No. 3), p. 33.

practical value. The reason is that a true risk-free asset, one of CAPM's assumptions, doesn't exist. Assuming a true risk-free security is useful for modeling purposes because it delivers a sharper focus on dissecting the risk-reward dynamic. But as a practical matter, the absence of a truly riskless security creates difficulties for empirically testing CAPM. Short-term government securities come close to the definition of a risk-free asset, but they fall short of the ideal. If the real-world proxy for the "risk-free" asset isn't fully liberated from risk, testing CAPM with actual prices may dispense skewed results in trying to find a seamless link between CAPM and the marketplace.

Black (1972) adjusts for the snag and reports that CAPM works rather well after all. That is, adding a restriction on borrowing and lending improves CAPM's description of risk and return. The adjustment focuses on the fact that investors trying to obtain an aggressive risk posture in their portfolios soon run up against the practical limits of borrowing. CAPM assumes that investors can borrow at no cost, which of course isn't true. The result, Black (1972) advises, is that aggressive investors are forced to own more high beta stocks than they otherwise would if borrowing costs were zero.

Imagine a world where borrowing was cost free. In that case, leveraged portfolios would be more accessible. Recall that MPT advises that everyone should own the market portfolio, but in different ratios relative to cash—a recognition of the varying risk tolerances among investors. More aggressive investors should own more of the market portfolio compared with the cash component. But what happens once the market portfolio comprises 100 percent of the investment portfolio? How does an investor increase risk exposure from there? Engineering a higher degree of risk at that point demands holding a leveraged market portfolio, according to MPT. But in the real world, leverage comes at a price, usually a fairly steep one. Adjusting for this fact leads to the view that investors bid up prices of high beta securities as a substitute for risk-free borrowing and levered portfolios. In turn, that real-world limit lessens returns for high beta stocks and raises returns for low beta stocks, relative to CAPM's predictions.

Such fine-tuning looks persuasive to some for salvaging CAPM, but the idea that we need to tweak the model to make it fit the facts looks damning to others. As the 1970s rolled on, researchers began emphasizing CAPM's limitations, a task that gained momentum in the 1980s. The critiques, though they take many forms, usually share a common theme: questioning the model's simplistic elevation of general market risk—beta—as the dominant factor for explaining asset pricing.

After years of investigations, it's now widely recognized that CAPM doesn't fully describe risk and return, and no amount of tweaking convinces skeptics. Deciding if this is a lethal blow, or simply a recognition that absolutes don't exist in finance, is the source of a vibrant and ongoing debate.

Then again, the terms of the debate may be inherently flawed. By some accounts, the premise of using CAPM to predict returns is misguided. Karnosky (1993) asserts that "CAPM has never claimed to be able to forecast expected returns. It is not a trading mechanism, and it does not indicate how to manage a portfolio actively." Rather, "CAPM attempts to explain relationships among variables over time. It is a framework that attempts to define the equilibrium conditions that dominate asset pricing. As such, it provides the foundation for development of models that generate expected future asset prices and returns."[1]

Regardless of how it's used, CAPM, at best, is a theory that only partly captures the dynamic of price formation. Supporters argue that the model's estimate of reality is close enough to make CAPM a practical, if imperfect tool for the design and management of investment portfolios. The fact that market-capitalization-based index funds have proven so hard to beat lends credence to the idea that CAPM captures a basic truism about the functioning of capital markets.

Yet there's no question that CAPM makes compromises, some of which look absurd. In a CAPM world, investors only care about price volatility and returns. There's also an assumption of a tax-free world where investors can borrow as much as they please at the prevailing risk-free rate, which is to say at a rate that's unavailable. Ludicrous as those rules seem, they don't necessarily invalidate the theory. If they did, market-cap-based index funds would have long ago imploded in the face of superior competition from active managers seeking to beat the market, which is to say market-capitalization benchmarks. In fact, quite the opposite has occurred. Indexing has proven durable. As such, the idea that indexing has succeeded in spite of CAPM is to misinterpret the vital link that binds one to the other.

Still, no one should confuse CAPM, or any other theory, with a thorough, definitive, and comprehensive explanation of the capital markets. Every stylized description of securities pricing is flawed, and CAPM is no different. Deciding if the flaws are grave, or simply marginal, is the task.

In that sense, choosing an investment strategy is effectively picking a model whose flaws are tolerable. Everyone must play the game, so it's unsurprising that everyone claims that their choice is enlightened. The truth is that no one can declare total victory since investing ultimately demands picking one's theoretical poison and rationalizing why the results fall short of the ideal.

## Refining CAPM

Critics charge that explaining risk and return is more nuanced than CAPM suggests. That persuades some to argue that the model should be abandoned entirely. The alternative view, and arguably a more reasonable and productive view, is that CAPM, while flawed, embraces a fundamental truth about finance and so there's value in trying to enhance it. In fact, much of the progress in recent decades for improving our understanding of markets and portfolio strategy has come from the various efforts to improve the basic intuition of CAPM and, by extension, the lessons of MPT.

An early reinterpretation of CAPM tells us that we should expect that there's more than a single market beta behind risk and return. Recognizing the presence of additional factors doesn't annul CAPM's basic reasoning, although it suggests that the standard model requires adjustment. That's the message in the intertemporal capital asset pricing model (ICAPM) of Merton (1973). The original CAPM and ICAPM are equivalent in the sense that both assume that investors prefer high expected returns and low risk (low volatility), but the two part ways from there.

A key difference is that ICAPM recognizes that investment opportunities are always in flux, so long-term investors are concerned about the potential for future shocks that can ambush the best-laid plans of portfolio strategy. That's in contrast to CAPM, a static model that expects a fixed set of risk and return opportunities. ICAPM knows better and permits investors to hedge their portfolios against adverse and unexpected events that can take a toll on investment expectations.

Merton (1973) infers that some other factor or factors, are relevant for portfolio design, in part by looking to previous studies showing that beta doesn't fully explain risk and return. Citing Black et al. (1972), Merton observes "they found that portfolios constructed to have zero covariance with the market had average returns that significantly exceeded the riskless rate which suggests that there is (at least) another factor besides the market that systematically affects the returns on securities."[2]

In the original CAPM, investors want higher returns and lower standard deviations (risk) for their portfolios, and they seek to optimize the two variables at the end of the current investment period. ICAPM embraces this goal, but it acknowledges that investors care about other risks too, and beyond the end of the current period. In the language of ICAPM, investors focus on return and risk as well as how state variables—labor income, investment opportunities, etc.—will vary with their wealth through time.

To keep things simple, Merton (1973) uses interest rates as a proxy for the shifting landscape of risk. "Unfortunately, the assumption of a constant investment opportunity set is not consistent with the facts, since there exists at least one element of the opportunity set which is directly observable," Merton observes, taking aim at CAPM. "Namely, the interest rate, and it is definitely changing stochastically over time."[3]

The assumption only begins to consider the full range of factors that define risk through time. For instance, we can observe that investors usually worry about the threat of recession—the risk of losing one's job and the possibility that labor income may be reduced or eliminated. In light of this concern, investors may tolerate a bit less return in their portfolio (relative to a classic CAPM portfolio) if it holds up better during economic contractions. On that basis, an ICAPM-inspired view of portfolio design is one that maximizes expected return while minimizing volatility *and* the risk of recession. There are now three factors to optimize rather than two in CAPM.

In fact, ICAPM allows for four, five, or more factors. It does so by recognizing the shifting of opportunities and risk through time and permitting portfolio adjustments for hedging risk. With enhanced flexibility for assessing risk beyond return volatility, ICAPM anticipates the portfolio techniques of twenty-first century diversification strategies that use assets in addition to stocks and bonds. So-called alternative betas, some of which have low or even negative correlation with stocks and bonds, have been shown to bring additional diversification benefits to a standard investment strategy. Examples of alternative betas that have become popular in recent years include REITs, commodities, inflation-indexed bonds, currencies, and various trading systems such as long-short equity, merger arbitrage, and other strategies favored by hedge funds.

Merton's research on ICAPM is laden with dense mathematics, although buried in the formulas is a blueprint for extending the original CAPM into a world of multiple betas that are continuously managed over time. "Merton's paper [on ICAPM] inspired me the most to say that CAPM doesn't have to be one factor," says Harindra de Silva, president of Los Angeles money manager Analytic Investors. "It can be multiple factors, and our challenge is to find as many of the systematic factors as we can to build portfolios that are diversified across all these factors beyond the market factor." He adds that "what we call factors are basically other betas."[4]

Sharpe also recognizes that CAPM is only an approximation of the real world, an observation that opens the door for acknowledging that there's more to investing than the standard market beta. As he says in a 1998 interview, "I'd be the last to argue that only one factor drives market correlation. There are not as many factors as some think, but there's certainly more than one." CAPM, he explains, is "a very simple, very strong set of assumptions that got a nice, clean, pretty result. And then almost immediately, we all said, let's bring more complexity into it to try to get closer to the real world. People went on—myself and others—to what I call 'extended' capital asset pricing models, in which expected return is a function of beta, taxes, liquidity, dividend yield, and other things people might care about."[5]

CAPM, in other words, evolves, and so it also inspires and otherwise compels investors to think about investing in terms of what works, what doesn't, and why. As a basic framework, it has proven itself a durable standard for deeper explorations of how securities markets function. As Sharpe explains,

> The CAPM was and is a theory of equilibrium. Why should anyone expect to earn more by investing in one security as opposed to another? You need to be compensated for doing badly when times are bad. The security that is going to do badly just when you need money when times are bad is a security you have to hate, and there had better be some redeeming virtue or else who will hold it? That redeeming virtue has to be that in normal times you expect to do better. The key insight of the capital asset pricing model is that higher expected returns go with the greater risk of doing badly in bad times. Beta is a measure of that. Securities or asset classes with high betas tend to do worse in bad times than those with low betas.[6]

## Rolling in Betas

Before CAPM's debut in the mid-1960s, the evidence suggesting that risk arises from multiple sources began peeking out from the literature. In 1960, four years ahead of Sharpe's seminal CAPM paper, a study by S. F. Nicholson was published in the *Financial Analysts Journal* that previewed the future of research by reporting an apparent free lunch: stocks with low price-to-earnings (P/E) ratios generated higher returns than high-P/E stocks.[7]

The idea that shares sometimes traded at discounts, which led to above-average gains, wasn't new in 1960. Graham and Dodd

(1934) told us as much decades earlier. Value investing, *Security Analysis* advises, offers the potential for market-beating performance, but it takes work. Indeed, this rather lengthy and detailed book is testament to the complication and subjectivity of value investing as it applies to stock picking.

But the notion that a systematically above-average return was available for everyone, with minimal effort, was something new. Nicholson (1960) identifies a recurring source of risk premia that, while not necessarily present in every low-P/E stock, seems to exist in a cross-section of shares that are trading at relatively modest levels compared to earnings.

The prospect of looking for an abnormally productive source of risk premia proved to be a resilient research focus in the years ahead. Basu (1977), for example, revisits the relationship between price and earnings and finds that low-P/E stocks produce substantially higher returns compared with high-P/E stocks between 1957 and 1971. Basu's paper also counsels that the higher return from low-P/E stocks isn't fully explained by the beta of CAPM, suggesting that something other than market risk is driving equity return. If beta is the only relevant risk factor, there should be no difference in performance among stocks simply because of the variation in P/E. Yet Basu's research suggests otherwise.

The P/E ratio was the opening bid for raising doubts about CAPM and the one-factor model. Two years after Basu's paper, another study described a link between high dividend yield in equities and higher returns.[8]

The trend of reconsidering CAPM went into overdrive in 1976, when Yale's Steve Ross developed a new model for explaining risk and return.[9] The arbitrage pricing theory (APT) is an alternate methodology to CAPM's more restrictive, simplified view of asset pricing. CAPM tells us that securities prices are mostly a function of market risk (beta) and any remaining influences are lumped together as one non-market factor (alpha). The world of asset pricing is more complicated, according to APT, which advises that numerous betas are driving asset pricing. But while APT puts no limits on factors, the model is governed by a common force that determines prices: arbitrage, which brings any mispricing back into line with its expected return.[10]

With no formal constraint on factors, APT embraces a more nuanced view of asset pricing. Its broader perspective is arguably closer to reality compared with CAPM. But with a wider palette of betas comes new challenges. APT allows for multiple factors in pricing securities, but the factors are unidentified, leaving investors with the task of deciding which ones to accept or reject. APT's ambition, then, is also its challenge since recognizing more factors increases complexity and raises the stakes for figuring out what's relevant and what's not. A similar challenge awaits in Merton's ICAPM. In practice, however, the possibility of recognizing multiple betas isn't necessarily overwhelming because only a handful is meaningful.

APT factors generally fall into two broad categories: macroeconomic and company-specific. The leading macro influences include economic growth and interest rates. For company-specific factors, the key influences are earnings and variables that relate to a firm's operations, such as oil prices for an oil company or changes in consumer spending for retailers.

In the 1980s, the evidence that securities pricing was more complicated than a CAPM view of the world suggested continued to pile up. Banz (1981) identified a performance premium in small-company stocks, which generate substantially higher returns compared with the stock market generally. Between 1931 and 1974, the study advises, returns from stocks with low capitalizations deliver a robust return premium relative to large-cap companies.

A new line of attack in the war on the efficient market hypothesis and, by extension, CAPM, was offered by Shiller (1981), who details the evidence that stock market volatility is excessive relative to what can be justified by the market's dividends. "We have seen that measures of stock price volatility over the past century appear to be far too high—five to thirteen times too high—to be attributed to new information about future real dividends ...."[11]

Throughout the 1980s, the assault on CAPM expands. There appears to be no end to the possibilities for identifying new factors that raise questions about the model's validity. Rosenberg et al. (1985) finds a relationship between relatively strong performance in equities and low book-to-market ratios. Bhandari (1988) identifies leverage as a crucial source of return. And Jegadeesh (1990) shows that short-term price momentum is a key driver of equity returns. Stocks with relatively high returns in the recent past are more likely to post relatively high returns in the near-term future. The study also reports that shares with low or negative returns in the recent past tend to remain poor performers in the short-term future.

Two years later, several threads of the accumulating empirical research on equity pricing were consolidated and reconsidered in Fama and French (1992), the first in a series of papers by the authors that are among the more influential bodies of work for understanding how securities prices are determined beyond CAPM's interpretation. The basic conclusion: stock risk is "multidimensional," and the extra dimensions are primarily the small-company factor and the value factor (inexpensively priced shares relative to book value).

The small-cap value factor generally seems to explain much of the formerly anomalous behavior identified in the research literature. More generally, adding small cap and value to CAPM's market beta provides a richer explanation for describing what's driving securities prices, Fama and French (1993, 1996) advise. The implication for portfolio strategy is that the degree of emphasizing, or minimizing, small-cap and value stocks, along with exposure to the market generally, is the basis for determining risk and return for most if not all long-only equity portfolios.

In the wake of the Fama and French 3-factor model (FF3), much of the previous research that identifies various sources of outperformance relative to the overall market is rendered moot, analysts explain. Other than the momentum factor of Jegadeesh (1990), FF3 is considered a robust solution for identifying the primary drivers of equity return and risk. The strategic story is further enhanced after a follow-up study in Fama and French (1993) that considers bonds and stocks, resulting in a five-factor model that adds fixed-income maturity risk and default risk to FF3 for explaining portfolio returns.

Even more intriguing is the prospect that the small-cap value factor may reflect critical but unidentified state variables in Merton's ICAPM, or the unnamed factors of Ross's arbitrage pricing theory, according to Fama and French (2004).[12] If so, this is a key insight because it means that small-cap value is a true risk factor rather than an ephemeral trading effect that can be arbitraged away or a mispricing born of irrational investor behavior.

One implication is that CAPM isn't irrelevant after all, although it requires some assistance—the Fama and French 3-factor model, for instance—for describing how securities are priced.

Initially, the small-cap value beta identified by Fama and French is greeted with quite a bit of skepticism. For example, some argue that survivorship bias is really the force behind the apparent small-cap value factor.[13] Another complaint is that the limited time frame in the original research raises the possibility that the results are dependent on data mining, in which case small-cap value may be a nonrecurring source of excess return tied to a specific time period. If you look hard enough, you'll find almost anything you want to find, runs this line of reasoning. Since Fama and French (1992) looked only at 1963–1990 data, it was open to criticism that the time period was a fluke.

In fact, virtually all empirical studies are subject to the data mining critique, and to some extent the criticism can never be fully dismissed, regardless of how much data is analyzed. The future, after all, can always surprise. Searching through market history for satisfaction to explain the laws of asset pricing can mislead, even if the test results suggest clarity. One problem is that different historical periods have a habit of dispensing different results.

Sharpe warns against studying a particular stretch of time as a shortcut to the truth. "It's been my experience that if you don't like the results of an empirical study, just wait until somebody uses a different period or a different country or a different part of the market," he says. To minimize deception from data mining, he recommends developing investment strategies inspired by theory "that proceeds from sensible assumptions, is carefully and logically constructed, and is broadly consistent with the data." In other words, "You want to avoid empirical results that have no basis in theory and [that] blindly say, 'It seemed to have worked in the past, so it will work in the future.' That's especially true of anything that involves a way to get something for nothing. You're not likely to get something for nothing as long as you've got investors looking to get something for nothing."[14]

Good advice, though the Fama-French 3-factor model looks less like a free lunch than a true source of risk. There are at least two reasons: economic logic and additional confirmation in follow-up studies.

Intuition suggests that the small-cap value factor is compensation for economic risk. Small-cap value stocks tend to be the most vulnerable of companies, which makes them particularly risky during economic recessions. No wonder, then, that small-cap value may suffer bigger losses compared with the broad market in bear markets.

That's the price one pays for earning a relatively higher risk premia over multiple business cycles.

That seems to be the case when we review the market indices. For example, the Russell Small Cap Value Index reports a 6.0 percent annualized total return for the fifteen years through February 2009, well above the 5.1 percent for large cap stocks, as defined by the Russell 1000 Index, according to Morningstar Principia.

The small-cap value factor holds up well over much longer periods too, outperforming U.S. stocks overall as well as other style slices of the domestic equity market (large-cap value, small-cap growth, etc.) for 1928–2008.[15]

The notion of a risk premium tied to small-cap value stocks also looks persuasive if we consider how this stratum of equities fared against the broad market following recessions, a period when small-cap value might be expected to shine as the economy recovers. As an example, consider **TABLE 3.1**, which reports the return difference for the Russell 2000 Value Index (a small-cap value benchmark of U.S. stocks) less the performance of Russell 1000 (a benchmark of broadly defined large-cap U.S. stocks). Following each of three recessions (dates defined by National Bureau of Economic Research) for 1982 through 2001, small-cap value earned substantially higher returns than the broad market. For instance, for the year after the 1981–1982 recession ended in November 1982, Russell 2000 Value gained 41% versus 25.1% for the Russell 1000—a return premium of 15.9% in favor of small-cap value.

The economic logic of the small-cap premium isn't likely to be lost on investors. Although everyone prefers higher rather than lower

Table 3.1    Post-Recession Small-Cap Value Equity Premiums

Small-cap value excess % returns from end of recessions, as per NBER, based on Russell 2000 Value less Russell 1000 total return performances.

| Final Recession Month | 1-Year Return Spread After Recession's End | 3-Year* Return Spread After Recession's End |
|---|---|---|
| Nov-82 | 15.9 | 3.7 |
| Mar-91 | 10.8 | 10.2 |
| Nov-01 | 14.3 | 14.5 |

*Annualized.
Source: Author's calculations using data from Morningstar Principia.

returns, the burden of holding small-cap value may be especially costly during periods of general economic distress. These shares, after all, tend to be companies that, for one reason or another, are out of favor with investors, as suggested by their relatively low prices compared with book value. Adding to the potential burden is the fact that many small-cap value stocks are thinly traded. As such, their illiquidity makes them unattractive to most investors. These characteristics aren't likely to fade away. Even though the word is out on small-cap value, periods of economic stress typically encourage (or re-encourage) investors to seek relative safety. Human nature, in other words, is likely to keep the small-cap value premium intact through time.

Of course, investors shouldn't be complacent. Small-cap value stocks can and do endure periods of underperformance relative to the market. Expecting this source of return premia to arrive consistently, in a timely manner, is expecting too much. In the 1990s, for example, the extraordinary bull market in large-cap stocks meant that the small-cap value premium was missing in action for a time, convincing some observers to declare that the Fama and French 3-factor model was dead. But that was premature, as suggested by the return of the small-cap value premium at times in the twenty-first century.

What's more, small-cap value has held up under additional academic scrutiny. Chan et al. (1995) reject the idea that the small-cap value factor is a product of survivorship bias. Meanwhile, Barber and Lyon (1997) show that data mining and survivorship bias don't infect the small-cap value premia. And Fama and French (1998) extend their analysis to international markets and find evidence that the small-cap value premium exists outside the U.S. In addition, the U.S. dataset for small-cap value stocks has been extended back to the 1920s, revealing that the original findings in Fama and French (1992) remain intact when viewed over longer periods.

## What Does It All Mean?

In the four decades–plus of analyzing CAPM, financial economists have uncovered a few fundamental facts. That starts with the evidence that CAPM is less than a perfect model for describing the behavior of capital markets. The market beta is important, perhaps even dominant, but it's hardly the only factor. Notably, small-cap and value factors appear to be important drivers of stock returns, too. For bonds, much of the return premia appears to be linked to the degree of maturity risk (long vs. short maturities) and default risk (corporate bonds vs. government bonds). If you want to understand what's driving a stock/bond asset allocation, the five-factor model of Fama and French is a powerful tool.

Does that mean it's time to abandon CAPM? Not quite. As Jagannathan and Wang (1996) counsel, "we have to keep in mind that the CAPM, like any other model, is only an approximation of reality. Hence, it would be rather surprising if it turns out to be '100 percent accurate.' The interesting question is not whether a particular asset-pricing model can be rejected by the data. The question is: 'How inaccurate is the model?'" [16]

Arguably, the answer is more encouraging than some critics allow. Is that a subjective view of CAPM's relevance? Perhaps, although it's also true that absolute objectivity in evaluating CAPM is probably impossible at this point. Certainly no one will confuse the views of financial economists generally as reflecting a consensus one way or another when it comes to the subject of CAPM—even after more than forty years of studying, debating, and testing.

Where does that leave us when it comes to the task of building portfolios? In pretty good shape, as it turns out, as detailed in coming chapters. Years of testing CAPM and investing generally have led to a broader understanding of markets and portfolio theory. There's still no secret formula or magic shortcut that delivers easy success in the money game. But the academic literature has imparted a valuable guide for thinking about investing and what constitutes intelligent portfolio design.

That starts with the recognition that risk can't be avoided, so it should be managed in the service of an investor's strategic goals. That's good news since risk can be controlled and predicted to a greater degree compared with trying to forecast and manage returns directly.

Does that mean the market is inefficient? No, as the next chapter explains. The market is still efficient generally, especially over the long run, but that doesn't mean it's entirely unpredictable, as researchers have discovered. That sounds like a conflict of terms, but it's not. In fact, it's the basis for enlightened portfolio strategy. A growing body of research tells us that these two states of market behavior can and do coexist. Explaining why that's so, and what it means for portfolio strategy, is at the heart of how modern portfolio theory has evolved and why it's still relevant for investing.

## Chapter Notes

1. Karnosky (1993), p. 56.

2. Merton (1973), p. 883.

3. Ibid., pp. 878–879.

4. Interview with author, 2007.

5. Burton (1998).

6. Ibid.

7. Nicholson (1960).

8. Litzenberger and Ramaswamy (1979).

9. Ross (1976).

10. APT is built on the theory of arbitrage, which is known as the law of one price. That is, any two identical investments cannot trade simultaneously at different prices. For example, let's say that gold is trading at $500 an ounce in New York and $505 in London at the same time. The price difference allows an arbitrageur to sell gold at the higher London price and buy at the lower price in New York, producing a $5 profit. What's more, that's a risk-free profit since the underlying asset is identical and trades at two different prices. But the theory of arbitrage says that market forces will narrow the spread and thereby eliminate the arbitrage opportunity. Market forces, in other words, adjust prices to eliminate the availability of risk-free trades.

11. Shiller (1981), pp. 433–434.

12. Fama and French (2004), pp. 37–41.

13. Survivorship bias refers to calculating returns without properly accounting for the firms that have failed, in which case the companies aren't accurately represented, if at all, in a database and so the reported returns are erroneously high.

14. Burton (1998).

15. *Ibbotson* (2009), p. 124.

16. Jagannathan and Wang (1996), p. 36.

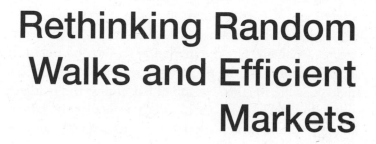

Chapter 4

# Rethinking Random Walks and Efficient Markets

JUDGING BY SAMUELSON's and Fama's seminal 1965 papers on the efficient market hypothesis (EMH), investing is simple. Perhaps too simple.

The simplicity arises from the idea that price changes are random. They're random because the primary catalyst behind fluctuating prices—new information—arrives haphazardly. News is unpredictable, erratic, and more or less arbitrary in its debut on the world stage. The best estimate of future prices, then, is the current market price. Some of the forthcoming news will raise prices, some of it will lower prices, and some will elicit mostly yawns. But if we can't routinely predict the news, then hedging our bets by riding with the market is attractive in the long run.

If the fundamental driver of new prices arrives randomly—news—it follows that price changes will be random. As we learned in a previous chapter, Fama's research tells us that a careful study of the evidence suggests no less.[1] Meanwhile, Samuelson (1965) lays out a proof that "properly anticipated prices fluctuate randomly."

By that standard, there's no point in trading for reasons based solely on price forecasts. The exception is if an investor is in possession of relevant information not generally known to the market. Otherwise, if expected prices are as likely to rise or fall, and if no one has reliable insight about the future, intelligent investors should favor middling results over time. In that case, logic suggests buying and holding the market from the start and forgoing all the associated costs and risks of trading. That is, bet on the long-run results of market beta. In a market that's truly random, this will be the superior investment strategy for most investors over time.

That would certainly make life easier for designing portfolio strategy, namely: buy the market portfolio and hold it for the long run. By definition, the market portfolio holds all the assets in their market-value weights. As an added bonus, the market portfolio is self-adjusting because each asset's influence is a function of its market value, which determines its weight in the portfolio. Accordingly, owning the market portfolio is a strategy that minimizes, if not eliminates, trading costs, tax consequences, and the burden and expense of analyzing securities and even asset classes.

Yes, that's the best strategy if the market is completely random. By "random" we mean that the return series—the monthly historical returns, for instance—are "normally" distributed à la a bell-curve distribution. Alas, the world isn't quite so simple because market returns aren't perfectly random. As a result, investing is more complicated than a random walk suggests.

## A Slight Complication

Equity returns aren't always normally distributed, and that means that returns aren't stable. Indeed, historical equity returns have been quite volatile—more so than a random walk allows. That implies that investors shouldn't simply buy and hold the market portfolio.

The reasoning starts by recognizing that so-called fat tails distributions are common in the historical record. Markets endure extreme changes at times—both up and down—and these extremes arise more frequently than a random distribution predicts, as a number of researchers have documented over the years. Mandelbrot (1963) shows that a random walk doesn't fully capture the statistical properties of securities prices. Fama (1965a) discusses Mandelbrot's research and the evidence that the random walk doesn't completely explain the behavior of securities prices. That leads EMH's leading advocate, Eugene Fama, to conclude from the start that the non randomness in stock prices appears "indisputable."[2]

Indisputable, perhaps, but many have still chosen to use randomness as a working assumption. Why? Partly because a random walk model, while not strictly accurate, works a fair amount of the time, perhaps even most of the time, as an accounting of market activity. The markets, in other words, are sufficiently random so that dismissing the random walk model completely incurs risk.

Nonetheless, there's also a considerable amount of danger in thinking that the random walk model will always describe market behavior. It doesn't. Markets don't behave according to pure randomness, Mandelbrot and Hudson (2004) remind. "If they did, you should be able to run any market's price records through a computer, analyze the changes, and watch them fall into the approximate 'normality' assumed by Bachelier's random walk. They should cluster about the mean, or average, of no change." But it's not so statistically simple:

> In fact, the bell curve fits reality very poorly. From 1916 to 2003, the daily index movements of the Dow Jones Industrial Average do not spread out on graph paper like a simple bell curve. The far edges flare too high: too many big changes. Theory suggests that over that time, there should be fifty-eight days when the Dow moved more than 3.4 percent; in fact, there were 1001. Theory predicts six days of index swings beyond 4.5 percent; in fact there were 366. And index swings of more than 7 percent should come once every 300,000 years; in fact, the twentieth century saw forty-eight such days.[3]

The statistics speak loud and clear about the limitations of looking at markets through random-walk-tinted glasses. The practical implications for money management, however, may not be so lucid.

Accepting that returns aren't normally distributed all of the time poses a number of statistical challenges for quantitative-oriented strategists intent on modeling market behavior. As Fama (1965a) observes, common statistical tools can be used to great effect for profiling markets if prices follow a random walk. By contrast, modeling prices in a non-random walk environment requires a different and more complex set of statistical measures.

A non-random walk world is not only different from a random walk world, it's also more complicated. There are no obvious or easy quantitative solutions for dealing with non randomness. That hasn't stopped researchers and money managers from trying, but no one should expect that there's a silver-bullet alternative to the classical risk measures developed under the modern portfolio theory umbrella.[4]

Despite the evidence that markets aren't always and purely random, Fama (1965a) isn't convinced that investors should abandon the general assumption of a random walk world and the related statistical metrics, such as standard deviation for measuring price volatility. "Getting along without these familiar tools is not going to be easy, and before parting with them we must be sure that such a drastic step is really necessary."[5]

The preference for favoring a random walk perspective is partly one of convenience. Economists have been "reluctant" to accept the tests showing that stock returns are normally distributed, Fama (1970) reports, "primarily because of the wealth of statistical techniques available for dealing with normal variables and the relative paucity of such techniques for non-normal stable variables."[6] More than three decades after Fama's observation, financial economists have become more flexible in using alternative statistical tools, but the general reluctance remains intact, as the widespread use of standard deviation, for instance, suggests.

Assuming that stocks follow a random walk certainly makes life easier for the quantitatively inclined investor. But given the theory's limits as a full and accurate description of market behavior, does that mean that embracing the random walk as an operating principle nsures failure in portfolio design and management? Not at all, at least not for those who understand the limitations of the random walk and invest accordingly.

Some market strategists argue that over very long periods using annual return data, the stock market's returns are close to being normally distributed. William Bernstein (2002), for example, reviewed annual U.S. stock returns from 1790 through 2000 and advised that the performance distribution approximates a random walk.[7] That is, extreme price changes are quite rare and the more middling returns are more frequent, persuading him to conclude that "the pattern of annual stock returns is almost totally random and unpredictable."[8]

And so, the relationship between return and standard deviation (i.e., risk), which assumes a random distribution of data, is still useful even if it's not a perfect. French et al. (1987), for example, demonstrate a positive relationship between the risk premium for stocks and stock market volatility. That's also clear from looking at a simple history of risk and return for stocks and bonds. **FIGURE 4.1** shows that for the eight decades through 2008, higher return has been associated with higher risk (standard deviation of returns). It's not a seamless connection, but it's a reasonably good description of how markets work in the long run: higher returns are associated with higher standard deviation, or return volatility.

The linkage isn't absolute across every security and every asset class at all times. In the short term we're asking for trouble if we mindlessly predict risk and return based solely on historical standard deviation. Looking at the long sweep of history and thinking that the dynamic will hold over the next week, month, or even next year is expecting too much. But standard deviation remains a prudent rule of thumb for thinking about long-term relationships among asset classes when developing portfolio strategy, assuming we recognize its limits in the short term. Yes, additional analysis is required for designing and managing asset allocation, as later chapters explain. But investors can start with the basic paradigm illustrated in Figure 4.1 for developing some perspective about market behavior among the various asset classes.

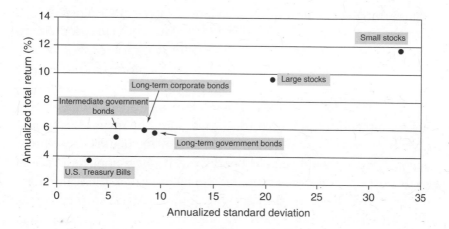

**Figure 4.1    Return and Risk: 1926–2008**

Over the long term, higher return usually comes at the price of higher risk

Source: Author's chart using data from *Ibbotson* (2009).

As Fama (1965b) explains,

> It is unlikely that the random walk hypothesis provides an exact description of the behavior of stock market prices. For practical purposes, however, the [random walk] model may be acceptable even though it does not fit the facts exactly. Thus, although successive price changes may not be strictly independent, the actual amount of dependence may be so small as to be unimportant.[9]

Malkiel (2003) makes a similar observation, explaining that "while the stock market may not be a mathematically perfect random walk, it is important to distinguish statistical significance from economic significance."[10] Identifying non randomness in tests is one thing. The question is whether it's possible to systematically profit from the non randomness, above and beyond what's available from a passive holding of the market and after adjusting for taxes and trading costs.

Unimportant or not, the limits of standard deviation as a descriptive tool are no longer an obscure reference buried in a handful of research papers. In the twenty-first century, Mandelbrot's 1960s-era counsel that markets aren't a pure random walk is widely recognized. "I think everyone accepts that [Mandelbrot's] basic point is true," Fama says in a 2002 interview—even though over longer time frames the market shows a closer relationship to randomness.[11]

A statistician might quibble, but expecting a bell curve for returns over the long run has its uses as a proxy for market behavior. Nonetheless, sophisticated strategists are hungry for more. Unfortunately, a complete and accurate statistical profiling of market behavior offers no practical alternative to the random walk assumption, at least not for most individual investors. To be sure, the quest for identifying a better model for describing and exploiting markets continues, and investors should remain open to using new applications and strategies as they become available. So far, however, the search for a better alternative that's fully accurate *and* pragmatic for the average investor remains elusive. Even Mandelbrot admits the shortcoming. His own efforts, based on fractal modeling of securities behavior, are intriguing and suggest a rich array of possibilities. A variety of other researchers have made headway as well. But the fact remains that a true alternative solution has yet to arrive, nor is it clear that one is imminent, or even possible. "This 'post-modern' finance has yet to yield real success," Mandelbrot admits. "Nobody has hit the jackpot."[12]

## Fluctuating Opportunity... and Risk

Deciding if a random walk does or doesn't define market behavior is more than an academic question. The answer directly influences how we should think about expected returns and risk in the design and management of asset allocation.

If randomness describes market performance, expected returns in the long run are constant. That means that asset allocation should remain static too. For example, if stocks generally are expected to deliver 10 percent annually in a random-walk world, that translates into keeping the appropriate equity allocation for a long-term investor unchanged as well. On the other hand, if the random walk model doesn't completely explain the behavior of prices, expected returns are less than constant, which lays the foundation for asset allocation that's at least partially dynamic and opportunistic.

The stakes are high in determining if the random walk is or isn't accurate, since the answer will dictate a fair amount of portfolio strategy. Fortunately, financial economists continue to shed light on the finer points of how markets operate. But you don't need a PhD in finance to recognize that stability isn't standard operating procedure when it comes to market returns. The basic evidence against the random walk, and the idea that expected returns are stable, is apparent to even a casual observer, argues Jahnke (2004):

> Just how poorly the random-walk model fits empirical data can be gleaned from the Ibbotson Associates publication *Stocks, Bonds, Bills, and Inflation* [a popular annual reference book for financial professionals that surveys historical investment returns and risk]. Among the derived statistics are asset-class returns and standard deviations by decade, and rolling sample mean returns, standard deviations, and correlations. How can anyone looking at the tables and charts not be struck by the lack of stability? How can anyone believe that the average return, standard deviation, and cross correlation computed with all the data, whether inflation adjusted or not, provide accurate forecasts for the purposes of financial planning and asset allocation?[13]

If you look at the stock market's history through the decades, the volatility in performance is obvious, even over long stretches of time. Consider rolling twenty-year holding periods starting in 1926–1945, followed by 1927–1946, 1928–1947, and on up through 1989–2008. Surveying all sixty-four of these twenty-year blocks of time reveals a shifting history of return. The worst twenty-year period is 1929–1948, when the U.S. stock market's annualized total return (measured by the Standard & Poor's 500 Index) is a relatively spare 3.11 percent. By contrast, the best twenty-year stretch is 17.88 percent a year for 1980–1999. The majority of twenty-year periods, however, are relatively middling next to those extremes, generally falling in the 7 percent-to-12 percent range.[14]

If we look at shorter periods—rolling five-year periods, for example—the variability of returns is even greater. Surveying the 1926–2008 sweep of U.S. stock market history through the prism of five-year periods reveals that the best phase is a 28.56 percent annualized gain for 1995–1999; the worst is –12.47 percent for 1928–1932. Once again, the bulk of the gains for most five-year periods is in the middle, or roughly 5 percent to 15 percent annualized returns.[15]

There's no reason to expect that the future will be any less volatile. The underlying forces that influence investment returns are still intact: changing economic, political, and financial conditions, along with varying degrees of investor reactions and expectations. Since all those factors—and more—will remain fluid, so too will market returns. Volatility, we can say with a high degree of confidence, is here to stay. We can argue about the causes and what it means, and when high volatility will dominate versus low volatility. But volatility is a constant.

If future market returns are likely to vary, strategic-minded investors should take the hint and embrace a degree of active asset allocation for exploiting the fluctuations. Easier said than done, of course, because the future is never perfectly clear, nor do expected returns arrive on a predictable time schedule. Yet the caveat also works in reverse: There's no guarantee that a buy-and-hold strategy will best a dynamic one. Much depends on the starting and end dates for determining success or failure, and there's no sure way to optimize this choice either.

What we do know is that future returns will vary, although we can never be certain of the timing or degree. As a result, we need some help in managing our asset allocation by putting the variability into strategic context. The help boils down to looking to a mix of familiar investment strategies that have long been part of the money management canon: contrarianism and value investing. Although these aspects of investing aren't new, their value is strengthened in the wake of a new era of financial economic research published since the 1980s. Investing is still risky, and it always will be. What's changed is our understanding of how the risks interact and behave, which gives us additional insight into managing the risks and thereby improving, if only slightly, our odds for successful investing.

The journey for understanding the deeper insights uncovered about risk and what it means for asset allocation begins by taking a closer look at the efficient markets hypothesis (EMH), how it fares with the new research, and what it all means for modern portfolio theory (MPT).

As a preview, both are alive and well, albeit in somewhat modified interpretations relative to their original incarnations in the mid-1960s and early 1970s. Yet many investors in the twenty-first century still equate EMH and MPT with the standards of yore, much as if the state of financial economics was stuck in, say, 1965. The erroneous belief inspires some to abandon EMH and MPT, along with asset allocation and the concept of diversification generally, particularly in the wake of the market upheaval of 2008. That's misguided. EMH and MPT are still relevant because our understanding of these theories has evolved. The evolution isn't widely recognized, or understood, which isn't surprising. As the finance literature has progressed, it has grown more complex.

Perhaps the biggest confusion revolves around the efficient market hypothesis and the random walk theory. Many investors mistakenly associate one with the other, thinking that the two are one and the same. Clearing up this confusion is the first step in understanding how modern portfolio theory has evolved and why its lessons for investing in the twenty-first century are now more valuable than ever.

## Valuation and Reversals

The hints that markets aren't perfectly random have been bubbling for decades. Mandelbrot's research in the 1960s offered a glimpse at the evidence. Another clue early on in the literature comes from Alexander (1961), who demonstrates that non-randomness (and therefore a degree of predictability) reveals itself in the short run and that it coexists with random behavior over longer periods. In addition, as we learned in the previous chapter, so-called anomalies—market returns that aren't explained by conventional finance theory—have been formally studied in the research literature since at least the 1960s.

But it wasn't until the 1980s that the study of anomalies became more than an intriguing but largely obscure field of inquiry. An early paper that helped launch the new era is Shiller (1981), who finds that stock market volatility exceeds the level implied by dividend changes. His paper's title summarizes the point by asking: "Do Stock Prices Move Too Much to Be Justified by Subsequent Changes in Dividends?" No, the study concludes. LeRoy and Porter (1981) also assert that stock market prices appear to be excessively volatile relative to the underlying fundamentals of publicly traded corporations.

One interpretation of the excess volatility data is that the market goes to extremes and is therefore "irrational." In other words, speculative bubbles arise from time to time, driving valuations to excessive heights. The process works in reverse during bear markets, when investors become overly pessimistic, which leads to repricing assets far below their intrinsic values. This line of reasoning says that in an efficient market, price changes in the stock market shouldn't be larger than the change in dividends, for example.

Shiller (1981) set off a furious debate in finance that continues to this day. The paper inspired a new generation of researchers to examine market behavior in the context of how prices fluctuate relative to fundamentals. Although it's fair to say that many researchers have published supporting studies, others have taken issue with Shiller's methodology for establishing that stock prices exhibit excess volatility relative to reported dividends. Critics point to a number of perceived flaws, including narrowly defining cash flow as dividends and underestimating expected changes in real (inflation-adjusted) interest rates.[16]

Regardless of one's interpretation of Shiller's study, the extreme behavior of price relative to dividends offers opportunity, at least for investors who have the discipline and skill to muster a degree of value-inspired contrarianism. Rozeff (1984) explains that dividend yields can be used to time purchases. He advises caution about reading too much from specific dividend levels for establishing buy and sell signals. He also warns about the hazards of trying to profit from dividend-yield signals in the short term. Nonetheless, the basic premise, if not exactly original, reflects economic common sense, Rozeff argues:

> My evidence indicates that returns increase *continuously* and monotonically as dividend yield in the prior year increases. My theory that the dividend yield is a measure of the ex ante risk premium explains why this is so. High returns tend to occur when the environment is perceived to be so risky that investors demand a high premium for holding stocks. Low returns tend to occur when the environment is perceived to hold such little risk that investors demand a low risk premium for holding stocks.[17]

Subsequent research also finds that valuation levels are unstable. For example, Summers (1986) observes that market valuations differ substantially and persistently from fundamental values based on the present value of cash flows. Campbell and Shiller (1998) report that the excess volatility documented previously in Shiller (1981) is fundamentally related to return predictability. And Poterba and Summers (1988) document the evidence that stock prices are mean reverting. That is, after a period when returns have exceeded their long-run average, they tend to drop back toward the historical benchmark. The process works in reverse too: when returns have been below average, at some point they begin rising toward the long-run average.

Fama and French (1988) acknowledge the growing evidence that stock returns are predictable, albeit only partially so. Studying autocorrelations (a statistical test to identify if nonrandom behavior exists or not) for stock returns for 1926–1985, they estimate that "25–45 percent of the variation of 3–5-year stock returns is predictable from past returns." In addition, the predictability factor for small stock returns tends to be higher than it is for large stocks.[18]

Shiller (2000) argues in favor of return predictability based on valuation parameters. One example comes by way of a diagram in his book that plots price-to-earnings ratios against subsequent ten-year returns based on buying the S&P Composite Index (a proxy for U.S. stocks) at various P/E ratios. The relationship, which draws on more than one hundred years of market history through 1989, shows a "moderately strong" link between low P/E ratios and relatively high returns, and vice versa. "Our confidence in the relation derives partly from the fact that analogous relations appear to hold for other countries and for individual stocks." Overall, the connection between P/E and return—valuation and subsequent performance— "confirms that long-term investors—investors who can commit their money to an investment for ten full years—do well when prices were low relative to earnings at the beginning of the ten years and do poorly when prices were high at the beginning of the ten years."[19]

Malkiel (2003) tests the idea of using valuation to forecast performance by comparing dividend yields for the U.S. stock market (measured by the S&P 500) for each quarter from 1926 relative to subsequent ten-year total returns through 2001. The result "shows that investors have earned a higher rate of return from the stock market when they purchased a market basket of equities with an initial dividend yield that was relatively high and [earned] relatively low future rates of return when stocks were purchased at low dividend yields."[20]

Valuation, in short, matters, just as Graham and Dodd taught in *Security Analysis*. But dividend yield, as valuable as it's been at times in forecasting future returns, isn't foolproof, Malkiel warns. Seemingly profitable trading strategies ebb and flow in their effectiveness as market-beating strategies over time, he observes. That's no surprise. There can be no sure things when it comes to investing. There are, however, varying degrees of risk and, as a result, varying levels of expected return.

Financial economists generally agree on the basic idea that future returns can and do vary. Why they vary, and what it means for portfolio strategy, remain controversial. The disagreement leads to two main interpretations about why returns fluctuate or, as the economists say, returns mean revert, i.e., high returns lead to low or negative returns, which then leads to high returns.

Some analysts assert that mean reversion, and the associated fluctuation in valuation levels and returns, is the direct by-product of investor irrationality. This view falls under the so-called behavioral school of thought in finance, which argues that stocks and other assets become overvalued/undervalued at times. Why? Because investors make investment decisions that are disconnected from the underlying economic fundamentals.

Looking to speculative passions for insight into the nature of market volatility is hardly a new area of study. Charles Mackay's *Extraordinary Popular Delusions and the Madness of Crowds* remains a standard read on the topic of crowd behavior and investment crazes ever since it was first published in 1841. In the twentieth century, British economist John Maynard Keynes refers to "animal spirits," or the shifting passions and moods of investors, as the dominant element in market pricing in his celebrated tome of 1936, *The General Theory of Employment, Interest and Money*.

The modern era offers a library of choice in the study of financial and economic bubbles and how they relate to investor psychology. Among the more popular treatments is a theory from hedge fund legend George Soros, who offers his "theory of reflexivity," which asserts that investors' perceptions of markets alter market conditions, and the shift further changes investors' perceptions, and so the cycle goes around and around.[21] Another twist on the bubble idea comes from Taleb (2005), who argues that extreme events that are generally unexpected tend to occur with more frequency than the crowd assumes. Meanwhile, formal academic inquiry abounds.[22]

Certainly the behavioral finance view of asset pricing can't be dismissed. The full body of research for this line of analysis in its modern form is deep and broad, a by-product of decades of work by acclaimed economists and researchers. Some even manage money based on behavioral finance research and reportedly have done quite well. One example: Fuller and Thaler, a San Mateo, California–based institutional money management firm that seeks to profit from so-called behavioral biases in financial markets. One of Fuller and Thaler's principals is Professor Richard Thaler, professor of behavioral finance at the University of Chicago.[23]

Undoubtedly, this branch of economics deepens our understanding of investing. At the same time, there's disagreement on whether behavioral finance has a monopoly on explaining markets and pricing behavior, or if it's even practical as an investment tool. Clearly, there are challenges to consider in terms of implementing a sophisticated behavioral-based investment strategy, particularly for the average investor.

At its core, behavioral finance extends and expands the premise that greed and fear are at the root of all market behavior and that those mood swings cycle to extremes on a semi-regular basis. As a result, behavioral finance creates a new framework focused on investor psychology for concluding that markets are inefficient and investor behavior is irrational.

Or so economists and money managers of this persuasion say. Yet the strategic lessons for managing portfolios based on the evidence of varying return premia and its partial predictability are the same regardless of whether markets are efficient or not. If expected returns fluctuate, and the variation is partly predictable, there's a case for adjusting asset allocation to take advantage of the shifting opportunities as they become available. That's true if you embrace behavioral finance or favor an updated view of market efficiency.

How does all of this fit in with the evidence that the random walk model isn't fully accurate as a description of market behavior? Superficially it suggests that markets aren't efficient. But let's not be hasty. As we'll discuss, the evidence in favor of a dynamic approach to asset allocation doesn't kill the efficient market hypothesis. In fact, the two seem to complement one another. To explain this nuance, we need to take a closer look at why EMH's viability isn't dependent on the random walk model.

## Efficiency Without Random Walks

Many observers of the financial scene equate a random walk with the efficient market hypothesis, mistakenly thinking that the two are one and the same. Under that flawed assumption, any questions and limitations that apply to the random walk hypothesis negatively reflect on the feasibility of EMH. But contrary to popular perception, the two aren't identical. The distinction permits us to question or even reject the random walk model without condemning the efficient market hypothesis.

Consider the perspective of Lo and MacKinlay (1999), who provide some of the more compelling research of recent vintage in favor of the idea that markets are *not* random walks. The book republishes papers under the title *A Non-Random Walk Down Wall Street*, an obvious counterpoint to Burton Malkiel's best-selling *A Random*

*Walk Down Wall Street* (originally published in 1973), which was the first book to make the case for index-based investing to a mass audience. In the newer book, Lo and MacKinlay outline the evidence that stock prices don't walk the random walk. They also state that "these results do not necessarily imply that the stock market is inefficient or that prices are not rational assessments of 'fundamental' values."[24]

The idea that the market may be partly predictable *and* price assets efficiently sounds contradictory. Under the original outline of EMH, as per Fama (1965a) and Samuelson (1965), predictability and efficiency are generally incompatible in that one or the other prevails. But the old EMH said that prices are random, which means that price patterns don't exist in the short term, at least not sufficiently to offer robust trading profits.

But after several decades of additional research, we now have a more nuanced view of markets, and that view allows for both efficiency and predictability (up to a point) under the same theoretical roof. Fama and French (1988) advise that the predictability of long-horizon returns, while it may be the result of irrational pricing bubbles, "can also result from time-varying equilibrium expected returns generated by rational pricing in an efficient market."[25] How so? One explanation is that investors discount stock prices in relation to expected dividends and that the discounting evolves to reflect changing economic and financial conditions. In that case, current prices may be reassessed because of a change in expected returns for the near term (perhaps because of a change in interest rates or some other variable) without a commensurate change in expected dividends or long-term expected returns.

Malkiel (2003) argues that predictability by way of dividend yield isn't necessarily inconsistent with efficiency. He hints that shifting economic conditions generally may be the underlying source of changes in market valuations. "Dividend yields of stocks tend to be high when interest rates are high, and they tend to be low when interest rates are low. Consequently, the ability of initial yields to predict returns may simply reflect the adjustment of the stock market to general economic conditions."[26]

The idea of pricing stocks by discounting expected cash flows boasts a long history, including the value investing techniques of Graham and Dodd (1934) and the dividend discount model of

Williams (1938). Modigliani and Miller (1958) offer a related but more generalized economic framework for seeing equity returns as a function of discounting the cost of capital. In this context, a firm's cost of capital is the expected return for its shares. As a result, it's certainly rational to adjust expected returns as discount rates change, which can shift for any number of reasons, such as a change in risk tolerance, a reassessment of the economic outlook, or a rise or fall in interest rates.

Market efficiency and predictability aren't incompatible after all. Unsurprisingly, not everyone agrees, and so the debate about efficiency rolls on, and probably always will. One reason is that proving or disproving efficiency directly is probably impossible, thanks to the joint-hypothesis problem.

When critics cite damning evidence against EMH, it's unclear if the source is the market itself or the pricing model that's used to identify the apparent inefficiency. Fama (1991) explains that "market efficiency per se is not testable. It must be tested jointly with some model of equilibrium—an asset-pricing model," such as the capital asset pricing model or the arbitrage pricing model. "We can only test whether information is properly reflected in prices in the context of a pricing model that defines the meaning of 'properly.' As a result, when we find anomalous evidence on the behavior of returns, the way it should be split between market inefficiency or a bad model of market equilibrium is ambiguous."[27]

Is the market inherently inefficient? Or do we simply need a better pricing model to identify the efficiency? It's difficult to say for sure. If your pricing model is broken, it's going to be impossible to use it to make definitive conclusions about the nature of the market. But how would you know if your model's broken? There are no easy answers because there is no neutral and universally accepted way to assess pricing models. Even when there's consensus, it may not be the smoking gun, pro or con, that it appears to be. "Academics largely agree on the facts that emerge from the tests [that raise questions about EMH], even when they disagree about their implications for efficiency," Fama notes.[28]

That's a reminder that moving beyond MPT as an investing framework isn't easy and why adjusting it, rather than throwing it out entirely, remains so compelling. If EMH can't be summarily dismissed, neither can MPT. Proving a negative, in other words, is difficult.

Some economists have called for a truce of sorts by arguing that the terms of the debate should evolve to reflect a more nuanced view of EMH. Economist Paul Samuelson, one of the intellectual fathers of EMH, has observed that markets can be simultaneously microefficient *and* macroinefficient. "Markets are becoming more microefficient," he says. "Pricing of securities, such as pricing a convertible one to straight bonds or equities, will improve. We have fast computers, bigger databases, better regulation.... But in terms of macroefficiency, pricing the Standard & Poor's 500 stock index or the Wilshire 5000 stock index, markets won't stay close to a predictive value. There will still be big swings above and below a fundamental value. I don't see any signs of any convergence in that."[29]

The observation that the market overall may suffer periods of inefficiency, combined with a simultaneous efficiency in the pricing of individual securities, is what's known as Samuelson's dictum. Jung and Shiller (2005) note that there's "substantial evidence" in favor of Samuelson's dictum.[30]

Meanwhile, Santa Clara University finance professor Meir Statman has written that "market efficiency" has two meanings. One is that investors can't systematically beat the market; the other is that security prices are "rational" in that they reflect only fundamental intrinsic values. He recommends that the finance industry accept that investors can't beat the market, but he also rejects the idea that prices are always at or near fundamental values.[31]

Making distinctions about efficiency dates to Fama (1970), who recognizes three subsets: weak, semi-strong, and strong. Weak form efficiency is a state where prices reflect all known information about securities; semi-strong pricing reflects all public information; prices in strong-form efficiency are based on all information, publicly known or not.

But it all comes back to the dilemma of definitively proving or disproving the idea. Fama (1970) observes, "The definitional statement that in an efficient market prices 'fully reflect' available information is so general that is has no empirically testable implications."[32] Samuelson (1965) also comments that his theorem "is so general that I must confess to having oscillated over the years in my own mind between regarding it as trivially obvious (and almost trivially vacuous) and regarding it as remarkably sweeping."[33]

In fact, Samuelson warns that his theorem "does not prove that actual competitive markets work well."[34]

If proving efficiency is virtually impossible, rejecting it completely isn't any easier. That leaves supporters and skeptics to review the end result: prices. One might assume that studying the historical record would dispense definitive answers, but it's not so simple. There's now a large body of research that demonstrates what some interpret as market inefficiency. This tempts critics to close the book on EMH and declare victory.

But one can argue, as this book does, that the apparent inefficiency calls for embracing a more nuanced view of EMH and MPT. There is quite a bit of evidence showing that expected returns in the market vary through time, and that this variation is quite rational. One reason for thinking it's rational is that the fluctuation of risk premia tends to be common across securities, which implies that the fluctuation is systematic and therefore a reflection of a larger force—the business cycle, for instance—that influences investor behavior.

Alternatively, one can argue that investors price securities irrationally but in a recurring and largely consistent pattern. Perhaps, but the idea that the market reprices risk as economic conditions evolve is hardly inefficient. It's convenient to equate fluctuating dividend yields, to take one example, as prima facie evidence of inefficiency, but labeling such fluctuations inefficient doesn't necessarily make it so. Indeed, some of this is a debate about semantics since the investment implications are the same regardless of whether the time variation of return premia is rational or not.

Critics of EMH are quick to note that the dramatic price swings in the capital and commodity markets in 2008 thoroughly discredit the notion of efficiency. But the only way that could be true is if EMH tells us that prices shouldn't change, or that prices shouldn't change dramatically. EMH says nothing of the kind.

At its core, the EMH asserts that an efficient market generates equilibrium prices—prices that reflect supply matching demand. When buyers and sellers agree on a price, and securities change hands at a given price, the market is in equilibrium, which arises from decisions by investors using the available information up to the time of the trade. Inevitably, the information changes, and the new information will generate new equilibrium prices. When the arrival of new information is chaotic and dramatic, as it is during a financial crisis, the resulting change in equilibrium prices is likely to be volatile. That's hardly evidence that markets are inefficient.

## Rational Versus Random

As for binding EMH to the random walk theory, that's even more of a stretch. Reichenstein and Dorsett (1995) advise that a random walk is but one version of the efficient market hypothesis. Another interpretation of EMH arises from what some call the rational markets story. This notion allows for varying expected returns in the context of an efficient market. The flexibility in expected returns contrasts with stable expected returns via a random walk model. The random walk says that

> ... markets are always in equilibrium, required returns never change, and returns are not predictable. According to the rational markets story, markets are always in equilibrium, but required returns vary through time and long-horizon returns are partially predictable. When required returns are above average, returns during the next few years will likely prove generous, and vice versa. Both the random walk view and rational markets story imply that short-term (weekly and monthly) returns cannot be meaningfully predicted, but they give different opinions about the predictability of long-term (one year and longer) returns.[35]

The source for embracing a degree of dynamic asset allocation is the market itself, suggests Bill Reichenstein, a professor of investments at Baylor University who holds a CFA.[36] When the stock market has fallen over, say, a period of months, he explains that "from this point forward, the risk premium that's embedded in stocks is higher than the risk premium of a few months ago. There's nothing inefficient about that." That doesn't mean that the next three months are going to deliver well-above-average returns, he adds. What it means is that over the next five or ten years, the *expected* return on your stock investment is higher than if you bought equities before the correction.[37]

Even dramatic market events that appear irrational to the casual observer aren't necessarily the by-product of market inefficiency. Take the technology stock bubble of the late-1990s. With the benefit of hindsight, it looks like investors went overboard in assigning high valuations to companies. But that fact alone isn't necessarily proof of irrationality or inefficiency. As Malkiel (2003) reminds,

> ... sharp-penciled professional investors argued that the valuations of high-tech companies were proper. Many of Wall Street's most respected security analysts, including those independent of investment banking arms, were recommending Internet stocks to the firm's institutional and individual clients as being fairly valued. Professional pension fund and mutual fund managers overweighted their portfolios with high-tech stocks.[38]

The analysts were wrong, of course, although clarity and confidence are always obvious in hindsight. Thus the distinction between expected returns and historical returns. Looking backward, we can say with absolute certainty that prices were excessive, fairly valued, or deeply discounted. Looking ahead in real time, however, is invariably risky.

The fact that investors make mistakes isn't necessarily evidence of irrationality. One line of research even explores the seemingly contradictory notion of "rational bubbles" as a possible explanation for what appears to be mindless pricing behavior. In fact, LeRoy (2004) suggests that equating bubbles with irrationality may ultimately be a way of avoiding the harder work of explaining such events.

Hall (2001) studies the idea that what appears to be an irrational bull market in stock prices in the late-1990s may have had a rational economic basis after all, or at least partially so. He finds an apparent link between the discount rate (as set by Treasuries) and the pricing of stocks. "Movements of the observed levels of discounts for Treasury bonds may provide some information about the movements of discounts for claims on corporations," he writes.[39] That suggests that the combination of relatively low interest rates and the stability of expected cash-flow forecasts from the late-1980s onward set the stage for the powerful bull market in equities in the late-1990s. As Hall explains,

> Though the evidence is hardly conclusive, the idea that the stock market values the property owned by corporations seems to stand up reasonably well in data for the United States for the past 50 years.

The volatility of the aggregate stock market in relation to other broad measures such as GDP is substantial, but not out of line with the movements of cash flows accruing to corporations after paying all their costs and satisfying all nonshareholder claimants including governments. Even some of the most puzzling episodes in the stock market, such as the collapse of values by 50 percent in 1973 and 1974, seem within the grasp of rational understanding, given the sudden reversal in cash-flow growth that followed soon after.[40]

Cash flow, in short, "is the key factor in understanding movements in the stock market," Hall (2001) concludes. "It is illogical to condemn astronomical price/earnings ratios as plainly irrational without investigating the prospects for growth in future earnings. Streams of future cash growing at high rates are hugely valuable."[41]

The fact that the market continually reassesses the value of expected cash flow isn't inherently irrational, although that doesn't preclude the possibility, indeed the likelihood of miscalculation at times. So while the market's assessment may be less than perfect, there's an apparent link between an assumption about the market's capitalization factor for cash flow and the five-year forward growth rate of real cash flow, as depicted in **FIGURE 4.2**. The relationship isn't flawless, but then why would we expect it to be? Judgments

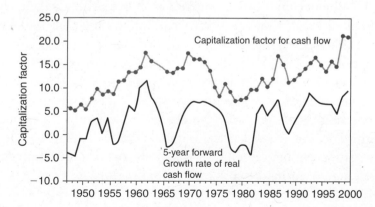

**Figure 4.2**  Discounting the Future

Capitalization factor for cash flow and 5-year forward growth rate of real cash flow

Source: "Struggling to Understand the Stock Market," by Robert E. Hall, *American Economic Review Papers and Proceedings*, 2001 (Vol. 91, No. 2), pp. 1–11.

about the future, which is to say the unknown, are necessarily risky and subject to fluctuation. As economic variables change, such as interest rates, inflation expectations, the economic outlook, etc., rational investors will modify their valuations of cash flow.

But what of the October 19, 1987, stock market crash? Surely the magnitude of the drop indicates investor irrationality and market inefficiency. What shift in economic or financial fundamentals could rationalize a one-day 20-percent-plus decline in stock prices? Nothing, some economists say. The market, as a result, must be inefficient.

But there are competing explanations. One example comes from Mitchell and Netter (1989), who argue that the market decline of October 1987 should be viewed in context with the preceding political activity. The authors assert that the selling of October 14–16, 1987, was a reasonable response to the surprising proposal from Congress via the House Ways and Means Committee to restrict interest rate deductions on corporate debt, which would make mergers and acquisitions and other corporate actions more expensive. The news on possible changes to the tax code for companies led to waves of portfolio-insurance-related selling on October 19—selling that the exchanges weren't prepared to process on a technological level. By this reasoning, the dramatic selling in October 1987 stems from pragmatic analysis of new information and its influence on future profits rather than market inefficiency.

Malkiel (2003) makes a similar point, noting that seemingly minor changes in such variables as interest rates and investor perceptions about risk can lead to big changes in securities prices within a rational pricing framework. As an example, he demonstrates mathematically how a rise in government bond yields to 10.5 percent from 9 percent, with no change in inflation, can imply a one-third decline in stock prices if investors also demand a modestly higher risk premium on equities—2.5 percent versus 2.0 percent.[42] Large changes in market prices, in other words, aren't necessarily irrational.

But if pricing is rational, how can long-run returns also be predictable? Let's recognize that the literature finds evidence that returns are *partially* predictable, and only when we look out several years. That still leaves the risk of being wrong, so predictability isn't certain. Yet even partial predictability raises questions about the existence of a rational-pricing framework. In search of common ground, Fama and French (1988) sketch out the economic logic for linking the two under a single conceptual framework:

> Expected returns correspond roughly to the discount rates that relate a current stock price to expected future dividends. Suppose that investor tastes for current versus risky future consumption and the stochastic evolution of the investment opportunities of firms result in time-varying equilibrium expected returns that are highly autocorrelated but mean-reverting. Suppose that shocks to expected returns are uncorrelated with shocks to rational forecasts of dividends. Then a shock to expected returns has no effect on expected dividends or expected returns in the distant future. Thus the shock has no long-term effect on expected prices. The cumulative effect of a shock on expected returns must be exactly offset by an opposite adjustment in the current price.[43]

Simply put, varying and somewhat predictable returns need not be the enemy of a market that prices assets efficiently. Of course, if you think of an efficient market as it was laid out in 1965 or earlier, including the notion that expected returns are constant and unchanging, then the idea of time-varying risk premia and rational pricing sounds radical. And, in fact, the new thinking on market efficiency is radical, but radical in the sense that it provides fresh insight into the functioning of securities markets.

That's not to say that valuing future cash flows in the present is easy or immune to miscalculation. But Mr. Market's estimates can be rational even if anecdotal evidence suggests otherwise. The fact that the market can be wrong about the future doesn't violate the efficient market hypothesis. Everything is clear in retrospect, and that includes recognizing mistakes. We might even go so far as to say that the market isn't efficient when looking backward. Hindsight, as they say, is 20/20.

The idea of efficient markets was never a concept that claimed omniscience. The market can and will be wrong at times, relative to the facts as they emerge in the future. So it goes in the game of estimating future values in the here and now. Nobody knows how or when the future may vary from the present, so it's never clear who'll be wrong or right, or when. Investment decisions, in the aggregate, reflect a range of opinion about an asset's prospective price. Handicapping the future is a dangerous business. The question is whether all the individual speculations—i.e., the market—will collectively offer reasonably good estimates of what the future will bring over time. In other words, is the market price a rational estimate based on the available facts and reasonable expectations of the moment?

Yes, or so the empirical evidence suggests. If it were otherwise, beating the market would be far easier than it appears to be. But how does that square with the research that finds that the market is partly predictable? Predictability implies that smart investors should be able to profit from the opportunity. Certainly that should be true for professionals who trade for a living, many of whom have access to sophisticated technology and research. These investors should be able to display evidence of market-beating performance.

Where should we look for such evidence? Mutual funds are an obvious choice. Mutual funds have been around for decades, so they have long track records available for study, dating back to the first half of the twentieth century. In addition, the mutual fund industry is highly regulated, so these portfolios' publicly reported track records are accepted as unbiased and statistically reliable accounts of active management. Investors can buy and sell at a mutual fund's net asset value, providing real-world validation that the mutual fund returns are genuine. If the reported net asset values were inaccurate or manipulated, mutual fund companies wouldn't be willing to make a daily market based on erroneous prices year after year.

Mutual funds represent the front line in the quest to document securities-picking talent. But the evidence that mutual funds are able to systematically exploit so-called market inefficiencies is slim. Instead, middling performance is common. In fact, researchers have been making this point for decades. Although some studies conclude otherwise, many if not most find that actively managed mutual funds underperform their benchmarks. A few of the many examples published over the years:

Jensen (1968) analyzed 115 mutual funds and found that, on average, they failed to beat a passive buy-and-hold-the-market strategy during 1945–1964. Gruber (1996) concludes that the average mutual fund lags its benchmark by 65 basis points annually. Carhart (1997) reports that net returns of mutual funds tend to fall as expenses and trading activity rise. That's a problem for actively managed portfolios, which generally incur higher levels of expenses and trading compared to passively managed index funds. And Arnott et al. (2000) observe that the Vanguard 500 Index fund outperforms the average equity mutual fund and that the outperformance rises after adjusting for taxes.

Simple mathematics also supports the empirical evidence that beating the market is difficult and that the pursuit of middling returns (index funds) is likely to favor investors generally in the long run. Sharpe (1991) makes this point, explaining,

> Over any specified time period, the *market return* will be a weighted average of the returns on the securities within the market, using beginning market values as weights. Each passive manager will obtain precisely the market return, before costs. From this, it follows (as the night from the day) that the return on the average actively managed dollar must equal the market return. Why? Because the market return must equal a weighted average of the returns on the passive and active segments of the market. If the first two returns are the same, the third must be also.[44]

Of course, there are managers who "beat the market," at least for a time. Doesn't this damage the case for accepting EMH? Not necessarily. Once we compare apples to apples and adjust for various embedded bets in portfolios, such as leverage or concentration in a particular corner of the market, it's often the case that a seemingly winning portfolio is simply riskier than its benchmark. In that case, the higher return may be compensation for embracing higher risk. That's hardly evidence against EMH or modern portfolio theory. What's more, looking backward and singling out a handful of managers who beat the market isn't quite fair in the first place because there will inevitably be managers who trailed the market. An efficient market doesn't preclude the possibility, even the likelihood, that there will be market-beating managers. No less is true for expecting relative losers. After considering the winners in context with the losers, the big picture usually looks like the market.

That's not only unsurprising, it's fate. The pursuit of market-beating returns, or alpha, is a zero-sum game, as Sharpe reminds. For every investor who beats the market, someone must trail it. Because this balancing act describes how the money game works, there's a limited supply of alpha—which is to say something other than beta—for a given marketplace. And of this finite quantity of alpha, only half is positive. A world where alpha sums to zero implies a set of laws that constrain the productivity of active investment strategies. That leads to the expectation that indexing will fare reasonably well over time compared to a relevant pool of active funds that incur costs and make mistakes. Owning beta for the long run, in other words, looks like a compelling strategy if alpha sums to zero.[45]

## No Free Lunches

All of this creates a conundrum, or so it seems. On the one hand, the financial research suggests that the market is partially predictable, which implies that investors can create alpha. Why, then, isn't there more compelling evidence of investors who are exploiting the opportunity?

Let's return to what's known as Samuelson's dictum in search of a clue. In a letter, economist Paul Samuelson—a founding father of the efficient markets hypothesis—suggested that while the market showed "considerable *micro* efficiency" in the trading of individual stocks, there's a case for arguing that "*macro* inefficiency" exists for the stock market overall "in the sense of long waves in the time series of aggregate indexes of securities prices below and above various definitions of fundamental values."[46]

Applying statistical tests to study the idea that micro efficiency and macro inefficiency coexist, Jung and Shiller (2005) report that "there is now substantial evidence supporting Samuelson's dictum where market inefficiency is defined as predictability of future (excess) returns." Speculating as to why the market overall may be less efficient compared with trading in individual securities, Jung and Shiller hypothesize that far more information on individual company fundamentals is available compared with broad market analysis and investors seeking to exploit opportunities across asset classes.[47]

Perhaps that partly explains why active management's real-world results tend to be middling. By focusing on individual securities, as is practiced by most mutual funds and active managers, market-beating behavior is tough, Jung and Shiller (2005) suggest. Meanwhile, the overall stock market may be less efficiently priced at times, in part because the overwhelming focus in the business of active management is trading individual securities, as opposed to the market overall.

Of course, we should be careful about the term "inefficient" as it applies to the market. Using Jung and Shiller's definition, an inefficient market is one where there's a degree of predictability for future returns. But as work by Fama and others remind, there's a case, and arguably a persuasive case, that return predictability by itself isn't proof that markets are inefficient.

Markets offer a changing mix of prospective performance opportunities. That's in keeping with updated views of modern portfolio theory and the efficient market hypothesis. Market equilibrium remains in constant flux, adjusting to the constant changes in supply and demand forces that flow from investors, who are reacting to shifting economic and financial conditions.

Structural changes are also a factor in the fluctuation of return premia. As one example, in a world where capital flows become increasingly globalized, the process affects expected returns in markets around the world. As investors diversify across political borders and asset classes, "the market pressure of portfolio globalization should drive global risk premiums down," advises Karnosky (1993).[48]

Return premia, in other words, aren't set in stone. They fluctuate as conditions evolve. The fact that different markets offer different risk premia at different times isn't inefficient per se. In fact, it would be surprising—and inefficient—if markets operated otherwise.

But while returns may appear partially predictable, we still need to remain humble on thinking that the apparent opportunity offers easy profits. Fama (1998) argues that an efficient market will generate a series of events that, individually, offer clues about future returns. Behavioral finance explains the events as evidence that investors go to extremes by, for instance, assigning excessively high or low valuations to assets. As an example, a relatively high dividend yield on the stock market implies above-average expected returns. But over time, unusually high and low valuations seem to balance out, Fama explains. Looking at any one case of so-called excess in isolation (a high price-to-earnings ratio, for instance) may be misleading because it obscures the evidence that suggests that anomalies are randomly occurring events. If the incidence of anomalous pricing behavior is more or less split evenly among overvaluation and undervaluation in the long run, as it appears to be, that implies that the market is efficient.

Regardless of whether one accepts that the market's efficient or not, there's no getting around the fact that indexing has proven itself a successful strategy for tapping risk premia and beating quite a large share, perhaps a majority, of active managers. Perhaps that's why Professor Richard Thaler—a founding member of the modern theory of behavioral finance—acknowledged in 2004 that most of his retirement assets were in index funds. Why? As he tells *The Wall Street Journal*: "It is not easy to beat the market, and most people don't."[49]

Super investor Warren Buffett—who's built a well-deserved reputation as one of the best active managers in history—has made similar statements over the years. In his 1993 letter to shareholders of Berkshire Hathaway, where Buffett is CEO, he counseled: "By periodically investing in an index fund, for example, the know-nothing investor can actually out-perform most investment professionals. Paradoxically, when 'dumb' money acknowledges its limitations, it ceases to be dumb." He repeated the advice ten years later, in the 2003 letter to shareholders, advising that "those index funds that are very low-cost...are investor-friendly by definition and are the best selection for most of those who wish to own equities."

One academic suggests that investors generally must learn to coexist with the practical virtues of the efficient market hypothesis, whatever its limitations. "To some, market efficiency means that there is no systematic way to beat the market," observes Meir Statman, a finance professor at Santa Clara University and a card-carrying member of the behavioral finance club. "To others, it means that security prices are rational—that is, reflect only 'fundamental' or 'utilitarian' characteristics, such as risk, but not 'psychological' or 'value-expressive' characteristics, such as sentiment. The market efficiency battle is being fought as if the believers can win only if the nonbelievers lose. But I argue that finance scholars and professionals would do well to accept market efficiency in the beat-the-market sense but reject it in the rational-prices sense."[50]

It's debatable if the distinction has any substance for designing and managing portfolio strategies with real money. The lesson, however, is clear: indexing is a potent weapon for capturing risk premia, a point that even some behavioral finance supporters concede.

Even if we accept that the market is efficient, or reasonably close to efficient for the long haul, that doesn't rule out the possibility, or even the necessity, of dynamically managing a mix of index funds that represent different asset classes. EMH suggests that we shouldn't try to beat a given market as it relates to a single asset class. Yet the fact that return premia vary, and perhaps predictably so, implies that we should adjust the relative weights of asset classes in a multi-asset class portfolio to take advantage of the fluctuating price of risk. In other words, we should exploit the lessons of EMH by owning index funds, and at the same time we should manage the relative weights of those funds.

Alternatively, we could simply own a passive proxy for the true market portfolio, which is an allocation in all the major asset classes, each weighted by its respective market value. But as we'll learn in upcoming chapters, the passively allocated portfolio across the spectrum of asset classes is optimal only for the average investor in the very long run. That's a good benchmark as we begin to think about designing and managing portfolios, but it's not necessarily the ideal strategy for any one investor. That's not a comment about market efficiency. Rather, it's simply recognizing that each investor has a particular objective, risk preference, time horizon, etc.

The priority, then, is customizing the market portfolio for each investor and dynamically managing the resulting asset allocation. But before we take a closer look at asset allocation strategy, we must familiarize ourselves with the asset classes, both individually and how they interact with one another.

## Chapter Notes

1. Fama (1965a).
2. Fama (1965a), p. 42.
3. Mandelbrot and Hudson (2004), pp. 12–13.

4. There have been a number of attempts at developing more sophisticated (i.e., more accurate) statistical tools for profiling risk in the securities markets over the years. These efforts have brought mixed results to portfolio management, however. Meanwhile, the newer techniques require a higher level of mathematical competence and analytical skills compared with using conventional statistical tools, such as standard deviation. Although the jury's still out on the practical relevance for money management, the newer metrics are intriguing and so they're worthy of ongoing study in the quest to discover post-modern risk measures. The growing list of post-modern techniques includes a family of tools based on what's known as autoregressive conditional heteroscedasticity (ARCH) metrics and its generalized counterpart (GARCH), which arise from Engle (1982) and Bollerslev (1986), respectively. Another effort at mining intelligence from the non-randomness aspects of securities markets comes from applications derived from the Hurst exponent, which seeks to evaluate the non-linear dimensions of data series for clues about the future. For more on the Hurst exponent and other concepts for modeling the "chaos" of the financial markets, see Peters (1996).

5. Fama (1965a), p. 44.

6. Fama (1970), pp. 399–400.

7. To distinguish William Bernstein from Peter Bernstein, hereafter we use William Bernstein in all text references for the former and continue to use Bernstein in reference to the latter.

8. Bernstein (2002), pp. 24–25 and footnote 1 and Figure 1-12.

9. Fama (1965b), p. 56.

10. Malkiel (2003), p. 62.

11. Herper (2002).

12. Mandelbrot and Hudson (2004), p. 16.

13. Jahnke (2004), p. 19.

14. Ibbotson (2009), pp. 46–47.

15. Ibid., pp. 42–43.

16. For critical reviews of Shiller (1981), see, for example, Ackert and Smith (1993), Marsh and Merton (1986), and Kleidon (1986).

17. Rozeff (1984), p. 74.

18. Fama and French (1988), p. 247.

19. Shiller (2000), pp. 11–12.

20. Malkiel (2003), p. 65.

21. See Soros 2003 and 2008.

22. The behavioral finance literature is vast. For an introductory overview of the concepts and literature, see Shleifer (2000), Shefrin (2002), and www.behaviouralfinance.net for additional references.

23. Thaler has written dozens of research papers and a number of books in the behavioral finance field. Investors interested in learning more about the discipline would do well to begin with a review of his work. An intriguing starting point that's accessible to the lay reader is Thaler (1992), a collection of papers focused on behavioral finance.

24. Lo and MacKinlay (1999), p. 18.

25. Fama and French (1988), p. 247.

26. Malkiel (2003), p. 65.

27. Fama (1991), pp. 1575–1576.

28. Ibid., p. 1576.

29. "Paul A. Samuelson," by Barry B. Burr, *Investment News*, June 28, 1999 (http://www.investmentnews.com/apps/pbcs.dll/article?AID=/19990628/SUB/906280709/1009/TOC).

30. Jung and Shiller (2005), p. 221.

31. Statman (1999), p. 18.

32. Fama (1970), p. 384.

33. Samuelson (1965), p. 45.

34. Ibid., p. 48.

35. Reichenstein and Dorsett (1995), p. 5, Footnote 6.

36. Chartered financial analyst, or CFA, which is the leading securities analyst degree, issued by the CFA Institute.

37. Interview with author, 2008.

38. Malkiel (2003), p. 75.

39. Hall (2001), p. 8.

40. Ibid., p. 11.

41. Ibid., p. 11.

42. Malkiel (2003), pp. 73–74.

43. Fama and French (1988), p. 248.

44. Sharpe (1991), p. 7.

45. A possible exception to the alpha-sums-to-zero rule arises by factoring risk into the analysis, as per Hill (2006). Alpha sums to zero only with a returns-only analysis. But investors have different time horizons, risk tolerances, objectives, etc., so risk-adjusted returns may not sum to zero. That leads to the possibility that more investors can outperform

(or underperform) the market in risk-adjusted terms than is possible when measuring results exclusively with straight returns. Thinking of alpha in risk-adjusted terms traces its intellectual origins to 1738, when mathematician Daniel Bernoulli laid out the foundations of expected utility (decision) theory in his famous solution to what's called the St. Petersberg Paradox. For an excellent overview of Bernoulli and his contributions to risk management theory, see Chapter 6 in P. Bernstein (1996).

46. Jung and Shiller (2005), p. 221.

47. Ibid., p. 221.

48. Karnosky (1993), p. 60. For additional analysis and perspective on the effects of globalized investing on risk premia, see Brinson (1995).

49. Hilsenrath (2004).

50. Statman (1999), p. 18.

Chapter 5

# The Market Portfolio Is
# the Benchmark

THE KEY LESSON of more than half a century of investment research is clear: diversify within and across the major asset classes. To the extent there's consensus in strategic investment ideas, it ends there, giving way to the great question that animates much of the debate about building and managing portfolios: how should we implement and manage a policy of diversification? For some investors that evolves into the question of which asset classes to hold or exclude. Beyond that, how should we weight the various asset classes? And how much and how often should we adjust the asset allocation?

There's no easy solution, nor is there likely to be one. The capital and commodity markets are resistant to the idea that an enduring truth will give us a silver-bullet answer to everyone's basic quest to earn above-average returns now and forever more. There can be no strategic solution that offers a guarantee of success for everyone at all times. The relentless feedback loop of risk and return is forever changing equilibrium prices and perceptions about what constitutes prudent discounting of expected events. The market's main output is price, which changes through time. The internal processing system that creates and modifies prices is largely a black box. Thanks to fifty years of research, it's less of a black box in the twenty-first century, but the mysteries of how the capital and commodity markets operate still overwhelm the thin sliver of what we can confidently identify as hard knowledge in the money game.

That shouldn't be surprising. If there was an obvious solution, the secret would soon leak out and everyone would pursue the strategy, which would reduce the return premium to zero. If such a thing as excess return relative to a risk-free rate exists, it must necessarily be risky, which is to say uncertain in some sense in terms of timing and the exact formula that generates the premium.

Even so, we're not entirely blind. Financial economics has revealed much about markets, investing, and what it all means for intelligently designed portfolios. Not everything, of course; not even close. What's more, the limited insight we have gleaned is even less useful for disclosing a one-size-fits-all investment solution. In fact, such a strategic epiphany, assuming one exists, is likely to remain indefinitely obscure. That's partly the nature of trying to deconstruct risk premiums, which are notoriously impenetrable beyond a basic understanding. Researchers are also at a disadvantage for identifying strategic solutions because of the distinctive needs of each investor.

Everyone has a singular objective and risk tolerance. That's partly due to who we are as investors, as workers, as family members. Some of us are wealthy, some aren't; some of us are retired, some young; some of us have children to put through college fifteen years from today, and some don't; some are frightened of the markets and can't sleep with more than a modest dose of risk; others have a more durable tolerance for short-term losses and instinctively seek to take advantage of turmoil. And on and on.

If everyone is different, each of us requires a customized portfolio strategy that satisfies a particular financial and psychological profile. The same is true for institutional investors. Even within the relatively homogeneous world of pension funds, for instance, there are variations in time horizons and liabilities tied to the existing and future pool of pensioners, for whom the pension funds are managing assets. The distinguishing set of factors that define each pension fund ensures that no one portfolio strategy is ideal for all institutional portfolios in this niche.

Common sense, perhaps, although the observation reminds us that most investors—probably all investors—should hold distinctive portfolios that satisfy a particular set of ambitions and preferences. The portfolio should also be managed through time with an eye on fulfilling those objectives.

Having distilled this basic lesson over the past decades into various theories, financial economists have turned the investment problem on its head. The money game, in other words, is one of managing risk rather than chasing return. The reasoning boils down to the recognition that the odds are better, if only modestly, for understanding and managing portfolios through a prism of risk compared with blatantly pursuing return. The two are intimately linked, of course, but fifty years of finance tells us that we have a better chance of achieving success by managing risk.

The wisdom of the advice may not always be self-evident. The focus on risk management looks superfluous most of the time for the simple reason that economic growth and positive investment performance dominate. That's not necessarily true for any one asset class, or country, or time period. But over the grand sweep of time, history is biased toward growth, even though it's punctuated by periods of stagnation or worse. As a strategic issue, the expansionary tendency is the source of our confidence that the market portfolio will post positive returns over time.

Accordingly, owning as broad a slice of the world's asset classes, weighted by their relative values in the global capital and commodity markets, is the default portfolio. This is the optimal investment for the average investor with an infinite time horizon. Why? In a word, growth. The market portfolio confers ownership in what we might think of as the beta of the global economy, which has expanded at a real (inflation-adjusted) annual rate of roughly 4 percent for the fifty years through 2006. Since 1820, the world economy's pace is lower, but still firmly positive through 2006 at a real 2.3 percent per year. [1]

Growth is the basic rationale for owning a piece of the global economy. The question is: how should an investor structure a portfolio to hitch a ride? Owning the beta for the world economy stands to benefit from the worldwide tailwind of economic expansion. It's also an investment strategy that's inexpensive and easy to assemble, thanks to the proliferation of index funds that serve as proxies for the various pieces of the global economic pie. Modern portfolio theory suggests that an index-fund-based investment portfolio, with the components weighted by their respective market values, will be the optimal portfolio in risk-adjusted terms for the long run. But what about the short run? Should investors pick and choose the pieces of the market portfolio? Should they emphasize some and minimize others at certain times? Should investors, in effect, build portfolios that differ from the investment fare offered by Mr. Market?

The standard solution in modern portfolio theory answers "no." The separation theorem of Tobin (1958) tells us that the market portfolio should be held by everyone. Customization is a function of simply varying the market portfolio's weight relative to cash: conservative investors hold a higher allocation of cash and lesser amount in the market portfolio; aggressive investors own a higher share of the market portfolio.

But a revised view of MPT suggests we should be more flexible when it comes to a strict definition of the market portfolio. One reason is that financial economics now tells us that risk premia aren't constant, as assumed in the first interpretation of MPT. In future chapters we'll analyze the evidence of time-varying risk premia in more detail. For now, we'll simply acknowledge the point and recognize that it provides a reason for considering that investors may want to own a variant of the market portfolio.

Meanwhile, even in a world of time-varying risk premia, investors should still build and manage portfolios that speak to their specific circumstances. Everyone has a different time horizon, tolerance for risk, investment objectives, etc., and so those factors should be considered when designing an investment strategy. The market portfolio is the right investment for the average investor for the infinite future, but since that profile describes no one specific investor, there's yet another reason for altering the market portfolio as passively offered to satisfy investment needs.

Investors, after all, are mortal. The market portfolio is optimal prospectively speaking, but the recognition doesn't preclude it from delivering suboptimal performance in the short run. The idea of simply buying and holding the market portfolio has its benefits. It's a low-cost strategy when implemented with index funds. It's also a strategy that effectively manages itself because after weighting the various components by their respective market values, the ebb and flow of market activity will forever keep the portfolio in balance in terms of reflecting the optimal mix implied by market equilibrium. The problem is that in the short run, the potential for inferior results are possible, perhaps even probable, depending on the time period and factoring in the idea that expected risk premia change.

That reality can complicate portfolio strategy for buy-and-hold investors who think they're completely immune to short-term volatility. The alternative is planning on taking advantage of the short-term shifts, i.e., managing the investment portfolio dynamically. For strategic-minded investors, this is a challenge that reduces to balancing the long-term bias for growth against short-term hazards and opportunities. The details of implementation are forever debated and constantly in flux, but at least we have a default position from which to begin our investment journey and consider the choices.

## Start with the World

Customizing the investment strategy is every investor's goal, but the process has a common starting point for analyzing the market landscape and the available menu of risk factors: the global market portfolio (GMP). This is the portfolio that holds all the world's assets in their market-value-based weights. It's the optimal strategy for the world's average investor for infinity, as the standard modern portfolio theory (MPT) suggests.

GMP may be inappropriate for most investors, but it remains a compelling portfolio in its own right by virtue of its attractive expected risk-adjusted return. Many investors in the long run, in other words, can do a lot worse than owning the GMP, which takes maximum advantage of the asset class choices.

Practical or not, GMP brings no preconceived expectations other than the decision to own everything in its market value weight. As such, it's the default portfolio, so it represents everyone's strategy benchmark for reviewing investment choices, customizing asset allocation, and analyzing risk and return generally.

Because GMP is a useful starting point for considering our strategic options in portfolio design, the first question is: should we build a portfolio that differs from the benchmark? If the answer is "yes," as it seems to be, then we need to ask: *how* should our portfolio deviate from GMP?

Markowitz (1952)—in writing the founding document of modern portfolio theory—sketched out the framework for considering the choices by raising the issue of asset classes as they relate to building optimal portfolios. Designing portfolios that maximize return for a stated level of risk, the paper advises, can be pursued with either individual securities or "aggregates," i.e., bonds, stocks, real estate, and other broadly defined asset types.[2]

A decade after the paper's publication came the development of the capital asset pricing model—a key piece of the theoretical foundation for index funds. CAPM further explored the concept of a multi-asset class portfolio as an integrated strategy, although the idea proper isn't fully outlined. Sharpe (1964) refers to the "capital market as a whole,"[3] although it's never explicitly defined; rather, the market portfolio is inferred via the discussion of developing "a *market* equilibrium theory of asset prices under conditions of risk."[4]

CAPM and MPT inspire us to consider the true market portfolio, which in theory encompasses all the world's assets weighted in proportion to their market value.

The idea in broad concept, however, has been downplayed. Subsequent reviews and applications of CAPM over the years favor identifying "the market" as the domestic stock market, or some other lone asset class. But defining the market portfolio as the U.S. stock market, or another asset class, runs the risk of misinterpreting the basic lessons of modern portfolio theory.

Applying CAPM via a narrow definition of the market portfolio can lead to erroneous investment conclusions. Why, then, is the preference for a constrained view of the market portfolio so popular? Probably because it's easy. Using the stock market as a proxy for the market portfolio has long been common, perhaps because data on the U.S. equity market is accessible and equity-oriented investing is widely considered the standard for a risk portfolio. Defining the market portfolio as a portfolio of stocks, then, is a natural extension of practice and habit.

Yet a closer reading of CAPM and the research it has inspired suggests defining the market portfolio more expansively as a multi-asset class concept. Broader, in other words, is better. Easy to say, hard to do because the true market portfolio holds all the world's assets—tradable *and* non-tradable assets. That means all the world's stocks and bonds, as well as real estate, commodities, labor income, and all the other assets of relevance in the global economy. Alas, measuring the true market portfolio, much less owning it, is hopelessly beyond the pale.

The good news is that even though the ideal remains elusive, we can still build a better market index by looking beyond a domestic stock market benchmark that too often serves as a proxy for "the market." This is hardly an academic exercise in the twenty-first century since we can invest in something closer to the true market portfolio, thanks to the proliferation of index mutual funds and their exchange-listed counterparts in recent years that tap a range of asset classes around the globe.

The theoretical reasoning behind building a more robust proxy of the true market portfolio has been discussed for decades in the literature. Black (1972), for example, demonstrates that the true market portfolio holds all the world's assets weighted by their market values. This is the classic efficient portfolio that maximizes expected return for a given level of risk à la Markowitz. Mayers (1976) advises that a better representation of the CAPM market portfolio includes "nonmarketable" assets as well as liquid assets, such as stocks and bonds, although he's skeptical that this offers practical value, and from the options available in 1976 he had reason to be cautious. There's still no obvious way to build a true market portfolio, but thanks to a wider array of index choices in the twenty-first century, we can afford to be somewhat more optimistic.

Meanwhile, Roll (1977) establishes that the only reliable test of CAPM and the implications for risk and return requires the use of a true market portfolio proxy, which by definition must hold all assets. Using a market proxy that's incomplete runs the risk of dispensing faulty results. The implication: expanding the set of tradable assets beyond stocks is productive, even if the expansion isn't absolute.

But we can't prove it. According to Roll's critique, a valid and definitive test of CAPM is impossible since building a fully comprehensive market portfolio is impractical. A number of asset classes are difficult to measure, much less trade, such as human capital and private equity, due to the lack of liquid trading markets in those areas. Even the most ambitious notions of securitizing assets must concede that much of what's valued on planet Earth must remain beyond the capacity of trading in conventional brokerage accounts.

That leaves investors to consider the *investable* asset classes as the next-best option in an effort to capture as full a range as possible of the world's betas. The compromise inevitably comes at a price: some, perhaps most asset classes will be missing from a market portfolio proxy in real-world portfolios. In addition, some of the available asset classes in mutual funds and ETFs are proxies and perhaps poor ones at that. Commodities and real estate, in particular, while available as index funds, exist as compromises relative to the true profile of their underlying assets. For instance, replicating commodities by way of futures contracts, the standard practice, is problematic for a number of reasons, as explained by Erb and Harvey (2006).

The limitations of building an investable market portfolio are obvious, although the incentive to expand the investment portfolio as broadly as possible is inspired by theory, even if we're destined to fall short of the ideal. Perhaps it's a leap of faith in thinking that broader is better, but faith is always part of investing. There are no guarantees in money management. Risk of one sort or another is a constant in investing strategies. The challenge is identifying and managing the risks intelligently and efficiently. Owning a global market portfolio is one way to satisfy that ideal to some extent and arguably the superior way.

As it turns out, theory, real-world track records, and prudent investment instincts provide a compelling case for building a global market portfolio that takes advantage of the asset classes available via low-cost index funds. In turn, this globally diversified portfolio should be designed to satisfy each investor's particular risk and return demands. But before we go down this path, we must become familiar with how the pieces interact and what clues are available for thinking that we can manage the mix productively. History has limits for telling us what's coming, so we must be careful about looking at the past as a guide for seeing the future. Yet in some respects history is all we have, and we can't afford to ignore it or misinterpret the few clues it offers. As such, strategic portfolio analysis begins with a review of history, although it doesn't end there. Looking backward is a useful exercise, as long as we don't allow it to dominate our efforts at designing and managing asset allocation.

## History Is a Guide, Not a Shortcut

A customized investment portfolio is everyone's goal, but it starts with Mr. Market's portfolio, which leaves out nothing (at least nothing based on what average investors can buy). This default strategy takes a passive stand on weighting the various components, i.e., owning assets based on their market values. This is a portfolio strategy that's available to everyone because it demands no investment skill or rebalancing decisions, and everyone can own it since it's based on equilibrium, meaning that everyone can buy the assets in accordance with their relative value in the portfolio without moving prices. If stocks represent half of the world's investable assets, all investors can put 50 percent of their portfolio in equities to replicate the benchmark. In addition, it's a strategy that's economically priced if implemented through index funds. It is, in short, the ideal benchmark for a long-term risk portfolio, at least in theory.

How might this benchmark fare in the real world? As Roll (1977) and others point out, definitive answers are hopelessly obscure because the true market portfolio is unobservable. But if the true market portfolio exists in concept only, theory and intuition suggest we can build a reasonable proxy with the available index fund and ETF choices, which can be summarized as stocks, bonds, real estate (REITs), and commodities.

The four asset classes and their primary subcategories are the building blocks for all conventional investment strategies. By slicing up these financial genes, we can clone an array of customized portfolios with an array of risk levels. To do so intelligently, we should first familiarize ourselves with the major components.

Let's begin with the long-run history of large-company U.S. stocks from the early nineteenth century through 2008. Domestic equities generated an annualized total return of slightly more than 8 percent a year during 1825–2008.[5] A long-term view of U.S. equities is informative since it offers perspective on how the asset class performs over the sweep of history. Yet we should remember that looking at a summary for nearly two centuries of equity prices is also a bit like looking at the Earth from space: useful, but limited. We also need a closer, more informed inspection.

In fact, no single review of return or risk is "correct" in the sense that one study tells all. That's partly because risk premia fluctuate. We usually encounter a broad range of historical results for each asset class depending on the time period. That's a reminder that we need a deeper understanding of asset classes in order to make informed decisions about estimating expected return and risk. We can and should look to the past for context about considering the future, but we need to do so prudently, cautiously, and only as a first step in our strategic analysis. In short, we can't blindly extrapolate the past into the future.

As an extreme example, it's the height of folly to take the annualized total return for U.S. stocks for 1825–2008 and assume that it will hold true in the next twelve months, or even the next five years. Analysis of asset class return and risk can start with a long view, but it shouldn't end there. We should also consider the current economic and financial climate as well as the price of risk for each asset class—topics that we'll discuss in more detail in later chapters.

Meanwhile, large-cap U.S. stocks generated an annualized 9.6 percent total return in the modern era (1926–2008), well above the 5.4 percent for intermediate-term U.S. government bonds.[6] How do the other asset classes compare? Looking at a variety of time periods reminds, once again, that return and risk are closely linked. Higher returns through time are generally a function of higher risk. The relationship isn't perfect, nor should we expect it to be, particularly over shorter periods in the future. But as a basic working assumption, the message that return comes by way of higher risk serves as a useful guide for thinking about stocks and bonds.

Once we look beyond U.S. stocks and bonds, the extent and quality of historical data varies to a greater extent and so our inquiries into the past face additional challenges. For, example, looking at real estate in its securitized form is convenient, but real estate investment trusts date only from the 1970s. Meanwhile, commodities are widely proxied by their respective futures contracts, but that solution leaves many questions about how to calculate a relevant bogey. Summaries of historical risk and return, as a result, are problematic, so the data records should be reviewed cautiously. With that in mind, it's still useful to consider REITs as far back as the data goes: for 1972–2008, REITs generated an annualized 11.2 percent total return.[7]

Calculating historical returns for commodities is also problematic, starting with the fact that defining the asset class is open to quite a bit of subjectivity. That hasn't stopped researchers from designing benchmarks. One of the more widely cited measures of commodities broadly defined is the Goldman Sachs Commodity Index (now known as S&P GSCI), which is also traded in its own right and serves as the basis of a number of index funds. Idzorek

(2006) reports GSCI's annual return as 12.5 percent for 1970–2005.[8] Meanwhile, Gorton and Rouwenhorst (2006) advise that an equally weighted, annually rebalanced mix of commodity futures contracts earns an annualized 11.2 percent return for the forty-five years through 2004.[9]

Rounding out our review of the historical perspective for the major asset classes, consider that equities in foreign developed markets posted a 9.7 percent annualized total return for 1970–2008.[10]

Now let's turn to mixing asset classes and how that affects portfolio returns and risk. We'll begin with a broad measure of the U.S. stock market (Russell 3000) and compare it to an index of three-month Treasury bills (a proxy for cash that's widely considered a "risk-free" asset) with a summary in **TABLE 5.1**.

Note that stocks outperformed cash by a comfortable margin— roughly 8.8 percent for equities versus 4.5 percent for three-month T-bills on an annualized total return basis for this twenty-one-year period. That's hardly surprising. Modern portfolio theory teaches that higher returns accompany higher risk in a diversified portfolio, and U.S. equities overall certainly harbor far more risk than short-term government debt securities whose principal is guaranteed. The annualized risk, or standard deviation, of the monthly total returns for stocks is 14.5 for the twenty-one years through 2008—dramatically higher than the volatility in Treasury bills over those years.[11]

Note too that the return on stocks per unit of risk—the Sharpe ratio—is 0.29. This risk metric—first outlined in Sharpe (1966) and revisited in Sharpe (1994)—calculates performance above the risk-free rate relative to its standard deviation. Higher Sharpe ratios

**Table 5.1    Return and Risk: U.S. Stocks**

Total return, volatility, and Sharpe ratio

|  | 21-Year Annualized Total Return | 21-Year Annualized Risk* | 21-Year Sharpe Ratio[†] |
|---|---|---|---|
| Russell 3000 | 8.8% | 14.5 | 0.29 |
| Citi 3-Month Treasury Bill Index | 4.5 | 0.6 | – |

*Annualized standard deviation of monthly total returns.
[†]Annualized total return less risk-free return (3-month T-bill) divided by the annualized standard deviation.

Note: data based on 21-years of monthly data through 12/31/08.

Source: Author's calculations using data from Morningstar Principia.

equate with higher risk-adjusted performance and so an investment with a 0.6 Sharpe ratio is superior to one with a 0.3 Sharpe ratio. In isolation, this risk measure isn't all that useful. On the other hand, the metric offers richer perspective when compared with Sharpe ratios on other investments or in context with other periods for a single portfolio, as we'll see. Meanwhile, like any one risk measure, Sharpe ratio should be used with other analytical tools, although for simplicity we use it throughout this chapter as a basic example of reviewing asset classes and portfolios for strategic insight.

Let's reflect on U.S. equities as an investment. Does the performance in Table 5.1 suffice? The return premium over cash is significant. Also, the equity return for 1987–2008 is comparable to the 1825–2008 performance, suggesting that the later period was unexceptional despite the fact that 2008 witnessed an extraordinary loss in the stock market. Meanwhile, it's clear that the higher return on equities in 1987–2008 came bundled with a much higher volatility relative to Treasury bills.

There's nothing exceptional about an 8.8 percent annual return over two decades, according to research firm Ibbotson Associates. If anything, it's a bit low compared to the experience for 1926–2008. There are sixty-four overlapping instances of twenty-year periods from 1926 through 2008 (1926 through 1945, 1927 through 1946, etc.), and 8-to-15-percent-plus annualized total returns dominate.[12] Yet expecting a particular return based solely on the past is premature if not dangerous. Depending on when you invest, and under what economic and financial conditions, results can and will vary. As such, the performance history you choose to focus on may be misleading—an anomaly, perhaps—in which case the odds of a repeat performance anytime soon, if ever, may be far lower than recent or long-term history suggests.

In short, we must consider return records cautiously and suspiciously as a guide to the future. Risk premia, after all, aren't set in stone, which is why they're called *risk* premia. It bears repeating: much depends on when you invest, and at what price—topics that we'll discuss again in later chapters. But let's assume for the moment that the 1987–2008 record is a fair representation of equity behavior. Could we do better? That depends on what we mean by "better."

If the goal is simply finding a higher return regardless of risk, identifying a superior opportunity beyond a broad U.S. equity index is easy. There's never a shortage of investments with higher expected returns than the stock market overall. A small company with a promising new technology is a candidate. We can also look to other asset classes—commodities, real estate—as possible investments that will beat stocks over some period.

In theory, the potential for market-beating returns is always vast. The problem is risk. If we're blind to risk, the opportunities for enhancing results are everywhere. The goal of finding higher returns at comparable if not lower risk levels is more challenging. In fact, the latter is every strategic-minded investor's goal. Risk and return are closely linked, and investors ultimately care about both, so neither can be ignored at the other's expense. Instead, the two must always be assessed simultaneously. As a result, most performance-boosting ideas don't pass muster after adjusting for risk.

How, then, should we approach portfolio design? Finance theory tells us that we must hold multiple asset classes. But which ones should we hold? And in what ratio relative to the others? Should the mix remain static? Or should we periodically change the asset allocation? If so, how often? And what factors should influence our decisions to change the asset allocation? Market conditions? The particulars of each investor's investment goals and risk tolerance?

Portfolio strategy, to put it mildly, is complex, and there are no easy solutions. But we can and should start the analysis from a point of simplicity to gauge what's appropriate, or not, for each investor's portfolio. We must walk before we can run, as the old saw goes. That leads us back to MPT, which teaches that owning the market in its entirety, in a market-value weighted mix, is the optimal choice for the long run. That makes the market portfolio the ideal neutral strategy for investigating and comparing our choices for customizing asset allocation.

One lesson embedded in the market portfolio is that we must look beyond U.S. stocks for opportunities to enhance risk-adjusted return. With that in mind, consider what happens when we add U.S. bonds to U.S. stocks in proportion to their market value, which leads to a 50/50 weighting for domestic bonds and stocks, based on market values for each at the close of 1987.[13]

As the numbers in **TABLE 5.2** show, the unmanaged, passively allocated stock/bond portfolio's performance wasn't quite as high as the stock-only portfolio for 1987–2008. The balanced portfolio

**Table 5.2**   Return and Risk: U.S. Stock/Bond Portfolio

Total return, volatility, and Sharpe ratio

|  | 21-Year Annualized Total Return | 21-Year Annualized Risk* | 21-Year Sharpe Ratio† |
|---|---|---|---|
| 50/50 Domestic Stock/ Bond Portfolio | 8.2% | 9.6 | 0.37 |
| Russell 3000 | 8.8 | 14.5 | 0.29 |
| Citi 3-Month Treasury Bill Index | 4.5 | 0.6 | – |

*Standard deviation of monthly total returns.
†Annualized total return less risk-free return (3-month T-bill performance) divided by the annualized standard deviation.

Note: based on 21-years of monthly data through 12/31/08.
Source: Author's calculations using data from Morningstar Principia.

trailed with an annualized 8.2 percent total return versus 8.8 percent for equities. On the other hand, the stock/bond portfolio's risk was quite a bit lower: 9.6 versus 14.5. As a result, the stock/bond portfolio gave up a small amount of performance relative to owning just equities, but the two-asset-class mix more than made up for the loss with a much larger decline in volatility. The net improvement in risk-adjusted terms is reflected in a higher Sharpe ratio for the stock/ bond portfolio compared to stocks alone: 0.37 versus 0.29.

Can we further enhance risk-adjusted results by expanding our investment possibilities? How, for example, does the portfolio respond by adding foreign stocks and foreign bonds?[14] Once again, we begin by weighting the components based on their market values as of December 31, 1987, with the unmanaged results shown in **TABLE 5.3**.

Notably, the average return for the International Stock/Bond Portfolio falls to 7 percent from a bit more than 8 percent in the domestic stock/bond mix. Risk, meanwhile, remains essentially unchanged at a standard deviation of around 9.7. But the combination of lower return and similar volatility pulls down the risk-adjusted score, as indicated by the lower Sharpe ratio relative to the portfolio of U.S. equities and fixed income. Is this a sign of the failure of international diversification? No, but before we discuss why, let's look at one more portfolio that adds commodities, REITs, and domestic high-yield bonds to the international stock/bond mix (see **TABLE 5.4**). Real estate and commodities are key parts of the global economy,

**Table 5.3**    Return and Risk: International Stock/Bond Portfolio

Total return, volatility, and Sharpe ratio

|  | 21-Year Annualized Total Return | 21-Year Annualized Risk* | 21-Year Sharpe Ratio[†] |
|---|---|---|---|
| International Stock/ Bond Portfolio | 7.0 | 9.7 | 0.25 |
| 50/50 Domestic Stock/ Bond Portfolio | 8.2 | 9.6 | 0.37 |
| Russell 3000 | 8.8 | 14.5 | 0.29 |
| Citi 3-Month Treasury Bill Index | 4.5 | 0.6 | – |

*Annualized standard deviation of monthly total returns.
[†]Annualized total return less risk-free return (3-month T-bill) divided by the annualized standard deviation.

Note: data based on 21-years of monthly data through 12/31/08.
Source: Author's calculations using data from Morningstar Principia and Standard & Poor's.

and both are available in index funds and ETFs. As a result, the asset classes are practical as well as integral for building a diversified investment portfolio that moves closer to the true market portfolio.

Adding REITs, high-yield bonds, and commodities in weights based on their respective market values appears to have no impact on risk-adjusted performance compared with owning just equities and bonds on an international basis. Indeed, the global market portfolio (GMP) doesn't outperform a 50/50 mix of domestic stocks

**Table 5.4**    Risk and Return: Global Market Portfolio

Total return, volatility, and Sharpe ratio

|  | 21-Year Annualized Total Return | 21-Year Annualized Risk* | 21-Year Sharpe Ratio[†] |
|---|---|---|---|
| Global Market Portfolio | 7.0% | 9.7 | 0.25 |
| International Stock/ Bond Portfolio | 7.0 | 9.7 | 0.25 |
| 50/50 Domestic Stock/ Bond Portfolio | 8.2 | 9.6 | 0.37 |
| Russell 3000 | 8.8 | 14.5 | 0.29 |
| Citi 3-Month Treasury Bill Index | 4.5 | 0.6 | – |

*Annualized standard deviation of monthly total returns.
[†]Annualized total return less risk-free return (3-month T-bill) divided by the annualized standard deviation.

Note: data based on 21-years of monthly data through 12/31/08.
Source: Author's calculations using data from Morningstar Principia, Standard & Poor's, and Citigroup.

and bonds. The not-so-subtle message: we're better off in U.S. stocks and bonds. That's a tempting conclusion, but it may be erroneous as a general rule.

As we expand the assets in the portfolio and approach the true market portfolio, we're likely to move closer to the optimum return and risk levels that are generated over time. It's no surprise that risk-adjusted returns improve sharply for a stock/bond mix relative to stocks alone. But as we continue to add asset classes and hold a diversified portfolio, the benefits necessarily become increasingly marginal in terms of long-term results. That's one indication for thinking that beating the market portfolio will be difficult over time without making aggressive bets with asset allocation.

Remember, too, that once we move beyond stocks and bonds on a global basis, the remaining asset classes, or at least those that are widely available as index funds, represent a small share of the capital markets when measured as liquid securities. The individual passive weights for REITs, high-yield bonds, and commodities, for instance, are all well under 5 percent each relative to a global portfolio of equities and fixed income. The tiny allocations may deserve higher weights, particularly if we look at the true economic value of real estate and commodities. But in the example above, we use the passive weights based on liquid markets as stated as a neutral example, so the influence on the total portfolio is minimal.

Separately, we should be wary of reading too much into the twenty-one-year slice of history analyzed above, or any one time frame. A particular stretch of time may not be, and probably isn't, representative of the future. Like all periods of time, 1987–2008 was distinctive, reflecting a particular set of political, economic, and financial trends that aren't likely to return in similar fashion.

History doesn't repeat itself, but sometimes it rhymes, Mark Twain said. We can and should consider the past as a guide, albeit as a naïve guide for considering the future. But we must do additional analysis for estimating expected risk and return. Consider, for instance, that 1987–2008 witnessed a sharp decline in inflation in the U.S. and much of the West, which allowed interest rates to fall and remain low for most of the period. Meanwhile, the Soviet Union collapsed, China and other developing nations embraced capital-ism and globalization, and economic growth was unusually strong prior to 2008. It was, in short, an idyllic time for earning risk premia. But there's no assurance that the future will echo the past. Every period is distinctive in some way.

Comparing U.S. stocks versus foreign stocks in developed markets, for instance, shows a history of changing leadership. In the 1970s, the dollar-based performance of foreign stocks handily beat U.S. equities: a 10.1 percent annualized total return for foreign equities in the decade versus 5.9 percent for U.S. stocks. The 1980s gave foreign stocks a decisive performance edge over U.S. stocks, too, although the trend reversed in the 1990s and the U.S. was the clear winner. For the twenty-first century through the end of 2008, foreign stocks took the lead once more, albeit in relative terms by losing less than U.S. equities.[15]

If we knew which slice of the equities markets would outperform, we wouldn't need to diversify globally. But we don't, at least not with a high degree of confidence, so it's misleading to draw absolute conclusions from any one period. Certainly the idea of betting heavily on one region or asset class to the exclusion of others is extreme if we're less than confident about the future, which is always the case.

With that in mind, let's reanalyze our global market portfolio and the domestic stock/bond portfolio by looking at how the two strategies fared relative to one another through time. **FIGURE 5.1** shows the difference in the five-year rolling returns for the two portfolios. When the line is above zero, GMP has outperformed the domestic stock/bond portfolio for the trailing five years, measured by annualized total returns. When the line is below zero, the domestic stock/bond portfolio is the leader. For example, the chart starts at the end of 1992, when GMP's trailing annualized five-year total return was 9.4 percent versus 13.7 percent for the domestic equity/bond strategy. The 4.3 percentage point lag for GMP is indicated by the line at just below −4. By contrast, GMP was leading the domestic equity/bond portfolio by more than two percentage points in late-2006. The message is that cycles prevail.

Figure 5-1 encourages the idea that an investor could have improved results dramatically by owning a domestic stock/bond portfolio from 1992 through 2003 and then switching to a broader global portfolio. But why stop there? Not only do different portfolios of asset classes wax and wane as performance leaders; so do individual

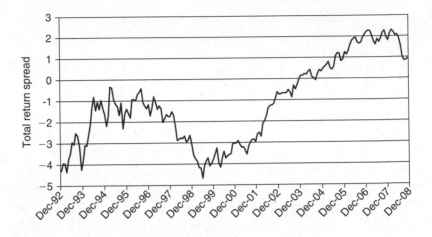

**Figure 5.1** 5-Year Rolling Annualized Total Return Spread

Global market portfolio 5-year % total return less domestic stock/bond portfolio 5-year % total return

Source: Author's calculations using data from Morningstar Principia and Standard & Poor's.

asset classes. Stocks often beat bonds, but sometimes the latter wins the race. And if we survey the history of foreign stocks and bonds, commodities, and REITs, a constantly evolving list of winners and losers emerges.

Surveying history promotes the illusion that the future will be clear. But it's the past that's transparent. The future is always different, always murky, and always surprising to some degree. That leads to the ancient problem of trying to consistently identify leaders and laggards in advance, with perfect or near-perfect timing. The task is virtually impossible on an ongoing basis. If we could correctly anticipate winners and losers with any consistency, there would be no need for holding multi-asset class portfolios. Diversification within and across asset classes would be pointless in a world where forecasting winners and losers was routine for mere mortals. But such powers of prognostication are the stuff of dreams. The ubiquity of mediocrity, and worse, in professional money management suggests as much.

If predictions are suspect, multi-asset class diversification looks like an essential alternative. We can also make a case for modest adjustments in the asset allocation to take advantage of changes in valuations or to rebalance the investment mix when market fluctuations throw our strategic blend out of whack. The extent and frequency of such changes are forever open to debate, and much depends on one's confidence in the current reading of market conditions. But as future chapters will argue, leaving an asset allocation untouched isn't riskless either, even in a world where forecasting is difficult.

The critical point for the moment is that the factors that make owning asset classes in isolation so hazardous—volatility, unpredictable performance in the short term—are turned into valuable risk management tools when asset classes are intelligently combined. The fundamental reason: broad asset classes generally move with varying degrees of independence from one another. When one suffers a negative period, another may deliver positive performance. There's no guarantee, particularly over a few months, and so there may be times when many, perhaps most of the major asset classes show unusually high correlations simultaneously during extreme bouts of selling, as 2008 reminds.

But momentary bouts of volatility, even extreme ones, don't change the strategic goal of managing risk. The reasoning is that with intelligent portfolio design we can maximize return while minimizing risk, as Markowitz first detailed in the 1950s. Chasing return without analyzing risk, by contrast, is misguided and prone to failure. Investors have more control over managing risk, so this is where strategic efforts are likely to be most productive.

## Risk Management 101

There are countless ways to measure and manage risk on the journey to building and managing an investment portfolio. As an introduction, let's begin by considering the annual total return histories of ten broad asset classes for the ten years through 2008 in **TABLE 5.5**. Note the fluid trend among leaders and laggards among stocks, bonds, REITs, and commodities. It's not uncommon to find leaders in one year succumb the next, and vice versa. In 2008, for instance, one of the worst calendar years ever for the global capital and commodity markets, there were three asset classes that posted gains: foreign bonds in developed markets, U.S. bonds, and, of course, cash.

There's enough randomness in the trends to keep investors guessing. That includes long stretches of positive results for longer than investors expect. REITs, for example, posted consistently strong

## Table 5.5 Annual Total Returns

Calendar year total returns for the major asset classes, ranked in descending order

| 1998 | 1999 | 2000 | 2001 | 2002 |
|------|------|------|------|------|
| U.S. Stocks 24.1 | Emerging Market Stocks 64.1 | Commodities 31.8 | REITs 12.4 | Commodities 25.9 |
| Foreign Developed Market Stocks 19.9 | Foreign Developed Market Stocks 27.0 | REITs 31.0 | U.S. Bonds 8.4 | Foreign Developed Market Government Bonds 22.0 |
| Foreign Developed Market Government Bonds 17.8 | Commodities 24.4 | Emerging Market Bonds 12.8 | Emerging Market Bonds 7.6 | U.S. Bonds 10.3 |
| U.S. Bonds 8.7 | U.S. Stocks 20.9 | U.S. Bonds 11.6 | U.S. High-Yield Bonds 5.8 | Emerging Market Bonds 8.8 |
| Cash 5.0 | Emerging Market Bonds 16.8 | Cash 6.3 | Cash 3.7 | REITs 3.6 |
| U.S. High-Yield Bonds 0.6 | Cash 4.9 | Foreign Developed Market Government Bonds −2.6 | Foreign Developed Market Government Bonds −3.5 | U.S. High-Yield Bonds 3.1 |
| Emerging Market Bonds −5.3 | U.S. High-Yield Bonds 3.3 | U.S. High-Yield Bonds −5.2 | Emerging Market Stocks −4.7 | Cash 1.7 |
| REITs −17.0 | U.S. Bonds −0.8 | U.S. Stocks −7.5 | U.S. Stocks −11.5 | Emerging Market Stocks −8.0 |
| Commodities −27.0 | REITs −2.6 | Foreign Developed Market Stocks −14.2 | Commodities −19.5 | Foreign Developed Market Stocks −15.9 |
| Emerging Market Stocks −27.7 | Foreign Developed Market Government Bonds −5.1 | Emerging Market Stocks −31.9 | Foreign Developed Market Stocks −21.4 | U.S. Stocks −21.5 |

Indices: 3-month T-bill; Citigroup ESBI-Cap Brady; Citigroup Non-$ World Government; CSFB High-Yield; Lehman Bros Aggregate; MSCI EAFE ($); MSCI EM ($); Russell 3000; Wilshire REIT; Dow Jones-AIG Commodities; iBoxx High-Yield.

Source: Author's ranking using data from Morningstar Principia and Indexco.com.

| 2003 | 2004 | 2005 | 2006 | 2007 | 2008 |
|------|------|------|------|------|------|
| Emerging Market Stocks 51.6 | REITs 33.1 | Emerging Market Stocks 30.3 | REITs 36.1 | Emerging Market Stocks 36.5 | Foreign Developed Market Government Bonds 10.1 |
| Foreign Developed Market Stocks 38.6 | Emerging Market Stocks 22.5 | Commodities 21.4 | Emerging Market Stocks 29.2 | Commodities 16.2 | U.S. Bonds 5.2 |
| REITs 36.1 | Foreign Developed Market Stocks 20.3 | REITs 14.0 | Foreign Developed Market Stocks 26.3 | Foreign Developed Market Government Bonds 11.5 | Cash 2.1 |
| U.S. Stocks 31.1 | Foreign Developed Market Government Bonds 12.1 | Foreign Developed Market Stocks 13.5 | Emerging Market Bonds 24.7 | Foreign Developed Market Stocks 11.2 | Emerging Market Bonds −10.9 |
| U.S. High-Yield Bonds 27.9 | U.S. High-Yield Bonds 12.0 | U.S. Stocks 6.1 | U.S. Stocks 15.7 | U.S. Bonds 7.0 | U.S. High-Yield Bonds −23.9 |
| Emerging Market Bonds 24.3 | U.S. Stocks 12.0 | Emerging Market Bonds 5.8 | U.S. High-Yield Bonds 11.9 | Emerging Market Bonds 6.3 | Commodities −35.6 |
| Commodities 23.9 | Emerging Market Bonds 11.3 | Cash 3.3 | Foreign Developed Market Government Bonds 7.0 | U.S. Stocks 5.1 | U.S. Stocks −37.3 |
| Foreign Developed Market Government Bonds 18.5 | Commodities 9.2 | U.S. Bonds 2.4 | Cash 5.1 | Cash 5.1 | US REITs −39.2 |
| U.S. Bonds 4.1 | U.S. Bonds 4.3 | U.S. High-Yield Bonds 2.3 | U.S. Bonds 4.3 | U.S. High-Yield Bonds 2.3 | Foreign Developed Market Stocks −43.4 |
| Cash 1.1 | Cash 1.4 | Foreign Developed Market Government Bonds −9.2 | Commodities 2.1 | REITs −17.6 | Emerging Market Stocks −54.5 |

returns during 2000–2006, marking an extraordinary run of strength for an asset class. Streaks also work in reverse, such as the three straight years of losses for U.S. stocks during 2000–2002.

Momentum, up or down, is a factor in the short-term movements in markets, and it's obvious in hindsight. But it's notoriously hard to predict before the fact. A year or two of stumbling may lead to a quick rebound, but not always. Meanwhile, a strong performance in one or more calendar years may lead to another win, but not consistently. Overall, erratic behavior appears to characterize the broad asset classes when we review prices alone in the historical record on a year-by-year basis. We may be confident that a given asset class will post positive performance over the long haul, but the prediction often looks speculative in the short run.

What looks like random and unpredictable patterns on a case-by-case basis, however, can be a powerful and benevolent force in the aggregate. Combining asset classes enhances stability for an investment portfolio compared with owning just one, or even two or three, just as Markowitz, Sharpe, and others counseled in the founding documents of modern portfolio theory. The challenge is finding a sufficiently broad array of asset classes and weighting them in a way that leads to superior risk-adjusted outcomes over time.

Theory tells us that the optimal portfolio—the point at which return is maximized for a given risk level—will be the best choice. Applying this concept to multiple asset classes brings us closer to the true market portfolio, or at least a reasonable proxy. Financial research suggests that the closer we move to the market portfolio, the more robust the risk-adjusted performance will be in the long run.

## Correlations and Diversification

A principal reason why the market portfolio is expected to offer competitive risk-adjusted returns over long stretches of time is that it always owns a variety of assets that move with varying degrees of independence. Correlation is a statistical tool for measuring the degree of independence.[16]

Markowitz was one of the first researchers to quantitatively explore the benefits of holding assets with low and negative correlations. A review of the numbers reminds us why. The relationship between any given pair of asset classes fluctuates: returns move with varying degrees of independence through time. For some asset classes the independence is quite large. Stocks and bonds, for instance, have a high degree of independence compared with U.S. and foreign stocks, which generally exhibit a much tighter relationship.

Imagine a simplified world where only correlations matter and you have a choice of five securities to build your portfolio—we'll call them Alan, Bobby, Cathy, Donna, and Edward. Let's also assume that you've decided that you must own Alan, but it's unclear if the remaining four should be held in the portfolio too. Again, correlations are the only relevant distinguishing characteristic in our imaginary universe, and your goal is to build a portfolio that's as diversified as possible. With that in mind, let's say that the remaining quartet have the following correlations with Alan:

Bobby: 1.0
Cathy: 0.7
Donna: 0.0
Edward: –0.4

Bobby looks unattractive because a 1.0 correlation with Alan tells us that there's no diversification benefit. Owning Bobby would be redundant since the two securities move in lockstep with one another. If one rises, the other rises; when one falls, the other falls. One is a proxy for the other. To the extent we're looking for diversification, there's not much point to owning Alan *and* Bobby, at least from a correlation-only perspective.

Cathy, by contrast, offers modest diversification benefits, as indicated by its reading below 1.0. Donna looks even better on that front; in fact, the zero correlation reading tells us that Alan and Donna move independently and neither has a relationship with the other. Finally, Edward's negative correlation means that the security will move in the opposite direction of Alan a fair amount of the time. This simple analysis tells us that in addition to our predetermined decision to own Alan, we should also purchase some Cathy, Donna, and Edward and avoid Bobby.

Portfolio design and management decisions in the real world are far more nuanced and complicated, of course, and correlation is but one factor in the mix. The performance outlook for each security, its current valuation (dividend yield, for instance), the investor's risk tolerance and investment horizon, and other variables must be integrated into strategic decisions. Yet in context with other factors, correlation is useful because it provides a quick numerical reading of an asset class's diversification history, or lack thereof. But we must be wary of accepting correlation numbers at face value without deeper research. Like returns, correlations are clear only in hindsight. The past, to cite the standard caveat, may not repeat. We can't see the future with perfect clarity, but we can and should go the extra mile to understand the past. That's why it's best to review correlations in their historical context, looking at how they ebb and flow over time.

Consider **FIGURE 5.2**, which shows rolling thirty-six-month correlations for four asset classes relative to U.S. stocks, defined as the Russell 3000 Index. U.S. bonds, for instance, posted a 0.18 correlation for the three years through December 1998, indicating a high degree of independence relative to U.S. stocks. In the ensuing years, the bond/stock correlation waxed and waned, offering varying degrees

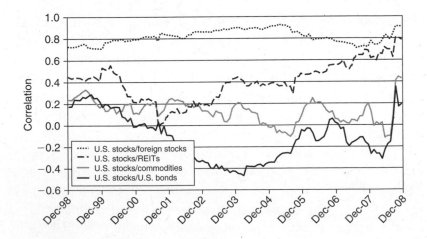

**Figure 5.2    Evolving Relationships**

Rolling 36-month correlations through 12/31/08 relative to U.S. stocks

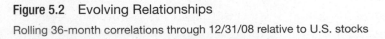

Source: Author's calculations using data from Morningstar Principia.

of diversification benefits born of mixing domestic equities and fixed income securities.

The primary message in Figure 5.2 is that correlations aren't static, so we should be suspicious of assuming that a fixed correlation for any pair of assets will hold. That's another way of saying that the benefits of diversification wax and wane. For example, for the ten years through the end of 2008, the rolling thirty-six-month U.S. stock/bond correlation has ranged from roughly 0.4 to –0.4. In addition, if the correlation is near the top (bottom) of the historical range, we might ponder the odds that a fall (rise) is coming. Additional insight can be mined by looking at longer periods, such as five- and ten-year rolling correlations and how they change over time.

Unfortunately, there's no sure thing when it comes to forecasting correlations and so no single methodology offers a perfect, unbiased look into the future. Why, then, review correlations from multiple perspectives? Rather than hoping for a crystal ball, the goal is becoming familiar with how correlations behaved in the past in order to develop reasonable expectations about what may be coming.

Keep in mind, too, that diversification benefits are present even when assets have high but still less-than-perfect correlation. Consider two asset classes with a correlation of 0.9. That's nearly 1.0, which implies there's a strong link between the two. Although the diversification benefits look minimal in this case, that's not the same as nonexistent. Depending on the context, and the available alternatives, adding another asset class that posts a 0.9 correlation with the existing holding may be superior to not adding it. In addition, because correlations fluctuate, a high correlation may not be destined to stay high and so adding the asset class may still be productive for diversification even if the past suggests otherwise. The process works in reverse as well so that an asset class that posts a low or even negative correlation with another asset in the past may become more correlated in the future.

## Harnessing Volatility

The decision to include, or exclude assets should rely on several factors. Correlation is a critical one, but it's hardly the only one. Volatility is another. The role of volatility is no less integral to our understanding of portfolio return and risk than correlation. To be sure, there are limits to what volatility (defined here and throughout as the annualized standard deviation of monthly total returns) can tell us, including what we can expect in the future based on volatility readings of the past. But it's a productive exercise, albeit as one piece in a broader risk management strategy.

As **FIGURE 5.3** illustrates, volatility, like correlation, is forever changing. Although these changes are largely unpredictable, particularly in the short term, there are broader cycles that convey valuable information for strategic-minded investors. Note that volatility was generally rising in the late 1990s. Early in the twenty-first century the volatility crested and then began falling, in some cases through 2007. Financial economics tells us volatility cycles may be partially predictable, as we'll discuss in more detail in future chapters. The implication: watching the trend in standard deviation is worthwhile for risk management.

History suggests that volatility tends to fall during bull markets and rise during bear markets. As bull markets progress, prices rise in a more consistent, less volatile manner. Meanwhile, prices tend to swing wildly in the throes of a bear market as sellers dump assets in a mad rush to raise cash. Casual observation reminds that market

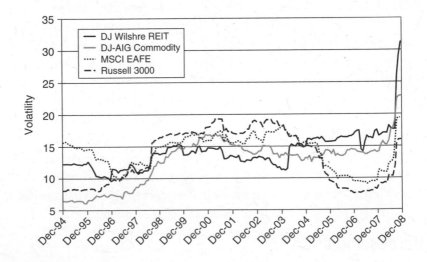

**Figure 5.3    Volatile Histories**

Rolling 36-month standard deviations of return (annualized, plotted monthly)

Source: Author's calculations using data from Morningstar Principia.

advances over a period of years can reverse course in a matter of weeks or months in severe corrections, a change of fortune that typically generates a surge in volatility. The intuition was confirmed anew in 2008, when severe corrections in the capital and commodity markets arrived, driving up return volatility to extraordinary highs from previously subdued levels.

The long-term record suggests that when volatility is at relatively low levels, it's a sign that the bull market may be nearing an end. In late 2006 and early 2007, for example, volatility for some asset classes dropped to levels last seen ten years earlier. As it turned out, the low levels of volatility in 2007 preceded a violent correction in all the major asset classes in 2008. At the very least, the low levels of volatility suggested it was time to begin reducing risk levels.

No, volatility trends alone aren't sufficiently reliable for use in market timing. But monitoring volatility across the various asset classes and understanding how current readings compare with history are critical inputs for designing and managing strategic-minded portfolios. All the more so when we combine volatility readings with other risk metrics.

Volatility, then, offers another layer of insight for assessing risk among the various asset classes. Although it's constantly changing, volatility tends to bounce around within a range for a given asset class. Since 1874, the U.S. stock market's three-year rolling annualized volatility has generally cycled within a 7.5-to-15 range, although at times it can and does rise beyond that range, as it did in 2008 and in the 1930s.

In addition, the range of volatility for asset classes differs. Volatility for equities, for instance, is consistently far higher compared to the volatility for U.S. bonds. Not surprisingly, many strategists argue that the higher volatility generally equates with higher expected returns. That's not always true for every period, but as a rule of thumb it tends to hold over long stretches of time.

In the short run, the relationship can fluctuate wildly. History suggests that the relationship will return to a "normal" range eventually, although we can't be sure of timing. Nonetheless, the historical bias has been that any substantial divergence from the long-term trend will likely be temporary, offering a strategic opportunity for rebalancing the portfolio's asset mix.

As an example, consider the volatility relationship for U.S. stocks and bonds. Equity volatility is generally higher than bond volatility. The average rolling thirty-six-month annualized standard deviation for stocks (Russell 3000) is 14.6, far above the 3.5 for bonds (Barclays Aggregate) for the ten years through the end of 2008. In the short run, the spread fluctuates—sometimes dramatically. But there appears to be a range relationship in the volatility between the two asset classes. As such, monitoring the relationship with an eye on looking for periods that appear to reflect peaks and valleys can be useful for risk management, particularly when used in connection with other risk metrics.

For example, consider a basic example that compares the trailing thirty-six-month volatility for U.S. stocks with U.S. bonds, as illustrated in **FIGURE 5.4**. The graph shows the rolling volatility for stocks (Russell 3000) less the volatility for bonds (Barclays Aggregate Bond). Note the troughs in 1994–1996 and 2005–2007. In each case, stock market volatility had fallen sharply and preceded sharp corrections in the equity market several years later.

As a short-term timing tool, the information in Figure 5.4 was of no value. Nonetheless, watching such trends is useful for assessing broad changes in relative relationships among the major asset classes.

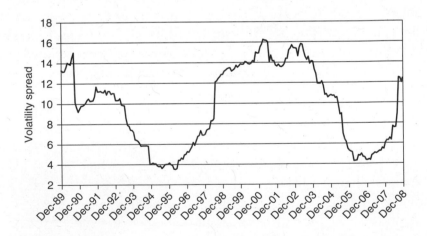

**Figure 5.4**   Stock/Bond Volatility Spread

Rolling 3-year U.S. stock market volatility less 3-year U.S. bond market volatility (annualized, plotted monthly)

Source: Author's calculations using data from Morningstar Principia.

The trend in Figure 5.4 is based on trailing data using monthly returns, but more granular readings using weekly or even daily data are more sensitive to current conditions, so they may offer more timely signals.

As we'll discuss later in the book, a growing body of financial and economic research offers some confidence for thinking that managing asset allocation in response to the various signals, including volatility, correlation, and other metrics, can help us improve risk-adjusted results over time. Dynamically managing asset allocation entails risk, of course, but so too does a buy-and-hold strategy. All investing strategies require that we pick and choose a set of risks.

Meanwhile, our benchmark is still the market portfolio, which is the ideal strategy for the average investor with an infinite time horizon. No one fits that profile, and so to the extent that an investor's risk and return requirements diverge from the average, modifying the market allocation is necessary and prudent, as we'll discuss in the next chapter.

## Chapter Notes

1. Author's analysis of data from Maddison (2009).
2. Markowitz (1952), p. 91.
3. Sharpe (1964), p. 442.
4. Ibid., p. 427.
5. *Ibbotson* (2009), p. 159.
6. Ibid., p. 32.
7. Ibid., p. 56.
8. Idzorek (2006), p. 9.
9. Gorton and Rouwenhorst (2006), p. 52.
10. Ibbotson (2009), p. 173.
11. The reader may wonder why twenty-one years of data are reviewed instead of a round number like ten or twenty years. Initially, I analyzed the twenty years through the end of 2007 and was prepared to use the results for the book. But after 2008's crushing losses I decided to add the year's extraordinary results to the analysis. In fact, the past twenty-one years offers a robust sample of what can go wrong as well as right in the capital and commodity markets and in that sense the period reviewed is productive. Ultimately, the choice of any one period is arbitrary and subjective, which

is why investors should look at multiple periods. Sampling twenty-one years is no better, or worse, than twenty years, or nineteen or twenty-two years, although each offers a distinctive snapshot of its time. For simplicity, I use a twenty-one-year review for the remaining portfolio analysis in this chapter, although readers shouldn't assume that the period studied is in any way superior or lesser to the alternatives.

12. *Ibbotson* (2009), pp. 46–47.

13. At year-end 1987, the Russell 3000's market cap was $2.2 trillion, virtually identical to the market value of Citigroup U.S. Broad Investment Grade Bond Index. Calculations for return and risk for bonds are based on Barclays Capital U.S. Aggregate Index.

14. Foreign stocks are represented by MSCI EAFE index for developed market stocks and MSCI Emerging Markets index for emerging market stocks. The proxy for foreign bonds is Citigroup Non-dollar World Government Bond Index in unhedged dollar terms. Along with the U.S. stock and bond indices, all markets are initially weighted by the relative market values to create the portfolio.

15. Ibbotson (2009), p. 173.

16. The possible correlation range is 1.0 to −1.0, with 1.0 being a perfect positive correlation and −1.0 being a perfect negative correlation. A correlation of 1.0 means that the two securities or asset classes move in perfect lockstep, which implies that there is no diversification benefit in holding both assets. A negative correlation of −1.0 indicates a tendency for one asset to move exactly opposite relative to the other. Midway between those two extremes is 0.0, signaling the absence of any correlation, meaning prices move randomly relative to one another.

## Chapter 6

# Rebalancing
## The Natural Extension of Asset Allocation

INVESTORS HAVE NEITHER an infinite time horizon nor infinite patience, which raises questions about the practical aspects of holding the market portfolio.

The unmanaged global market portfolio is a compelling benchmark of available risk premia, but as a real-world investment strategy, it's destined to run into challenges in the short run. The problem starts with the recognition that the market portfolio is probably ill suited to every investor's specific investment needs and risk profile. Another complication is the fact that risk premia vary through time, implying that investors can and should take advantage of the ebb and flow of market cycles by reassembling the market portfolio's asset allocation to build a customized strategy.

Yet we must be careful not to assume this is easy or that success is assured. For those who deviate from this benchmark, the risk of falling short of the market portfolio—perhaps far short—always looms, and the hazard grows as the time horizon lengthens. In the long run, outperforming the market portfolio is difficult, as suggested by the mediocre returns of active managers generally. Nonetheless, this is a risk worth taking for most strategic-minded investors, assuming we proceed intelligently by limiting our second-guessing of the market portfolio's asset allocation to those times and asset classes when the odds appear to be in our favor.

We start by considering the playing field: the market portfolio. In broad terms, there are four asset classes available in publicly traded funds: stocks, bonds, real estate (REITs), and commodities. If we think of cash and its equivalents as an asset class, there are five basic choices. We can further subdivide the first four into ever finer groups. Stocks, for example, can be separated into domestic and foreign categories, or value and growth stocks, small stocks and large stocks, or developed and emerging market stocks. Regional and sector distinctions are available as well. We can also overlay these categories on top of each other to produce, say, foreign value stocks in developed markets. But we must recognize that there's a danger of slicing the pie too thin with overly narrow definitions of asset groups. As the subcategories become narrower, the required effort of monitoring, analyzing, and managing the portfolio increases, and greater complexity raises the possibility of error.

For the moment, the crucial point is that we can identify the basic investment choices and subdivide them in an economically logical way to create opportunity for our portfolio strategies. The goal is managing these subdivisions intelligently to generate the investment results that satisfy our goals. The basic architecture for overseeing this task is commonly known as asset allocation.

## The Strategic Foundation

The modern literature on asset allocation dates to the dawn of modern portfolio theory in the 1950s. As detailed in Chapter 2, Tobin (1958) sets the basic asset allocation framework as choosing the ratio of cash to the market portfolio. In this simplified structure, every investor holds the market portfolio, with the amount of cash held, if any, as the distinguishing factor. The chosen mix reflects an investor's risk profile. A young investor may opt for a high weighting of the market portfolio relative to cash whereas a retired investor with little tolerance for short-term loss may choose the opposite: a high allocation to cash with a modest exposure to the market portfolio.

The definition of the market portfolio, as initially defined by Markowitz, is one of holding all the risky assets weighted in an "optimal" mix. Optimization is determined by the expected returns, volatility, and correlations of the individual components. On its face, these portfolios sit on the so-called efficient frontier by offering the highest expected return for a given level of risk. In designing such a portfolio, Markowitz (1952) also refers to "aggregates such as, say, bonds, stocks and real estate."[1] Building efficient portfolios by combining asset classes is a natural and intuitive extension of MPT.[2]

Starting with Sharpe (1964), the research advises that the market portfolio, with components weighted by their respective market values, is the super efficient portfolio that trumps all other possible combinations of assets on the efficient frontier. Everyone and anyone can own a proxy of the market portfolio. It requires no analytical skills, either initially or an ongoing basis. A number of narrowly interpreted applications of Sharpe (1964)—most notably in the large-cap U.S. equity space—have shown a high degree of practical success, i.e., the cap-weighted market index has proven itself competitive if not superior to most active management efforts intent on beating the stock market over time.

Everyone can own the market portfolio and thereby share the same asset allocation, but that's neither typical nor necessarily reasonable. Perold and Sharpe (1988) demonstrate that investors will favor different asset allocations partly because of perceptions and tolerances of risk that vary from one person to another. Yet the global market portfolio as per Sharpe (1964) is still useful as a benchmark for investigating the asset allocation alternatives. In effect, this is the passive asset allocation available to everyone. It provides a neutral starting point for considering the market's structure and asset allocation. The question is how can investors improve upon Mr. Market's asset allocation?

Our search for an answer begins by first reviewing the market's asset allocation. For example, using estimates from Bekkers et al. (2009), the breakdown for the capital and commodity markets for the end of 2008 is listed in **TABLE 6.1**.

Finance theory suggests that we use this mix as a neutral starting point for considering how to change the asset allocation. The rationale for focusing on the broad weights of components as the primary means of managing portfolio strategy begins with Brinson et al. (1986), which marks the start of the empirical explorations into the nature and relevance of asset allocation. Widely cited over the years, this influential paper has also been widely misinterpreted.

**Table 6.1**    Global Passive Asset Allocation

Market value % weights of major asset classes, as of 12/31/08

| | |
|---|---|
| Equities | 39.2% |
| Government Bonds | 30.4 |
| Corporate and Mortgage-Backed Bonds | 22.1 |
| Real Estate | 3.9 |
| Inflation-Linked Bonds | 2.3 |
| High Yield Bonds | 1.2 |
| Commodities | 0.9 |

Source: Author's calculations based on data from Bekkers et al. (2009).

At its core, Brinson finds that asset allocation is the primary influence on the variation of returns.[3] It reaches that con-clusion by studying the investment results of ninety-one large pension plans during 1974 through 1983. The key finding: investment policy—choosing the asset classes and picking the weights for the investment portfolio—"explained on average fully 93.6 percent of the total variation in actual plan return."[4] Market timing and security selection had relatively little influence on the variation of return. A follow-up study reaffirmed that asset allocation is the "overwhelmingly dominant contributor" of results in a diversified portfolio.[5]

As one of the first paper's co-authors explained later, "we found that the broad types of asset classes a fund includes in a portfolio and the proportions they represent have a profound effect on the *variability* of returns. These decisions also directly affect the returns themselves, of course, although we did not choose to stress that aspect. We concluded that asset allocation policy is an impor-tant component of the management process and deserves careful consideration."[6]

Other researchers have made similar observations, although there's a bit more nuance in the numbers and implications depend-ing on how the question of asset allocation's role is framed and the results interpreted. For example, Ibbotson and Kaplan (2000) report that asset allocation explains 40 percent, 90 percent, and 100 per-cent of investment performance. "The answer depends on how the question is asked and what an analyst is trying to explain."[7] In search of greater clarity about the role of asset allocation, Ibbotson and Kaplan (2000) study ten years of performance for ninety-four balanced mutual funds (funds that own stocks and bonds) and five years of data for fifty-four pension funds. The study then asks and answers three questions:

1. To what extent do funds' investment policy benchmarks explain the variability of returns over time?
2. How much of the investment policy decisions explains the difference in performance among the individual funds?
3. How much of a fund's return is explained by its investment policy return?

Ibbotson and Kaplan note that the two Brinson studies focused on the first question and conclude that asset allocation (i.e., the choice of policy benchmarks) explains most of the variability of returns. The result is reconfirmed in Ibbotson and Kaplan, which reports that about 90 percent of the variability of a fund's return is driven by the variability in policy returns.

The second question wasn't addressed in the Brinson studies, although many observers mistakenly thought otherwise, Ibbotson and Kaplan note. Clarifying this point, Ibbotson and Kaplan report that investment policy explains only 40 percent of the return differences among funds. The study asserts that this "relatively low" reading "must be the result of a large degree of active management."[8] To understand why,

> If all funds were invested passively under the same asset allocation policy, there would be no variation among funds (yet 100 percent of the variability of returns across time of each fund would be attributable to asset allocation policy). If all funds were invested passively but had a wide range of asset allocation policies, however, all of the variation of returns would be attributable to policy.[9]

Finally, how much of the return is determined by asset allocation? The answer varies, depending on how much market timing and security selection factors are used. For example, for funds that shun market timing and security selection and rely solely on the investment policy decisions, asset allocation explains 100 percent of the return. For context about why that's so, Ibbotson and Kaplan report that their analysis of balanced mutual funds and pension funds verifies the statement in Sharpe (1991): before costs, the aggregate of investors' performance equals the market's return. After costs, the average investor trails the market return. In short, Ibbotson and Kaplan find that "our results confirm this prediction," i.e., 100 percent of fund returns over time, as a general proposition, is explained by the investment policy return. Any one fund is likely to have different results, of course. But the average return for all funds will track the market, less expenses.[10]

The study adds that for investors with security selection and market timing skills, active management can be a positive contributor to fund return. In that case, asset allocation explains less than 100 percent of fund return. Nonetheless, this is the exception rather than the rule, according to Ibbotson and Kaplan, a point that effectively supports the central conclusion in the two Brinson studies.

Even so, Brinson et al. (1986) remains controversial by some accounts. Jahnke (2003) argues that the Brinson study is "seriously flawed" because of its focus on the quarterly variation of returns. "Investors fund their financial objectives from the accumulation of returns, not from the variation in quarterly returns," Jahnke asserts. "An analysis of the variation of quarterly returns tells us very little about how the investment choices affect cumulative returns, future portfolio values and the likelihood of funding financial objectives."[11]

Even if the Brinson studies aren't the last word on asset allocation's role in money management, we know from other research that investors imperil their long-term objectives by ignoring the management of asset classes. So-called style analysis from Sharpe (1988 and 1992), for example, shows that asset allocation casts a strong influence on portfolio results. Style analysis is a technique for identifying the sources of return in a portfolio. The process is one of decomposing portfolios returns against a series of benchmarks that are proxies for "factors," such as stocks, bonds, industries, and other identifiable sources of investment risk and return. Explaining portfolio returns via factors supports the idea that asset allocation is critical for investment results.

Discussing the research by Brinson et al. (1986), Sharpe says: "What that study said is if you put enough securities—in this case mutual funds or investment managers together—you're going to get something that's responsive to basic market factors. In other words, there isn't a lot that's going to impact the portfolio but what's going on in those basic factors."[12]

Analyzing the value of asset allocation from a different perspective, Booth and Fama (1992) quantify the performance advantage associated with diversification by showing that a portfolio's compound return exceeds the weighted average of compound returns for each asset in the portfolio. This is what's referred to as the return from diversification, and it argues for considering new purchases and sales of assets in a portfolio context rather than looking at assets in isolation, on a one-by-one basis.

Taking inspiration from Markowitz (1952 and 1959), Booth and Fama mathematically demonstrate the strategic benefits of focusing on the portfolio as a whole rather than on the components individually. The key point: investors shouldn't blindly build portfolios simply by choosing assets with the highest expected returns. Sometimes an asset with a relatively low expected return is the better choice if it also exhibits sufficiently low covariance (low correlation) with the rest of the portfolio. An asset's appeal, in other words, comes from its diversification and return contributions to a portfolio.

The basic message: asset allocation matters, and for most investors over the long run it's a critical factor for investment results. Ignoring asset allocation, then, is courting trouble. But recognizing the importance of asset allocation is only half the battle. The bigger challenge is deciding how to manage asset allocation.

## Variations on a Theme

The default choice for asset allocation is letting Mr. Market run the show by simply holding the market-value-weighted market portfolio composed of the major asset classes globally and letting the chips fall where they may. In broad terms, that works out to holding four asset classes: stocks, bonds, REITs, and commodities. There are others, but these four (including their subgroups) are the most liquid and easily replicable via mutual funds and ETFs.

The challenge of allowing the market to dictate asset allocation is that the strategy is only appropriate for the average investor with an infinite time horizon, which means that it's less than optimal for any one investor—perhaps radically suboptimal for some people. That raises the question: how should we customize the market portfolio to suit our particular investment needs and risk tolerances? That's another way of asking how we should design and manage asset allocation to match our individual circumstances.

Building the initial asset allocation and then managing it through time is the core of prudent investing and the essence of risk management. And like any sound risk management policy, deciding on the details will dictate results. So the real work begins by parsing the finer points of asset allocation's implementation.

Common sense and financial theory tell us to start by considering a broad range of asset class choices. "Although it is not always advisable to utilize all the investment alternatives in a given situation, it is always preferable to have more, rather than fewer, investment alternatives to choose," advises Gibson (1996), a financial planner, in his best-selling book on asset allocation. "Any time investment alternatives are artificially restricted, the risk is incurred that the investor will be confined to a choice along a lower efficient frontier than would otherwise be possible."[13]

Certainly the case for considering bonds in addition to stocks is widely understood. Owning a mix of equities and fixed-income securities is the foundation of building a diversified portfolio. The reasoning boils down to the fact that bond returns generally have a long history of independence from stock returns, and so holding the two asset classes concurrently stabilizes and strengthens a portfolio's risk-adjusted performance.

But what of the other two major asset classes—real estate and commodities? As it turns out, these are also worthy of consideration for a robust asset allocation strategy, as a number of studies demonstrate. For example, research by Lee and Stevenson (2005) and Idzorek et al. (2006) argue that the evidence is persuasive that real estate enhances asset allocation results. MacKinnon and Al Zaman (2009) make a similar observation, adding that REITs are a proxy for actual real estate because holding both is "redundant" in terms of portfolio results.

Researchers have also identified commodities (represented by futures contracts targeting raw materials such as oil, wheat, and gold) as productive for inclusion in asset allocation strategies. Gorton and Rouwenhorst (2006) show that commodities in the long run are an attractive asset class, offering an enticing profile of equity-like returns with comparable volatility and low to slightly negative correlation with stocks. An equally weighted mix of commodity futures contracts that's rebalanced annually generated an annualized 11.2 percent return for the forty-five years through 2004. In essence, the paper suggests that commodities overall can be considered as a distinct beta for portfolio construction purposes and one that offers powerful diversification benefits. Other researchers have made comparable points. Idzorek (2006), for example, shows that the attributes of a broad portfolio of commodities are useful for enhancing risk-adjusted results as a component in a diversified portfolio.

The strategic goal is ultimately building and maintaining a portfolio with the highest expected return for a given level of risk within the context of also satisfying an investor's risk tolerance and investment objective. Using a mix of different asset classes enhances the odds of achieving this goal. The reasoning goes back to the diversification lessons outlined in Markowitz (1952), i.e., intelligently blending assets that are less than perfectly correlated improves the portfolio's risk-adjusted return. As the investment set is broadened, the prospective risk/return profile improves, i.e., the portfolio moves closer to the optimal point on the efficient frontier, which is the best investment mix for maximizing return and/or minimizing risk.

## Rebalancing

We know that owning some mix of asset classes is generally preferable for enhancing our expected risk-adjusted results. We also know that while the market portfolio is a solid starting point for considering the options in portfolio design, we'll need to adjust this mix to suit our specific needs. That leads to the logic that we'll also need to dynamically manage asset allocation through time.

That doesn't mean we should engage in rank speculation and high levels of trading among the asset classes. But if we initially build a portfolio that differs from what the market offers, we should continue down this path by opportunistically intervening in the asset allocation process. Otherwise, why not simply buy and hold the market portfolio? If we decide to customize our asset allocation, we should also maintain the customization by managing the asset mix through time. In fact, the research literature tells us that managing asset allocation can enhance risk-adjusted performance.

But how should we manage asset allocation? For insight, let's begin by recalling Chapter 4, which reviews the evidence that market behavior isn't always a random walk, which implies a degree of predictability exists in the market. A number of studies starting in the 1980s find support for partial predictability, including a relationship between fundamental measures of market valuation (dividend yield and price-to-earnings ratio, for example) and future returns. To the extent that markets are partially predictable over longer-term horizons, asset allocation should partially exploit this opportunity by making portfolio adjustments based on what current market conditions suggest for expected returns and risk. That is, emphasize those assets with relatively high expected returns and minimize exposure to assets where expected returns are relatively low.

Another reason for deviating from the market portfolio is based on the theory that every investor is different, a fact that should be reflected in the portfolio. Recall that the central lesson of the intertemporal capital asset pricing model of Merton (1973) is that investors should build portfolios that are customized to their return and risk expectations and financial objectives, and that these portfolios should be managed through time as opposed to letting the initial design stand untouched.

Theoretically, the case for customizing an investment portfolio is clear, since the market portfolio isn't likely to suffice for any given investor. It follows, then, that a customized portfolio should be managed dynamically to avoid asset allocation drift, which threatens to create a portfolio that's inappropriate for a given investor. Further, given the evidence that asset allocation is a key driver of investment results, there's a strong case for arguing that asset allocation should be managed dynamically. Finally, both theory and empirical evidence make a strong case for using market value-weighted index funds to represent the asset classes.

In short, build custom multi-asset-class portfolios and manage the portfolios dynamically. But even if this strategy is grounded in theory and supported by compelling evidence that the markets are somewhat predictable, that alone doesn't tell us why we should expect any success in trying to beat the true market portfolio, even in risk-adjusted terms. But if we take a closer look at the mechanics of dynamic asset allocation, there's reason to think that intelligently managing the portfolio mix is more than uninformed speculation.

To understand why, consider a simple example: a customized portfolio of 60 percent stocks and 40 percent bonds. Assume that this is the ideal portfolio for John Smith, which implies that the primary goal is maintaining the 60/40 asset allocation in the face of ever-shifting markets. After setting the 60/40 mix, let's imagine that over the next year the stock market rises by 10 percent and bonds advance by 5 percent. Now the allocation has shifted to roughly 61/39. Over time, because stocks and bonds are likely to continue posting different returns, the original 60/40 allocation is likely to move further away from the target allocation, perhaps radically so in the long run.

The lesson is clear: an unrebalanced portfolio leaves the asset allocation to Mr. Market. If we decide to opt for something other than the market's asset allocation initially, it's logical to take charge of the asset allocation afterward too. If we've determined that a 60/40 mix is preferable, then we should manage the portfolio with an eye on maintaining that asset allocation until and if we decide on a new target mix. That's not to say that the 60/40 target should never be changed. But for as long as that's identified as the preferred allocation, the investor should plan on keeping the portfolio in line with the mix.

So-called rebalancing of the portfolio is the primary tool for preventing Mr. Market from commandeering our asset allocation strategy and thereby undermining our investment objectives. With a rebalancing plan, whenever stocks rise above or fall below the target weight, the portfolio is rebalanced back to the original equity allocation. The same rule applies to the other asset classes in the portfolio.

To the extent that the strategic asset allocation is the goal, rebalancing is the tool for maintaining this mix. In principle, rebalancing entails selling asset classes that rise and redeploying the proceeds to asset classes that have fallen. By design, it's a contrarian strategy, and to that extent it shares a bit of common ground with the value investing principles outlined by Graham and Dodd's *Security Analysis*.

The degree of contrarianism in rebalancing can be adjusted by altering the frequency of buying and selling and the threshold parameters (the rules that trigger and define the rebalancing activity). But at heart, this is a strategy that maintains the target asset allocation by preventing winners from taking full control of the portfolio allocation while making sure losers don't fade into irrelevance.

The underlying logic assumes the following for portfolios built with a mix of broadly defined asset classes: 1) cycles endure, and different asset classes move in cycles that tend to unfold on different time schedules from each other; 2) asset classes, broadly defined, don't disappear, so assets that are out of favor imply relatively attractive buying opportunities, and vice versa; and 3) every asset class suffers bear markets, perhaps unusually long ones, so putting a ceiling on portfolio weights for each asset class is a necessary risk-management tool.

The inherent tradeoff of rebalancing is potentially earning lesser, perhaps even negative returns in the short run compared with an unrebalanced portfolio. Yet the potential for earning a positive return in a rebalanced portfolio versus an unrebalanced portfolio is a possibility too, and we enhance the possibility of earning a profit by broadening our list of asset class investments. The point is that rebalancing reengineers portfolio risk and return, transferring more control to investors at the expense of the market, thereby giving investors an edge by enhancing their risk management powers.

Those powers arise from the basic proposition of rebalancing, which requires selling a portion of the winners to finance purchases in the losers. There are times when winning and losing are defined in relative rather than in absolute terms. If one asset class gains 10 percent as another rises by 5 percent, the rebalancing is financed by selling a portion of assets in the leader and investing in the asset class in second place. The same idea applies if all the asset classes post absolute losses. If stocks fall by 20 percent and bonds fall by a relatively mild 5 percent, rebalancing is financed by moving some money from bonds (the relative winner) to equities (the relative loser).

Rebalancing is especially useful if one asset class is likely to dominate the portfolio in terms of high performance relative to other parts of the portfolio. That's usually the case with equities versus bonds, for instance, or so history advises. Over time, the higher return in equities raises the asset class's portfolio weight relative to bonds unless we intervene with rebalancing. If history's a guide, a portfolio of stocks and bonds, left untended, will eventually become overwhelmed by the risk and return profile of equities.

Some might ask: what's wrong with that? Nothing, assuming that stocks live up to their historical role as the winning asset class relative to bonds in the long run. Granted, a fair amount of research encourages such thinking as a prudent view of the long-term future. "The superiority of stocks to fixed-income investments over the long run is indisputable," reports Siegel (1994).[14]

In that case, an investor with a time horizon beyond ten years may be tempted to hold only stocks and shun bonds and other asset classes too. Asset allocation, in other words, can be ignored for disciplined investors with a sufficiently long time horizon.

Perhaps, although there are some hazards one must be willing to accept in an equity-only portfolio. First, we must be awake to the possibility that there's no guarantee that stocks will beat bonds over, say, the next ten years, nor is there any assurance that stocks will even post a positive return over that horizon, or any other, for that matter. And while it's easy to declare oneself a long-run investor, there's enormous pressure to sell and take losses after sharp market declines.

Yes, waiting out the storm seems like a reasonable plan. But even the most battle-hardened investor may weaken if a bear market rolls on for longer than expected, or if the losses are unusually steep. Even the garden variety correction can test the mettle of steely investors. For most people, the risk of abandoning the long run in the face of a current loss is quite real.

Even if you were sufficiently disciplined to own equities through good times and bad, there's no guarantee that a stocks-only strategy would suffice. Equities are one asset class and so owning stocks alone is the equivalent of making an extreme bet relative to the true market portfolio. It may be a bet supported by history, and it may pay off, but it's still a bet, since the future is always unclear to some degree.

Portfolio theory and the limits of trying to identify winners and losers favor a diversified portfolio of multiple asset-classes. Yes, stocks have been the superior performer over most long periods of time. But we can't be 100 percent sure that the past will always repeat, particularly if we're looking at a specific period of time in the future.

What we do know is that bonds sometimes outperformed equities in the past. U.S. market history, for instance, shows several periods of superiority in fixed-income performance lasting for five to ten years relative to stocks since 1926, according to Ibbotson (2009). Arnott (2009) also reports that there are extended periods in U.S. financial history when stocks trailed bonds. In addition, commodities and other asset classes have been known to come out on top for several years at a time versus equities.

Waiting for equities to provide superior performance may look easy on paper, but in practice there are few who can tolerate the extended bouts of sharp losses that afflict the equity market from time to time. A two- or three-year bear market may look tolerable in concept, but it's something else to endure the pain as it unfolds day after day in real time.

Owning assets beyond equities to tame risk, it seems, has both academic and street appeal. In that case, a multi-asset-class portfolio that systematically rebalances the mix looks prudent. In sum, rebalancing is an essential component for winning the investment game if we consider the various risks, emotional and otherwise, that threaten to lay low the best-laid plans of investors.

## The Mechanics of Rebalancing

If rebalancing is a critical part of successful portfolio management, investors are well advised to familiarize themselves with the process. In concept, rebalancing is the essence of simplicity. Sell winners and buy losers. In practice, there's far more nuance to consider.

Rebalancing has several crucial facets, allowing investors to customize the process to fit their goals and the particulars of the portfolio. As with the initial setting of asset allocation, each investor should tailor a rebalancing strategy to match his particular expectations, risk tolerance, investment horizon, financial goals, and so on. In addition, each rebalancing program should be crafted with a particular portfolio in mind. Among the basic questions to answer in choosing a rebalancing strategy are:

- How often should a portfolio be rebalanced?
- Should the rebalancing occur with clock-like predictability? Or should it be more flexible to take advantage of, say, favorable valuation levels?

- What should the rebalancing triggers be? Should we allow a target allocation to drift five percentage points up or down before rebalancing? Ten percentage points? Twenty?

There are no easy answers. Different rebalancing strategies, like different asset allocations, deliver different results under different market conditions and different historical time periods. Certainly there is no rebalancing program that's always optimal. Some rebalancing strategies will shine at certain times and lag at others. And what's reasonable for one investor may be inappropriate for another because risk profiles and objectives differ.

One might wonder why rebalancing is useful. The superficial answer is that we want to maintain a particular asset allocation, and that requires intervention to prevent market forces from moving the portfolio off its course. But why should we expect rebalancing to provide value in the pursuit of our strategic investment goals? If the markets are reasonably efficient through time, which they appear to be, then there should be little if any opportunity to add value over the market portfolio.

And yet there appears to be a benefit from rebalancing. "The actual return of a rebalanced portfolio usually exceeds the expected return calculated from the weighted sum of the component expected returns," William Bernstein (1996) advises.[15] In other words, rebalancing is projected to yield a higher return than holding the same assets and not rebalancing. But the superior outcome with rebalancing requires assets that have both high volatility and low correlation. The market's trend, or lack thereof, is also a crucial factor.

The basic process that creates opportunity with rebalancing was examined in Perold and Sharpe (1988), which analyzed a simple portfolio of 60 percent stocks and 40 percent cash. For that mix, the paper finds that a rebalancing strategy that maintains that asset allocation will lag a nonrebalanced (buy-and-hold) strategy if there's an upward price trend in stocks. By contrast, in a trendless equity market, rebalancing will beat the unrebalanced strategy. In a persistently falling equity market, the buy-and-hold portfolio will lose less than the rebalanced portfolio. In fact, persistently falling or rising markets are the exception. More likely, markets reverse previous moves to some extent within a given time frame. Volatility, in short, is a factor, and it influences rebalancing results. Generally, reversals tend to give rebalanced strategies a performance edge over unrebalanced strategies, Perold and Sharpe find. If the equity market was flat over the investment period but endured a fair amount of volatility in the interim, rebalancing a 60/40 mix would probably exploit the equity volatility by generating a higher portfolio return relative to an unrebalanced strategy.

William Bernstein (1996) presents a formula[16] for quantifying the so-called rebalancing bonus, asserting: 1) a rebalanced portfolio usually outperforms an unrebalanced version of the same investments; and 2) the excess return generated by rebalancing can be predicted and measured with a high degree of precision. "The intrinsic rebalancing potential of any asset pair," the paper explains, "is the difference between its mean variance and covariance." The author tests the formula's accuracy for estimating the rebalancing bonus by analyzing 105 portfolios of 50/50 mixtures of asset pairs represented by fifteen indices for equities, bonds, REITs, and natural resources. The conclusion: the formula's theoretical forecast is typically close to the actual number that's based on market returns for 1988 through 1994.

Bernstein and Wilkinson (1997) note that a crucial factor for exploiting the benefits of rebalancing depends on the extent of divergence in the returns for each asset in the portfolio.[17] "Common experience demonstrates that rebalancing often yields significant excess returns when the return differences are small. Contrariwise, rebalancing penalizes the investor when asset return differences are large."[18]

Rebalancing a portfolio of virtually riskless Treasury bills and U.S. stocks, for instance, is likely to trail the performance of a stocks-only portfolio in the long run, assuming the historical trend of rising equity prices remains intact. By comparison, the rebalancing drag is likely to diminish with a mix of U.S. stocks and U.S. bonds; depending on the time period, rebalancing this asset allocation may even outperform a nonrebalanced mix of the same two asset classes. Why? Because the return spread between stocks and bonds tends to be smaller compared with the spread between stocks and T-bills.

The implication: rebalancing strategies should differ depending on the portfolio's composition. What's appropriate for a wide mix of assets—stocks, bonds, REITs, and commodities—may be less than ideal for a portfolio of cash and stocks.

William Bernstein (2002) analyzes rebalancing and shows that its application on diversified portfolios[19] offers three key benefits over time relative to not rebalancing: "First, it keeps your portfolio's risk within tolerable limits. Second, it generates a bit of excess return [relative to the same portfolio that remains unrebalanced]. And third, and perhaps most important, it will instill the discipline and mental toughness essential to investment success."[20]

Capturing these benefits through rebalancing relies on a systematic strategy for buying low and selling high. In theory, anyone can take advantage of the opportunity; in practice it's difficult because emotion makes contrarian-based financial decisions difficult for the average investor. Focusing on maintaining a rigorous rebalancing strategy helps exploit the benefits that accrue over time with a contrarian-based investment philosophy. "Rebalancing forces you to buy low and sell high," advises William Bernstein (2002). "It takes many years and many cycles of rebalancing before you realize that bucking conventional wisdom is a profitable activity."[21]

In concept, the evidence in favor of some form of rebalancing is clear. Research by Tsai (2001) finds evidence that rebalancing generally is superior to an unrebalanced portfolio. The paper analyzes four rebalancing strategies, each with varying parameters applied to multiple asset classes, and compares results against an unrebalanced portfolio. The return and risk differences are "small" among the four rebalancing systems, and no single rebalancing strategy emerges as an obvious winner for the study period 1986 through 2000. What's striking is the inferiority of never rebalancing when results are measured in risk-adjusted terms with Sharpe ratios.[22] "This paper shows that neglecting rebalancing produces the lowest Sharpe ratios across a wide range of risk profiles."[23]

Tokat (2006) notes that "the effect of a rebalancing strategy on a portfolio depends on return patterns over time. If security prices approximately follow a random-walk pattern, then rebalancing more frequently or within tighter bands reduces a portfolio's downside risk (absolute as well as relative to the target asset allocation). In a trending or mean-reverting market, the impact of rebalancing may be somewhat different when viewed on an absolute or relative-to-target basis."[24] The paper, summarizing results from previous studies, identifies four key factors that determine rebalancing's effects: return correlations, return volatility, return scale, and time horizon:

- Lower correlations between assets improve the expected value of rebalancing; higher correlations reduce the potential rebalancing benefit.
- When return volatility is higher for one or more asset classes, that "implies a greater need to rebalance" to keep the target allocations on track.
- A "high" expected return in a given asset class elevates the need for rebalancing to keep it from dominating the portfolio and thereby inadvertently raising the overall risk level. Also, the wider the spread in returns among the various portfolio components, the greater the case for rebalancing to maintain the target allocation.
- Time horizon is a critical factor too. "A long time horizon increases the likelihood of a portfolio drifting from its target allocation, which produces a greater risk of significant return deviation."[25]

These four factors are immutable in the sense that they can't be altered directly. For example, a portfolio holding assets with low correlations will produce different rebalancing results compared to a portfolio of high correlation assets. Only through indirect means—changing the assets—can we adjust the influence of correlation on rebalancing results.

The point is that expectations for what a rebalancing strategy can—or can't—deliver are largely grounded in the specifics of a portfolio's composition. Identical rebalancing strategies applied to different portfolios will necessarily produce different, perhaps radically different, results. To the extent that investors can take advantage of the four rebalancing factors above, the opportunity flows indirectly, by way of portfolio construction, i.e., asset allocation.

Although the specific asset allocation will determine much of a rebalancing strategy's results, the influence isn't absolute. We can also partly manage the results of rebalancing directly by focusing on another set of variables. This is a function of designing and managing the rebalancing strategy. The primary choices fall into two categories: frequency and threshold.

Frequency refers to how often rebalancing activity takes place, which in turn directly affects portfolio results. Rebalancing a portfolio once every quarter will lead to different results compared to annual rebalancing. Threshold relates to the rules that trigger a rebalancing action. For example, a portfolio with a 60 percent equity weight can be allowed to drift five percentage points above or below the target allocation before rebalancing kicks in. In that case, even if stocks rose to a 65 percent allocation, or fell to a 55 percent allocation, no rebalancing would take place. But if the equity weight climbed to 66 percent, or dropped to 54 percent, the stock allocation would be rebalanced back to the target 60 percent weight.

Blending the frequency and threshold variables will generate a range of portfolio results, even for otherwise identical portfolios. And so the challenge is customizing a rebalancing plan that's appropriate given 1) the portfolio's asset allocation and 2) the investor's objectives and risk tolerance.

Rebalancing strategies necessarily vary depending on the mix of assets too. A portfolio with a broad array of low and uncorrelated asset classes, several of which exhibit fairly high levels of return volatility, demands a different rebalancing strategy compared with a portfolio of, say, just stocks and cash or a portfolio of only investment grade bonds. Each asset class has a different risk and return profile, so a portfolio's risk and return composition is dictated by the asset mix. In turn, each asset mix requires a rebalancing program that's appropriate for the portfolio and sensitive to the investor's objectives and risk tolerance.

We must also remember that more frequent rebalancing activity isn't infinitely beneficial. At some point, increasing the frequency of rebalancing faces diminishing results, perhaps to the point of becoming detrimental to a portfolio compared with an unrebalanced strategy. That's because while a rebalancing strategy can look good on paper, in the real world rebalancing incurs the various costs associated with buying and selling securities, including brokerage commissions and taxes. Because these factors must be considered when crafting a rebalancing strategy, what look goods in concept may be less so in practice.

Leland (1985) establishes that, in the extreme, maintaining a constant target allocation requires constant trading, which would eventually generate expenses that would overwhelm the portfolio even with minimal transaction costs. Clearly, practical considerations demand something less than continuous rebalancing, particularly for taxable accounts. The presence of trading costs with rebalancing reminds that careful attention must be paid to the design and implementation of a rebalancing strategy in order to minimize the costs and maximize the benefits.

As a practical issue, capital gains taxes are the major challenge for a rebalancing strategy, argue Dammon et al. (2003). Accordingly, investors should seek to minimize the taxable consequences of rebalancing through a variety of techniques, such as directing new investment monies into underweighted asset classes and taking advantage of tax loss harvesting to offset any capital gains, Riepe and Swerbenski (2007) recommend.

Horvitz (2002) notes that the costs associated with taxes and trading, although sizeable, are typically underestimated when rebalancing. Recognized or not, taxes and trading costs triggered by rebalancing must be weighed against the expected benefits in search of the optimal tradeoff.

A number of studies have factored in the presence of trading costs in the study of rebalancing and found that creating no-trading bands around target allocations improves results. A target allocation for equities of 60 percent, for example, would be allowed to fluctuate in a band around the allocation before engaging in rebalancing trades. Instead of rebalancing once equities deviate from 60 percent, a rebalancing band would allow the allocation to drift. A band of five percentage points permits a 60 percent target allocation to drift to 65 percent or 55 percent before rebalancing commences.

After factoring in trading costs, Constantinides (1986), Dumas and Luciano (1991), and Leland (1996) demonstrate that the optimal rebalancing strategy usually requires a "no trade" band around the target allocation. Only after the allocation has moved outside the band should rebalancing commence, returning the allocation to the outer edge of the band as opposed to the original target. As an example of the "optimal policy" mechanics, according to Leland:

... the target stock/bond ratio is 1.5: a 60/40 stock-to-bond ratio. We show that no readjustments should be made when the ratio remains between 1.44 and 1.56. If the ratio moves (say) to 1.58, then trading should take place to restore the ratio to 1.56. If the ratio moves to 1.42, then the ratio should be restored to 1.44. Thus there may be extended periods with no trading (as the ratio remains inside the no-trade interval), followed by brief periods in which many trades may be required to keep the ratios at the interval boundary.[26]

Clark (2001a) explains the rationale for a non-trading region (NTR) as a buffer to insure that costs associated with rebalancing don't overwhelm the benefits. The reasoning inspires establishing an NTR around the target weights for each asset class. Assume, for instance, a 60 percent allocation to stocks and that the break-even point (rebalancing costs and benefits are identical) is five percentage points. That is, the break-even point is if stocks fell to a 55 percent weight or rose to a 65 percent allocation. Only if the equity allocation falls below 55 percent, or rises above 65 percent should rebalancing commence because at those points the benefit exceeds the cost.

Masters (2002) devises a formula[27] for identifying the trigger point where the net benefit of rebalancing exceeds the costs. "Rebalancing entails portfolio transactions, so the benefit has to be weighed against the costs incurred, including both direct trading expenses and indirect market impact." The costs tend to outweigh the benefits until the allocation has sufficiently deviated from the target allocation. The larger the spread between the target and current allocation, the more likely there's a net benefit to rebalancing.[28]

One qualification is that "the trigger point will not necessarily be the same for all asset classes," Masters adds. "If the benefit of rebalancing comes from avoiding tracking error [a measure of how closely a portfolio follows its benchmark index], then more volatile asset classes would tend to have lower trigger points for rebalancing, assuming all else is equal."[28]

## The Myth of the Perfect Rebalancing Strategy

The decisive variables for designing a rebalancing system are frequency and magnitude. Simply put, how often? And to what degree?

It's tempting to think that a rebalancing program can be optimized on these two factors along the lines of building optimal portfolios as per Markowitz. Unfortunately, the optimal rebalancing plan is elusive. What's optimal for one strategy, given the assets and the investor's profile, may be suboptimal for another portfolio owned by another investor.

"The question of how often to rebalance is one of the thorniest in investing," William Bernstein (2002) observes. Historical data suggests rebalancing every two to five years, depending on the asset allocation and the time period. "But you have to be careful in interpreting this data, because the optimal rebalancing interval is exquisitely sensitive to what assets you use and what years you study." A happy medium seems to be "about once every few years." That's partly to minimize tax and trading costs, which are exacerbated with more frequent rebalancing.[30]

In addition, William Bernstein reminds that for periods of one year or less, the financial literature finds evidence of price momentum, i.e., strong performance is followed by more of the same and vice versa. Over longer periods, studies find evidence of the opposite: the worst performers become the best and the best become the worst. Because rebalancing thrives on the latter, "you should not rebalance too often."[31]

But there's no consensus in the various rebalancing strategies analyzed over the years. Arnott and Lovell (1992) examine several rebalancing programs that vary by frequency and threshold with market data for the years 1968 to 1991 based on a stock/bond target allocation of 50/50. Among the different strategies reviewed: 1) calendar rebalancing with monthly, quarterly, and annual rebalancing frequencies; 2) rebalancing to an allowed range, e.g., a 60 percent target with five-percentage-point band so that a rise to 66 percent triggers a sale to reduce allocation to 65 percent; 3) threshold rebalancing so that a 60 percent target allocation that rises to 66 percent is returned to 60 percent; and 4) a drifting mix that applies no rebalancing.

Overall, "We find that more frequent rebalancing has been beneficial and that wide tolerance for departures from policy has not," Arnott and Lovell report. In essence, maintain the asset allocation and rebalance often, the study finds. The results also argue against letting a portfolio's asset mix drift. "Laxness has permitted excessive portfolio exposures at just the wrong times," which is to say that the unrebalanced portfolio posted discouraging results.[32]

Additional insights from Arnott and Lovell include these observations:

- Less restrictive rebalancing guidelines degrade results, particularly if we merely rebalance to the outer bounds of the allowed range.
- Threshold rebalancing performs very well, nearly matching monthly rebalancing, if we aggressively return to the normal portfolio. Surprisingly, the breadth of the thresholds seems to make no meaningful difference to returns.
- Effective rebalancing requires only slightly higher transaction costs since income reinvestment and allocation of cash flows can provide most of the necessary funds. Monthly rebalancing requires just 10 per cent annual turnover. If we assume that 6 per cent turnover can be achieved "for free" through reinvestment of income and targeting of portfolio cash flows, then we must incur only 4 per cent additional annual turnover. Such low turnover costs far less than failure to rebalance. The futures markets can help to make even these marginal costs smaller still.[33]

But we must be careful not to read too much into any one rebalancing study. Results can and will vary depending on the time period studied, the rebalancing rules, and the asset mix used in the analysis. A study that reviews rebalancing strategies for one twenty-year period may produce different results for another twenty-year period with the same assets. As a result, we should be wary about drawing definitive conclusions from one or even several rebalancing studies.

Israelsen (2001), for example, shows that the risk reduction benefits of rebalancing will vary over time. The study analyzes the historical returns for a portfolio with three equally weighted equity components: U.S. large-cap stocks, U.S. small-cap stocks, and foreign large-cap stocks. One strategy is an unrebalanced portfolio, the other uses annual rebalancing. Both portfolios are compared for three time periods: 1970–2000, 1991–2000, and 1996–2000. The result is that substantial risk reduction (defined as the percentage decrease in standard deviation) prevails in all three rebalanced portfolios. But only in one case (1970–2000) did annual rebalancing generate lower risk *and* substantially higher return relative to no rebalancing. In the other two periods, the risk reduction from rebalancing was accompanied by marginally lower returns, although just barely so.

Daryanani (2008) recommends "opportunistic rebalancing" as an alternative to the more popular fixed-calendar rebalancing program. "The problem with annual or quarterly rebalancing is that the dates chosen for rebalancing are arbitrary, and thus we cannot possibly expect to catch the juiciest buy-low/sell-high opportunities," the paper notes.[34] The author argues that a better choice generally— based on the study's results from various strategies using 1992–2004 market history—is one of rebalancing less often while looking more frequently in search of the superior opportunities. That doesn't mean you should rebalance more frequently; rather, you should favor those times when the opportunities look most appealing. Daryanani also finds evidence that "rebalancing benefits can be increased by using more uncorrelated assets, to increase the number of buy-low/sell-high opportunities."[35]

Tapping additional benefits from rebalancing is closely linked to choosing a superior rebalancing band, or the range of allocations permitted around the target allocation before rebalancing activity begins. "The new insight our data provides is that too narrow a band (0, 5, 10, 15 percent) curtail rebalancing benefits because it does not allow asset classes to ride the up or down trends," Daryanani explains. "On the other hand, too wide a band (25 percent or higher) misses buy-sell opportunities." The conclusion: favor 20 percent bands. And while looking more frequently is beneficial, this research suggests that there are diminishing returns on this front too. "A revelation from our study is that one does not need to go to the extreme of daily looking to capture these marked improvements; weekly and biweekly looking provides just as much in rebalancing benefits."[36]

Nonetheless, consensus is elusive in the rebalancing literature. Other researchers come to a range of conclusions with regard to the optimal timing for rebalancing activity. Examples from two extremes include:

- Buetow et al. (2002) find that shorter rebalancing frequencies improve performance versus longer intervals. Using Monte Carlo simulations, the study finds that daily monitoring and 5 percent trigger rebalancing produce the best results relative to less-frequent strategies. Generally, more frequent rebalancing periods are superior.

- Smith and Desormeau (2006) argue the opposite extreme, finding that deferring rebalancing for up to four years is preferable to monthly and quarterly rebalancing rules.

There are also conflicting results on the merits of pre-set calendar rebalancing versus opportunistic strategies that only rebalance when and if certain conditions are met. Similarly, different studies find a variety of results for setting threshold rules—how far allocations are allowed to drift from target weights before rebalancing commences.

Reviewing the expanding list of rebalancing studies reminds that a single optimal strategy probably doesn't exist, just as the perfect asset allocation plan for everyone is illusory because of varying preferences and objectives. That doesn't make rebalancing any less germane to managing the asset allocation process, although it highlights the difficulty of choosing a rebalancing regime.

Riepe and Swerbenski (2006) examine twenty rebalancing strategies plus a never-rebalance program for tax-deferred accounts and assuming no transaction costs. The rebalancing strategies varied by 1) the trigger, or the rule that sets the rebalancing actions in motion and 2) by the target, which determines if the rebalancing moves allocations back to the target weight or to the tolerance boundary, a range around the strategic allocation. Simulating results by using a Monte Carlo–based analysis, the study reviewed 5,000 ten-year histories for the examined asset classes: large-cap stocks, small-cap stocks, international stocks, bonds, and cash.[37]

Yet despite the range of strategies analyzed, no clear rule emerged from the study. The authors report that "no one technique resulted in a superior trade-off between risk and return."[38] That's not to say that the twenty-one strategies didn't produce a variety of outcomes—they did. But it's not obvious that the sets of trade-offs offer clear-cut choices about what's superior and what's not. For example, annualized monthly returns varied but in line with volatility. Higher returns from rebalancing strategies were generally available at the price of higher risk. The relationship, in fact, appears strikingly familiar with what modern portfolio theory predicts on the matter of tradeoffs between return and risk. Higher risk, then, is inherently neither good nor bad, which is to say that different investors will come to legitimately different conclusions about which rebalancing program is superior.

That leads the authors to advise: "Our conclusion is that the decision to rebalance is far more important than the decision of how exactly to do it."[39] To the extent one can intelligently make a selection, Riepe and Swerbenski explain that one should favor one rebalancing plan over another to the extent that it serves the strategic risk and return targets of the investor.

Rebalancing in some form is clearly advisable, if only to maintain the asset allocation plan. Indeed, there's not much point to designing an asset allocation that's specific to an investor and then letting the market take full control of the portfolio for managing asset weights thereafter. In that case, why not simply buy the true market portfolio in the beginning and be done with it? If that's unappealing, so too is the idea of forgoing the rebalancing process.

Rebalancing is a natural and necessary extension of any asset allocation strategy that differs from the market portfolio. A reasonable interpretation of the research calls for limiting the rebalancing transactions to those times when target allocations are altered by more than a trivial amount. How does one define "trivial"? Inevitably, different investors will cite different answers, although a 10 percent shift from the target allocation is a practical guideline. Aggressive investors may be inclined to lower the threshold; conservative investors may want to raise it. Alternatively, one could limit rebalancing in the portfolio to once a year, or every other year, breaking the rule if dramatic market moves inspire an early intervention.

Ultimately, the details of implementation must be driven by each investor's objectives and risk tolerance. The conundrum of asset allocation and rebalancing is that they are at once essential and yet immune to generic solutions.

## Chapter Notes

1. Markowitz (1952), p. 91.
2. The necessary calculations for building portfolios were tedious and impractical when Markowitz (1952) was written. In the computer age, the task has been greatly simplified, thanks to a broad array of software tools for building

optimal portfolios. A few examples include Zephyr Associates' Allocation Advisor (www.styleadvisor.com), Morningtar's EnCorr (corporate.monringstar.com), Hoadley Portfolio Optimizer (www.hoadley.net), and Mathworks' Financial Toolbox (www.mathworks.com). This list merely scratches the surface of the available choices. But with vast choice comes a variety of design, so results can vary, perhaps dramatically. Accordingly, investors should understand the assumptions and design methodology of a software product before using it to make investment decisions.

3. It's important to emphasize the word "variation" here. Many of the references to Brinson et al. (1986) over the years mistakenly report that the paper finds that asset allocation is the primary driver of investment returns. Actually, the study concludes that asset allocation is the main driver of the variation of quarterly returns. Although the two are related, the variation of returns and the actual returns are sufficiently distinct to treat each separately in portfolio analysis.

4. Brinson et al. (1986), p. 42.

5. Brinson et al. (1991), p. 40.

6. Hood (2005), p. 7.

7. Ibbotson and Kaplan (2000), p. 26.

8. Ibid., pp. 30–31.

9. Ibid., pp. 29–30.

10. Ibid., p. 32.

11. Jahnke (2003), pp. 26–27.

12. Vinocur (1995).

13. Gibson (1996), pp. 127–128.

14. Siegel (1994), p. 25.

15. William Bernstein (1996), p. 1. See Bernstein and Wilkinson (1997) for a formal treatment.

16. $X_1 X_2 (Var_1/2 + Var_2/2 - Covar_{1,2})$, where $X_1$ is the amount of asset 1, $X_2$ is asset 2; $Var_1$ is the variance of asset 1, $Var_2$ for asset 2; and $Covar_{1,2}$ is the covariance of assets 1 and 2.

17. Divergence here refers to the absolute level of return. Annualized returns of 9 percent and 10 percent, for example, are relatively similar compared to returns of 5 percent and 20 percent.

18. Bernstein and Wilkinson (1997), p. 3.

19. Diversification here is defined as owning a mix of assets with some degree of low and/or negative return correlations—i.e., multi-asset-class portfolios.

20. William Bernstein (2002), p. 286.

21. Ibid., p. 288.

22. A Sharpe ratio is a risk-adjusted performance measure calculated as an asset's return over the "risk-free" rate divided by the asset's volatility. Higher Sharpe ratios indicate higher risk-adjusted performance.

23. Tsai (2001), p. 110.

24. Tokat (2006), p. 2.

25. Ibid., p. 4.

26. Leland (1996), pp. 2–3.

27. $T = 2KC_i / \sigma_i^2 + \sigma_j^2 - 2\rho_{ij}\sigma_i\sigma_j$, where T is the trigger point; K is the variable kelly, a measure of an investor's risk tolerance that quantifies the trade-off between a unit of risk and a unit of return; C is the cost (including market impact) of trading the asset$_i$; $\sigma^2$ is the volatility of asset$_i$ and the remaining assets in portfolio$_j$; and $\rho_{ij}$ is the correlation between asset$_i$ and portfolio$_j$. Note: the volatility and correlation numbers are forward-looking estimates.

28. Masters (2002).

29. Ibid.

30. William Bernstein (2002), p. 290.

31. Ibid., p. 291.

32. Arnott and Lovell (1992), p. 2.

33. Ibid, p. 3.

34. Daryanani (2008), p. 49.

35. Ibid, p. 60.

36. Ibid, p. 56.

37. Monte Carlo analysis is a statistical process for simulating estimated results using large quantities of random sampling.

38. Riepe and Swerbenski (2006), p. 41.

39. Ibid., p. 41.

## Chapter 7

# Tactical Asset Allocation

## The Devil and the Details

INVESTING DEMANDS THAT investors make a fundamental choice: embrace the market portfolio or opt for something else. Most investors choose something else, which by definition translates into crafting an asset allocation policy that, consciously or not, differs from the market's allocation.

As we discussed in the previous chapter, the basic task of managing asset allocation—rebalancing—is necessary if we intentionally modify what's available passively in the market portfolio. There's not much point to customizing an asset allocation strategy only to abandon it to the market's whims for managing the mix. If there was reason to doubt or second-guess the market's asset allocation in the initial design of an investment strategy, no less is required for managing the asset allocation through time.

Rebalancing, then, is the required task that flows directly from embracing an asset allocation that departs from the passive mix available in the market portfolio. Rebalancing here is defined as responding to the asset allocation changes imposed on the portfolio by the fluctuations in the capital and commodity markets. As such, rebalancing is reactive and seeks to manage the market-driven shifts in portfolio structure.

If rebalancing is managing asset allocation by reacting to market events, what do we call changes to the portfolio structure that are based on forecasts? Sharpe (1987) distinguishes between strategic asset allocation (SAA) and tactical asset allocation (TAA). In SAA, the investor considers the asset choices and the possible outcomes for the various combinations of asset classes. The chosen allocation "constitutes the 'policy,' 'long run' or 'strategic' asset mix."[1] Inherent in SAA is rebalancing, or periodically adjusting the asset mix to return the allocation to the policy benchmark. The rebalancing, Sharpe explains, is done "after market moves change relative asset values."[2]

TAA also reflects ongoing management of the asset mix, but with the distinction of looking ahead. Instead of reacting to market-driven changes in the asset allocation, "tactical changes in asset mix are driven by changes in predictions concerning asset returns," explains Sharpe. Variations of TAA range from the basic, such as forecasting return, to more complex systems that incorporate predictions of volatility, correlations, and other variables in addition to performance projections.[3]

Strategic asset allocation is the fundamental choice of the asset classes to own and how much each should represent in the portfolio. In principle, all portfolios begin with SAA. The SAA may later be adjusted and replaced by a new SAA, as circumstances change, such as a reassessment of return and risk expectations for the long term and/or a change in the investor's personal financial circumstances. But initially, the basic choice of portfolio design for investors is the SAA.

Tactical asset allocation seeks to obtain superior results relative to strategic asset allocation alone. If successfully implemented, TAA will generate a more favorable risk-adjusted return compared with SAA. Think of two portfolios created on January 1, with identical strategic asset allocations. One is managed by focusing on SAA, so only rebalancing is employed. The other portfolio, which is identical at the outset, is managed with TAA. On December 31, if the TAA results are superior to SAA's results, TAA has succeeded. Otherwise, SAA has proven itself a better system.

Rebalancing, then, is an option for managing asset allocation, but it's not the only option. In fact, it may be combined with TAA or abandoned entirely and replaced by TAA. For most investors, rebalancing is appropriate and will suffice. But we must at least consider the primary alternative: tactical asset allocation. To do so, let's review the fundamental difference in the mechanics.

Imagine an investor who thinks stocks are overvalued, based on some yardstick, such as a low dividend yield. Interpreting the low yield as a sign that stocks are expected to perform poorly relative to bonds, the investor reduces the equity allocation and raises the portfolio weight in bonds. Another investor, using only a standard rebalancing strategy, would wait until the equity allocation moves outside its target range before making a change in the portfolio mix.

Some of the preference for rebalancing versus TAA is a function of temperament and expectations. Some investors are more comfortable anticipating trends and believe they have the skill to do so. Others prefer to react to market events, perhaps because they don't think forecasts are reliable or because they decide they don't have the ability to make accurate forecasts. Skill level, or the absence thereof, then is also a factor in choosing TAA versus rebalancing.

Clearly, some ability to monitor, measure, and analyze markets is required to implement TAA if it's to be even mildly successful. Rebalancing, meanwhile, demands no skill per se, since the strategy is a system for responding to market activity rather than anticipating it. As such, rebalancing requires only discipline and a well-designed rebalancing strategy.

Inevitably, the results of rebalancing strategies differ, but that's a function of design rather than the investor's skill in managing the strategy. Of course, one can argue that skill is required to design a successful rebalancing strategy. But assuming the rules for rebalancing are productive, running the plan isn't dependent on analytical talent.

What, then, is the case for using TAA, either in combination with or as a replacement for rebalancing? Critics charge that TAA is really just market timing in disguise. If so, why consider TAA, given the evidence that making investment decisions based on forecasting is fraught with risk, perhaps unusually high risk?

As it turns out, TAA is more than just another market timing device, although the details are critical for explaining why it's different. TAA is a nebulous concept, with rules and parameters that float and change depending on who's writing the definitions. A fair and informed judgment requires an understanding of how TAA evolved and how it's treated in the financial literature.

## Inventing TAA

William Fouse's legacy in financial history was assured when, in the early 1970s, he helped transform indexing from an intriguing idea into a practical strategy. Yet indexing was only a prelude in his money-management innovations.

In 1971, Fouse and others launched the first index fund at Wells Fargo.[4] From there it was a short leap into the realm of managing multiple asset classes dynamically in one portfolio. Fouse's leadership in devising the concept evolved into a technique that became known as tactical asset allocation, or TAA.

Initially, TAA focused on three asset classes: domestic stocks, domestic bonds, and cash. The weight of each in the portfolio changed, depending on the expected returns. The essence of TAA is favoring assets with higher expected returns while shunning those with lesser prospects. As Fouse recalls, "In 1972, I designed a formal, computer-based, utility maximization model to allocate assets actively that was consistent with both classical value theory and capital market theory."[5]

It was a revolutionary idea, in part because TAA linked the value-investing concept outlined by Ben Graham to the modern portfolio theory concepts designed by Markowitz, Sharpe, and others. Fouse isn't shy about promoting the linkage between the two dominant yet seemingly incongruous schools of thought in the world of investment strategy. On the one side is an investing focus on securities that trade at discounts to fundamental value, a notion that was reengineered in a quantitative chassis via John Burr Williams' dividend discount model. On the other side of the investing aisle is modern portfolio theory, including indexing the market portfolio.

Two different investment concepts, each at odds with the other. Yet the apparent differences aren't fatal, according to Fouse, who points to these two seemingly contradictory parts to synthesize a new whole. "What influenced the pioneers in asset allocation?" Fouse asks. "Certainly John Burr Williams' *Theory of Investment Value* and Harry Markowtiz's 'Portfolio Selection' were influential. So was an article by Bill Gray of Harris Bank in the *Financial Analysts*

*Journal* entitled 'The Application of Discount Rates in Forecasting Returns for Stocks and Bonds.'"[6]

Fouse goes on to explain the basis for the dynamic management of multiple asset classes, observing that there is usually a gap between the expected return of one asset class versus another. The difference varies and so the gap, or expected return spread, can be relatively wide at times. Such a gap suggests changing the asset allocation to exploit the apparent opportunity.

In a 1987 conference presentation, Fouse offers an example, pointing to the fluctuations in the expected return spread during 1973–1985, based on the forecasted performance of stocks less the prediction for bonds. The spread varied over those years from a low of roughly 1 percent up to nearly 7 percent, he reports. The implication: investors should favor a relatively heavy equity weighting when the anticipated return on stocks was high and reduce the equity allocation when the outlook turns less favorable.

Combining the dividend discount model with the theories of Markowitz, Sharpe, and others may sound like an uneasy union, but in fact the two sides share common ground. Consider a 2001 review of TAA as practiced by Fouse, whose strategy

> … assumes that the expected return on a stock index equals the implied discount rate for the stocks in the index (that is, the rate of return that equates expected future earnings with today's price). The expected equity return, thus calculated, is compared with the expected return on bonds as measured by their yield to maturity. With these expected return estimates plus some assumptions about correlations and the utility of high and low returns to pension plans, the model determined the "optimal portfolio" of stocks and bonds.[7]

By the standard of Fouse's track record, TAA proves itself worthy with an extraordinary twenty-three-year run of excess return through 2000 relative to an unmanaged 60 percent stock/40 percent bond benchmark. TAA's record under Fouse's guidance, according to one rating, merits membership in the "exclusive society of all-time best performers."[8]

TAA's application by others has been identified as productive as well. Weigel (1991), for instance, reviews seventeen U.S. TAA managers and finds that "the vast majority provided positive timing ability at a statistically significant level. This holds for both managers' simulated and actual market returns."[9]

Perhaps, although one might wonder if the impressive, albeit limited run with the TAA model reflects a fundamental truth about dynamically managing asset classes. Is there reason to think that adjusting the asset allocation through time, based on risk and return projections, constitutes sound investment policy? Or is it just one more speculative approach to investing without a fundamental basis? In search of an answer, let's take a fresh look at the literature published over the years that supports the case for some form of dynamic asset allocation beyond periodically rebalancing the strategic asset allocation exclusively by reacting to market trends after the fact.

## A Tactical Foundation

Our review begins with a series of research papers published from 1969 through 1973—Samuleson (1969) and Merton (1969, 1971, 1973). These four studies collectively make a powerful case for seeing the optimal portfolio concept first discussed by Markowitz (1952 and 1959) as a strategy of holding two funds. The mean-variance investment portfolio of Markowitz is one portfolio, but an incomplete one, since it's designed as a one-period optimization. In other words, building a portfolio based on Markowitz's optimization strategy is myopic, as financial economists like to say. As such, a strict reading of the Markowitz model applies only if you're building a portfolio today with the intention of holding it, unchanged, for the period ahead.

But investors often manage portfolios beyond the immediate period ahead, and so a more realistic view is one of a multi-period strategy, which implies dynamic management of asset allocation. That, of course, creates a bit of a problem with the conventional one-period Markowitz framework, which is static and doesn't look beyond a single end point. In a Markowitz world, returns, volatility, and correlations are projected and a portfolio is crafted based on those expectations. Given the information on hand, the resulting portfolio is optimal—i.e., it maximizes return for a given risk (volatility). But it's optimal only for the period considered and so the question becomes: what to do in the next period? Or, for that matter, in the interim for the current period ahead?

In the simplified one-period world of Markowitz, the complication of managing a portfolio through time isn't addressed. That's hardly a surprise. At the dawn of portfolio theory's creation, laying out the basic framework of the revolution was the priority. But portfolio design must be flexible in the real world. The practical realities of finance demand no less since the ebb and flow of markets and economies ensure that yesterday's optimal portfolio is at risk of becoming suboptimal tomorrow.

A critical piece of the evolution that formally recognized the dynamism in portfolio theory arrived in the late 1960s and early 1970s with the Samuelson and Merton papers. These articles discussed and analyzed the task of managing a portfolio through time, including the crucial challenge of maintaining an optimal mix in a dynamic setting. As such, portfolio theory was upgraded from one suited to a myopic, one-period time frame to a continuous-time application.

Simply put, the fundamental theory for dynamically managing a portfolio arrived with these four papers. The idea that an investor could build an optimal portfolio once, and it would remain optimal indefinitely, was challenged, examined, and to an extent, resolved in the Samuelson and Merton papers. A crucial discovery is that the solution for portfolio choice in the short term can and does change over the long term.

"The key is to recognize that optimal portfolios for long-term investors need not be the same as for short-term investors," advise Campbell and Viceira (2002). "Long-term investors, who value wealth not for its own sake but for the standard of living that it can support, may judge risks very differently from short-term investors."[10]

Time horizon alone changes the real and perceived risk inherent in a given asset class. Cash and inflation-indexed bonds, for example, have different imputed risk levels for investors, depending on their plans for how long the portfolio will be held. Campbell and Viceira offer some basic examples: "Cash…is risky in the long term even though it is safe in the short term, because cash holdings must be reinvested in the future at unknown real interest rates. Inflation-indexed bonds, on the other hand, provide a known stream of long-term real [inflation-adjusted] payments even though their capital value is uncertain in the short term."[11]

In practical terms, this means that an asset allocation strategy that's expected to work well over, say, the next twelve months may be less than ideal and perhaps even misguided if we consider its possibilities five or ten years on. Over time, risk changes. Meanwhile, there may be new hazards for a long-term horizon that aren't relevant in a short-term outlook. Indeed, interest rates, inflation, expected return premia, and virtually everything else is at risk of changing to some extent through time. The investor's financial circumstances can improve or worsen, too, which is likely to influence the design and management of a portfolio. In addition, an investor with a twenty-year time horizon becomes an investor with a nineteen-year horizon twelve months out, followed by an investor with an eighteen-year horizon, and so on.

The basic message is that as time passes, the higher the potential for required modifications in the original assumptions and forecasts. That implies that even an optimal portfolio requires adjustments through time.

## Change Is the Only Constant

The research from Samuelson and Merton is all the more persuasive when considered in context with the studies from the 1980s onward that observe a shift in risk premia over time. That's in contrast to expectations of static risk premia, as implied by a strict reading of the random walk theory for explaining the behavior of securities markets.

Over the very long term there's a case for seeing the capital and commodity markets as reasonably close to a random walk. But over shorter periods, something less than a pure random walk world applies. That fact lays the groundwork for seeing asset allocation as a dynamic process, perhaps to the point of using tactical asset allocation as a guiding principle.

Recall that TAA is proactive and anticipates market behavior. The question is whether there's any evidence for thinking that forecasting market activity is reasonable. Assuming the future is clear is always a dangerous proposition, if for no other reason than surprises continually trip up investors. But we're not completely blind when peering into the future, which opens the door for embracing TAA to a degree.

As we've discussed, there's a lengthening list of research papers published over the years that suggest 1) risk premia fluctuate through time and 2) returns are partially predictable for the medium- to long-term based on a range of variables, including dividend yields, price-to-book ratios, price-to-earnings ratios, and other factors. Long-term return market reversals are identified by Fama and French (1988), Poterba and Summers (1988), Campbell and Shiller (1998), and others. That is, the market has a tendency to decline under certain conditions; it also tends to rise under another set of conditions, as determined by market valuation and other factors. Fama and French, for instance, report that a mean reversion in stock prices during 1926–1985 indicates a predictable component of 25 percent to 40 percent for equity return variances for three-to-five-year periods. "Our results add to mounting evidence that stock returns are predictable...."[12]

Campbell and Shiller (1998) find that as much as 40 percent of the variance of future equity returns can be identified based on price-to-earnings ratios. Cochrane (1997) reports that 60 percent of the variation in stock returns can be forecast based on the price-to-dividend ratio when looking ahead by five years.

Quite a few other studies offer similar conclusions. Looking back from the vantage of the twenty-first century reveals a rich and growing body of evidence in favor of identifying some degree of medium-to-long-term predictability in stocks and bonds based on a number of accounting metrics. A few examples of the factors that have been found to offer clues about prospective equity performance include short-term interest rates,[13] spreads between so-called junk bonds and short-term interest rates,[14] long-term and short-term interest-rate spreads,[15] stock volatility,[16] and book-to-market ratios.[17]

There's a robust debate about what predictability implies about the efficient market hypothesis and, by extension, modern portfolio theory. Some say the ability to forecast returns based on historical measures indicates that the market is inefficient and that investors are irrational. But there's an alternative interpretation, and one that seems no less plausible: risk premia vary through time for rational reasons, a view that jibes with an updated interpretation of the efficient markets and MPT.

That may sound counterintuitive, but the efficient markets hypothesis asserts that prices reflect all known information. That doesn't mean prices won't or can't change, or that price changes are perfectly random, although that's one view. In any case, some economists argue that when new information arrives, it can and will affect prices, sometimes dramatically, and so prices will adjust through time in an efficient market.

Sometimes the price changes will be random, which is to say that new prices will be totally unpredictable. This describes the behavior of the equity market some of the time, perhaps even most of the time, and certainly over shorter periods. But not all of the time. Price changes aren't always random. That means that price changes are partially predictable. That opens the door for exploiting tactical asset allocation.

For instance, let's consider a simple example using the ten-year Treasury note. At the end of 1999, the ten-year Treasury closed the year at a 6.45 percent yield. An investor who bought a ten-year note expected a 6.45 percent return for the next decade. A year later, the yield on a ten-year Treasury note fell to 5.12 percent at 2000's close. Unsurprisingly, investors lowered their return expectations by 133 basis points for a ten-year Treasury note between December 31, 1999 and December 31, 2000. There's nothing inefficient or irrational per se in a change of expectations, even if it leads to an adjustment in asset allocation. Indeed, lowering expectations after the yield dropped was warranted because there was a high degree of confidence—a virtual certainty, in fact—that the ten-year note's lesser expected return would be realized.[18] The predictable component of the ten-year Treasury's return, in other words, approaches 100 percent. The fact that investors change their outlook as yields change is evidence neither that the Treasury market is inefficient nor that investors are irrational.

Calculating expected returns for stocks and other asset classes is, of course, subject to greater uncertainty and so confidence in forecasting returns is necessarily lower, perhaps quite a bit lower relative to Treasuries. Indeed, the ability to accurately predict future return varies widely, depending on the asset class and time horizon. As such, investors must act accordingly when making asset allocation changes.

Generally, there's a higher degree of confidence in longer-term horizons. The return for the stock market can and does fluctuate from year to year, as recent history clearly reminds. In 2007, for instance, the stock market as per the S&P 500 rose 5.5 percent; the next year—2008—it dropped by a crushing 37 percent. It's a safe assumption that few investors, if any, at the end of 2007 expected that the year ahead would deliver the worst calendar year for U.S. stocks since the Great Depression. Such dramatic reversals of fortune are rare from year to year, but it's clear that predicting what will happen in the immediate future is highly uncertain if not impossible.

The odds of being right improve for looking out, say, ten years or more. One reason is that history offers a useful, albeit imperfect, guide for what may be coming in the long-run future. The range of return outcomes falls sharply over longer horizons. The historical span of returns for one-year periods stretches from a high of nearly 54 percent down to a steep loss of more than 43 percent. The outcomes narrow considerably for ten-year periods and the performance range compresses further for twenty-year periods, according to data from *Ibbotson* (2009).

Another clue for developing reasonable expectations about future stock returns comes from looking at current dividend yields. Consider **FIGURE 7.1**, which compares the current yield through time and the subsequent ten-year price return on a $1 investment in the U.S. stock market from 1945 through 2008. For example, in

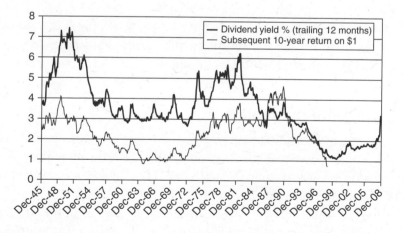

**Figure 7.1**   A Sign of Things to Come?

Trailing 12-month % dividend yield for S&P Composite U.S. Stock Index versus subsequent 10-year price return on $1 invested (monthly data)

Source: Authors's calculations based on data from Robert Shiller (www.econ.yale.edu/~Shiller).

December 1945, the trailing twelve-month yield was 3.8 percent. A $1 investment in the stock market at that point would have grown to $2.62 over the subsequent ten years before factoring in dividends. The basic relationship suggests a link between current yield and future return. Higher yields imply higher returns, and vice versa. It's not a perfect link by any means, although the association is close enough to warrant using dividend yield as one of several factors for estimating stock returns in the years ahead.

The idea of discounting cash flows based on dividends to calculate fundamental value dates back to Fisher (1930) and Williams (1938). From that foundation, Gordon (1959) introduces what's become known as the Gordon dividend formula or Gordon equation: current dividend yield added to the historical growth rate of dividends equals the long-term expected return for stocks. William Bernstein (2002) observes that the Gordon equation has been remarkably accurate over time. "For example, during the twentieth century, the average dividend yield was about 4.5%, and the compounded rate of dividend growth was also about 4.5%. Add the two together and you get 9.0%. The actual return was 9.89%—not too shabby."[19]

The relevance of dividends for estimating future return has been identified in a number of studies. Ibbotson and Chen (2003), for instance, decompose the U.S. equity return for 1926–2000 and find that the majority of the return is due to dividend payments and nominal earnings growth (including inflation and real earnings growth).

## Peering into the Future

If a degree of transparency exists in the financial markets, the visibility implies that the information can be used for managing asset allocation on a forward-looking basis. That suggests tactical asset allocation may be a practical tool.

Recall that in the previous chapter we established that rebalancing as a form of asset allocation management was limited to responding to market events after the fact. In a world of pure random walks, rebalancing would be the only logical strategy for managing asset allocation since the opportunity to add value is nil if forecasting is doomed to failure. But financial economists have documented that risk premiums vary through time, in a partly predictable way, and so the opportunity to exploit relatively higher expected returns, and shield the portfolio from relatively low or negative returns, emerges from time to time as a possibility.

Arnott and von Germeten (1983) document the merit of calculating expected return using the cash yield for projecting cash return; bond yield to maturity for long-term fixed-income return; and the dividend discount model for estimating long-term equity return. Using this framework, the estimated relative returns among the three asset classes are correlated with the posted relative performance over subsequent one-month and one-year periods. As the paper explains,

> From January 1, 1973 through December 31, 1982, each one percentage point difference in calculated relative returns was worth anywhere from 2.4 to 5.4 per cent in actual return over a subsequent year! This should not be surprising. If the markets are in equilibrium (with calculated returns remaining constant over time), then each 1 per cent in calculated expected return will be worth exactly 1 per cent in subsequent return. One per cent of expected return is worth *more* than 1 per cent in subsequent return simply because relative returns tend to move toward "normal" from extremes.[20]

If the markets are a perfect random walk, expected returns would be unchanging, in which case there would be little point to TAA. But if expected returns vary, and some of the variation can be projected using dividend yield, interest rates, and other factors, then TAA offers an opportunity to enhance results relative to a static buy-and-hold or even a straight rebalancing regime.

Projecting future results is widely accepted with fixed-income investing. Absent default risk, buying and holding bonds till maturity offers a high degree of transparency based on the reliability of future coupon payments. Buying an investment-grade bond with a 5 percent coupon offers a high degree of confidence that the expected return will be 5 percent for the life of the bond. Applying a similar methodology to calculating expected returns for stocks is less reliable, particularly in the short term, although the concept is justified, according to a number of investment practitioners with a value-oriented perspective.

"I look at the prospective return on stocks as a function of their valuation," says John Hussman, portfolio manager of the Hussman Funds, a boutique firm with several mutual funds with a respected track record and value-oriented focus. "There's a difference between trying to identify short-term direction and trying to identify prospective long-term rate of return." Hussman goes on to explain:

> It can't be market timing for an investor to say that he's more comfortable holding bonds when the yield to maturity is quite high, and that he's less willing to own bonds when the yield to maturity on bonds is extremely low.
>
> There's a direct corollary to stocks in that when stocks are richly valued, you have two things working against you. One is that the long-term prospective rate of return is very low, or unacceptable, when stocks are richly valued. On a historical basis that tends to be true when prices as a multiple of normalized earnings, or peak cycle earnings, are over, say, eighteen times peak earnings.
>
> The other feature is that when stocks are richly valued, the so called duration of stocks is commensurately high. In other words, stocks end up being a much more long-term proposition when they're richly valued, and a more reasonable long-term proposition when valuations are depressed. At the [equity market] peak in 2000, stocks were a ninety-year proposition in terms of getting your cash flows back through periodic reinvestment of those cash flows. Whereas in 1982, stocks were a sixteen-year proposition.
>
> There's no such thing as merit for an investment class. An investment class has merit depending on the relationship of the price to the future cash flows that the investment will deliver to investors over time. Investors do not receive reported earnings and certainly not reported operating earnings. They receive cash flows only to the extent that those cash flows are paid out as dividends or are profitably reinvested.[21]

Warren Buffett offers similar analysis, including a reference to equities as a "disguised bond." As he explains in an interview in *Fortune*, "A stock ... is a financial instrument that has a claim on future distributions made by a given business, whether they are paid out as dividends or to repurchase stock or to settle up after sale or liquidation. These payments are in effect 'coupons.'" Buffett notes that "gauging the size of those 'coupons' gets very difficult for individual stocks. It's easier, though, for groups of stocks." As an example, he recalls

> Back in 1978, as I mentioned, we had the Dow [Jones Industrials] earning 13% on its average book value of $850. The 13% could only be a benchmark, not a guarantee. Still, if you'd been willing then to invest for a period of time in stocks, you were in effect buying a bond— at prices that in 1979 seldom inched above par—with a principal value of $891 and a quite possible 13% coupon on the principal.
>
> How could that not be better than a 9.5% bond? [the yield on long-term corporate bonds at one point in 1978] From that starting point, stocks had to outperform bonds over the long term. That, incidentally, has been true during most of my business lifetime. But as Keynes would remind us, the superiority of stocks isn't inevitable. They own the advantage only when certain conditions prevail.[22]

Valuation, then, inspires adjusting the asset allocation in anticipation of varying expected return. In Figure 7.1, for example, the changing dividend yield suggests a commensurate shift in the equity allocation. Changes to the equity allocation are based on changes to expected return, which in this simple example is determined solely by dividend yield.

## Beyond Cash Flows

Discounting cash flows and analyzing prices relative to current and expected earnings, book value, dividends, and other economic fundamentals form the basis for projecting returns and estimating risk. A growing body of research in financial economics, stretching back decades, tells us so. The fact that value investors such as Ben Graham and Warren Buffett enjoyed investment success over long periods only strengthens the case for seeing the investment challenge as intimately linked to the fluctuations in fundamental value and price.

What's true for assessing the value for individual securities has application for analyzing asset classes and designing and managing portfolios. Asset allocation is grounded in the fundamental analysis of securities, financial economics assert, but it doesn't end there. Financial researchers continue to probe ever deeper into the investment challenge, peeling away the onion skin of mystery on countless fronts.

Modeling the relationship between return and various measures of risk, including volatility, correlation, skewness, and kurtosis, has become an increasingly productive research arena too. This is hardly surprising. Modern portfolio theory from its earliest days identified variance and covariance as contributing factors for determining risk premia. Estimating these two variables is at the heart of Markowitz's mean-variance portfolio optimization. Meanwhile, financial economists have appreciated since Mandelbrot (1963) and Fama (1965a) that return variance and covariance also fluctuate through time.

The modern era of modeling the time variation of variance and covariance dates to the early 1980s with Engle (1982), who outlined the so-called ARCH model for analyzing volatility. ARCH is short for autoregressive conditional heteroskedasticity, which has spawned a variety of statistical heirs, including the generalized application of ARCH, or GARCH, as outlined by Bollerslev (1986).

A large body of literature inspired by the ARCH/GARCH family of volatility now offers a deep pool of insight into estimating and forecasting volatility. This approach represents substantial progress over the basic approach of extrapolating historical volatility into the future. The problem with using a naïve sampling of past volatility is that it ignores the fact that volatility isn't constant.

It's tempting to use the historical record of annualized 20 percent standard deviation for the U.S. stock market as a long-term forecast for equity risk, in part because it's easy. It's arguably a good benchmark for thinking about stock market volatility as a long-term proposition. But there's no reason to think that such long-term historical measures of volatility offer much, if any, insight into, say, the next year to five years. The reason is that market return volatility is, in fact, volatile, particularly in the short run. In the jargon of statisticians, the changing level of return volatility exhibits the property of heteroskedasticity, a term that comes from the Greek: *hetero*, or different, and *skedasis*, which means dispersion.

ARCH/GARCH and its extended family factor in the volatility of standard deviation through time. The result is a more robust and reliable methodology for forecasting volatility compared with a simple linear approach. Although ARCH/GARCH is mathematically intimidating for the uninitiated, there are a number of software products available that streamline the necessary calculations.[23]

ARCH/GARCH offer substantial theoretical progress for estimating volatility, but the alternative methods of forecasting volatility are still worthy of consideration. Poon and Granger (2005) recommend that investors use an array of methodologies for predicting volatility since each technique has its own pros and cons. Indeed, some researchers find that the value of sophisticated volatility forecasting methods diminishes as time horizon lengthens. Figlewski (1997) reports that a simple historical data series is still useful, perhaps even superior to more sophisticated methodologies when forecasting volatility beyond twelve months.

Generally, the focus on volatility has been a fertile area that advances our understanding of market behavior. It's now widely accepted that forecasting volatility is easier than predicting return. Easier, but still difficult. As such, focusing on volatility is hardly a silver bullet, although it's clear that modeling volatility offers additional context for estimating returns and tactically managing asset allocation.

The basic analysis begins with the observation that the volatility of return tends to cycle through time. This is in contrast to many older models of volatility that operate on an assumption of stable volatility. In fact, the opposite is true, as you can see in **FIGURE 7.2**,

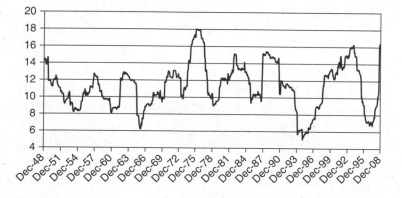

**Figure 7.2**   Volatility Cycles

3-year Rolling Annualized Standard Deviations of S&P Composite (price return, monthly)

Source: Author's calculations based on data from Robert Shiller (www.econ.yale.edu/~shiller).

which plots annualized volatility for U.S. stocks (S&P Composite) for the sixty years through 2008. The cyclical fluctuations clearly vary in a semi-routine fashion. High volatility leads to lower volatility, and lower volatility eventually gives way to higher volatility.

The first thing to note is the recurring oscillation of volatility. The fluctuations look like noise in the short run, but viewed in historical context the squiggles add up to more than a random pattern. There's a tendency for volatility to spike higher at times of market distress and fall in times of plenty. The process repeats itself, offering yet another metric for tracking cycles and estimating when the next phase will commence.

In mid-2007, for instance, as the bull market of the previous five years was coming to an end, volatility fell to its nadir for the cycle. Around that time, the U.S. stock market was basking in the wake of strong trailing returns for the past three years. Meanwhile, the market's dividend yield looked unattractive at roughly 1.8 percent. By comparison, a ten-year Treasury note offered a 5 percent-plus yield for a time in mid-2007. Even real (inflation-adjusted) yields for a ten-year TIPS bond at the time could be locked in at rates above 2.5 percent during the summer of 2007.

The alternatives to stocks, in short, were competitive if not compelling as one considered the investment landscape in mid-2007. The fact that volatility was unusually calm only strengthened the case for at least lightening up on equity allocations.

The signals emanating from volatility aren't perfect, of course, and sometimes the apparent message leads you astray. High volatility isn't always a sign of an imminent boom, nor is low volatility a flawless warning sign of trouble pending. That's why volatility can't be trusted in isolation. That's true for all market gauges, which is why monitoring a range of metrics is essential.

That said, watching volatility can offer useful clues about major turning points in the market, particularly when the trend goes to extremes and similar signs are coming from other metrics. Volatility is a complement to analyzing markets based on dividend yield, price-earnings, and other fundamental-oriented trends, offering strategists another tool for assessing the performance outlook. A nice idea, but is there an economic basis for seeing volatility as a tactical weapon in TAA's quiver?

Academic research is no stranger to volatility's potential value for peering into the future. The story begins with the observation that expected risk premia are generally higher at business cycle troughs compared to the outlook for premia at cyclical peaks. The empirical record supports this idea, and Hyman Minsky wouldn't argue otherwise.

Minsky was an economist who made a name for himself by writing passionately on the idea that in every boom lay the seeds for the next bust. Stability breeds instability, he argued.[24] His thesis that capitalism is inherently unstable is an idea that echoes Joseph Schumpeter's description of free-market economics as "creative destruction."[25] Schumpeter argued the point in the context that capitalism's evolutionary process was chaotic but integral for generating economic growth. In essence, Schumpeter advised that growth is messy.

Minsky's view was somewhat different in that he saw cycles as inherent to capitalism, quite apart from whether the process generated growth or not. As he explained, "over periods of prolonged prosperity, the economy transits from financial relations that make for a stable system to financial relations that make for an unstable system."[26]

The paradox is that capitalism is at once the engine of growth and the source of volatility. A growing body of research now relates the fluctuating level of stock market volatility to macroeconomic volatility. For example, Hamilton and Lin (1996) demonstrate that the stock market is more volatile at times due to economic recession. This factor alone accounts for more than 60 percent of the variance in the equity market. Analyzing the relationship, the paper advances a model that is "useful both for forecasting stock volatility and for forecasting economic turning points."[27] This is especially valuable information once we equate it with the research from the early 1990s onward that shows that the Treasury market yield curve imparts clues for projecting economic cycles—a topic we'll discuss in more detail in Chapter 9.

Another line of research ties market volatility to changes in return expectations. French et al. (1987), for instance, finds that volatility is a productive source for estimating future stock returns. Engle (1993) flatly states, "Financial market volatility is predictable.

This observation has important implications for asset pricing and portfolio management." Elaborating, Engle explains,

> Investors seeking to avoid risk, for example, may choose to adjust their portfolios by reducing their commitments to assets whose volatilities are predicted to increase or by using more sophisticated dynamic diversification approaches to hedge predicted volatility increases. In a market in which such strategies operate, equilibrium asset prices should respond to forecasts of volatility, as well as to the risk aversion of investors.[28]

This line of research lays the theoretical foundation for thinking that studying volatility cycles, market fundamentals, and economic trends can offer clues about prospective returns. Indeed, there's a small library of research telling us that equity return volatility is negatively correlated with stock market performance. To the extent that the relationship holds, and it often does, the former can be used to predict the latter.

That's partly due to the fact that volatility tends to exhibit what's known as clustering. A rise in volatility is usually followed by more of the same for a time. That provides a rationale for expecting that a new period of higher volatility will persist for some period of time before reversing. Low volatility levels have a tendency to cluster too.

No one should think that forecasting volatility is easy, or that it continually provides flawless clues about future returns. The greatest value of volatility appears to be when it's extremely elevated relative to the recent past. As Marquering and Verbeek (2004) note, "It appears easier to forecast returns at times when volatility is high."[29] This research documents that using velocity-related analysis for estimating future stock returns enhances results compared with efforts at forecasting returns without a volatility factor. Other researchers have found similar results as it relates to studying volatility and improving asset allocation decisions. Fleming et al. (2001) report that "volatility timing strategies outperform the unconditionally efficient static portfolios that have the same target expected return and volatility" for short-horizon investors.[30]

## Correlation

The study of variance and standard deviation naturally extends to covariance and correlation. That's unsurprising since both are the building blocks of modern portfolio theory, which assures that correlation is integral to analyzing, designing, and managing asset allocation strategies generally.

Modeling the correlation profile among the asset classes through time is less advanced in the financial literature compared to volatility, but it's no less promising for uncovering additional insight into the behavior of securities and commodities markets.

One of the key findings will be familiar to veteran investors: correlations among risky assets tend to rise, perhaps to the point of becoming one, during times of high volatility, that usually accompanies bouts of selling. That leads to another crucial message: correlations vary through time. The basic intuition is that when trailing correlations are low, and therefore diversification benefits are high, investors should consider the possibility of a future rise in correlations and then plan accordingly for asset allocation.

It's tempting to think otherwise. Assuming that correlations are stable makes the job of designing and managing asset allocation easier. But like volatility, correlations fluctuate, offering one more indication that asset allocation should be partly dynamic.

Longin and Solnik (1995) report that correlations among international equity markets are "unstable" through time, although a degree of predictability exists. The paper offers evidence of a link between high correlations among equity markets and periods of low and negative returns. Goetzmann et al. (2005) analyze 150 years of history for the world's major equity markets and also report that correlations vary through time and so the diversification benefits of global stock market investing fluctuate.

The instability isn't totally random, however. Kaplanis (1988) shows that correlations are mean reverting and so high correlations are followed by low correlations, and so on. The cyclical tendency in correlations appears partly predictable, Longin and Solnik (1995) suggest. "There is some preliminary evidence that economic variables such as the dividend yield and interest rates contain information about future volatility and correlation that is not contained in past returns alone."[31] And Moskowitz (2003) reports that portfolio return covariances are closely linked with recessions.

Coaker (2007) extends the study of correlation analysis to eighteen asset classes for the period 1970–2004 and reaches a number of conclusions for asset allocation:

a)   correlations change, sometimes dramatically
b)   mixing asset classes with consistently low correlations improves risk-adjusted returns, although he offers little encouragement that correlations are predictable
c)   low correlations for some asset classes become high correlations and so a distinction should be made between those assets with consistently low correlations versus low correlations that may be temporary

Coaker identifies five asset classes with relatively consistent levels of low correlation to the other asset classes, including equities:

1.   commodities
2.   long/short strategies
3.   U.S. bonds
4.   foreign bonds in unhedged dollar terms
5.   cash

"Natural Resources [commodities] have had the lowest average correlations—and the most consistently low correlations—to every asset in this study, including every category of stocks, bonds, and alternatives," Coaker advises. "Hence, natural resources have provided more diversification benefits than every other asset in this study." Meanwhile, foreign bonds offer a more robust level of low correlation in asset allocation than domestic bonds, although U.S. bonds are still quite potent in their own right. Nonetheless, "when mixed with U.S. equities, global bonds have provided more diversification benefits than U.S. bonds."[32]

Correlations among other asset classes, including real estate (REITs) and stocks, foreign equities and domestic equities, for example, can also be substantial at times. Yet Coaker warns that the correlations for these pairings aren't consistently low and so the related diversification benefits are more tenuous and require closer monitoring in the short term. The same is true for various subcategories within equities. Style distinctions of value and growth stocks, for instance, can offer less diversification benefits than the average posted correlations suggest.

The fact that all correlations change through time reminds us that investors can't be cavalier when estimating future relationships. At the very least, extrapolating the recent past as an estimate of the future is naïve and subject to substantial error. Even the conclusions of Coaker can't be assumed to hold indefinitely. At the same time, investors must make an assumption about correlations since this metric is at the heart of asset allocation.

Chow et al. (1999) offer a practical-minded framework for thinking about correlations that vary through time. The intuition arises from the fact that volatility and correlation tend to rise sharply in times of market stress. The challenge of using a straight reading of history is that markets are rarely in distress and so a naïve measuring of the long-run past will reflect the fact that periods of calm dominate the time series. Yet much of the incentive for analyzing the history of risk is preparing for the inevitable periods when market turbulence arrives—events that occur infrequently, which means that their influence in the historical record is slight. As a result, seeing history as one unified perspective is likely to underestimate the potential for future high-risk events.

Chow et al. address this dual challenge with a procedure for estimating risk parameters from so-called outlier periods, or those periods that are infrequent but likely to reflect high stress in the markets. The high-stress periods are integrated with the counterparts from "quiet" times for generating forecasts.

We then assign a probability of occurrence to each risk regime [i.e., the quiet period and the high-stress period]. Second, we allow investors to specify different degrees of risk aversion toward the two regimes. Investors can, of course, express a view about the relative likelihood of the two regimes and at the same time assign different risk aversions to them, but separating the two parameters is important: One is a forecast, whereas the other is a behavioral parameter. Too often, a forecast of risk is confused with an attitude toward risk.

Once we have estimated the quiet and stressful covariance matrixes, we blend them into a single covariance matrix that can reflect one's view about the likelihood of each regime and one's attitude toward each regime. We then incorporate this blended covariance matrix into the standard optimization algorithm for selecting portfolios.[33]

A number of other studies over the years offer encouragement, albeit with reservations, that estimating future correlations may be possible. A few examples include:

- Erb et al. (1994) report some success in predicting correlations based on analyzing historical trends and putting the results into context with business cycles and the mean reversion of return and the associated predictability of return based on dividend yield.
- Jacquier and Marcus (2001) establish a link between volatility trends and future correlations.
- Wainscott (1990) reports that the fluctuating difference between stock-market dividend payouts and bond-market interest payments "contains information about the future relation between stocks and bonds."[34]
- de Goeij and Marquering (2004) find support for dynamic asset allocation that takes advantage of the predictability components embedded in the tendency for variance and covariance in stock and bond returns to rise after bad news is reported.
- Huang et al. (2007) investigate the evidence that correlations change with some degree of predictability related to economic conditions and that acting on this information via a dynamic portfolio of monthly rebalancing offers a return premium over a static asset allocation.
- Andersson et al. (2008) find that inflation expectations cast a strong influence over stock and bond correlations. Stock and bond prices exhibit higher correlations in times of high-inflation expectations, while low-inflation expectations appear to correspond with negative stock and bond correlations.

Correlation, in short, is a critical factor for tactical asset allocation. It's not completely reliable, of course, particularly in the short term, and so correlation alone can't be trusted. But when analyzed in context with other metrics, including dividend yield, price-to-earnings ratios, price momentum, volatility, and other variables, correlation helps dispense a richer perspective for managing asset allocation.

# The Economics of Satisfaction

Another motive for considering TAA arises from what's known as utility, which is the relative satisfaction that allows one investor to embrace a level of return and risk that another investor finds less satisfying if not unacceptable. Utility theory dates to 1738 and the publication of "Exposition of a New Theory on the Measurement of Risk," a paper by Dutch mathematician Daniel Bernoulli. Bernoulli analyzed the question of how someone might "estimate his prospects from any risky undertaking in light of one's specific financial circumstances." He outlines an answer by way of a story:

> Somehow a very poor fellow obtains a lottery ticket that will yield with equal probability either nothing or twenty thousand ducats. Will this man evaluate his chance of winning at ten thousand ducats? Would he not be ill-advised to sell this lottery ticket for nine thousand ducats? To me it seems that the answer is in the negative. On the other hand I am inclined to believe that a rich man would be ill-advised to refuse to buy the lottery ticket for nine thousand ducats. If I am not wrong then it seems clear that all men cannot use the same rule to evaluate the gamble ... But anyone who considers the problem with perspicacity and interest will ascertain that the concept of *value* ... may be defined in a way which renders the entire procedure universally acceptable without reservation. To do this the determination of the *value* of an item must not be based on its *price*, but rather on the *utility* it yields. The price of the item is dependent only on the thing itself and is equal for everyone; the utility, however, is dependent on the particular circumstances of the person making the estimate. Thus there is no doubt that a gain of one thousand ducats is more significant to a pauper than to a rich man though both gain the same amount.[35]

Bernoulli's hypothesis challenged the conventional wisdom of the era for making decisions under conditions of uncertainty. Rather than picking the strategy that offered the highest expected value, Bernoulli's model favored the highest expected utility. As a result, two people faced with the same decision and looking at the same price expectations could reasonably come to different conclusions in Bernoulli's world. Why? Because expected utility varies depending on a person's preferences. That leads to the idea that people may place a diminishing value on additional wealth under risky conditions. In short, risk matters when assessing the allure of return and deciding how to invest.

Analyzing the theory of choice under uncertain conditions was expanded considerably in the twentieth century with the mathematical approach in the expected utility hypothesis described by von Neumann and Morgenstern (1944).[36] The authors formalized the idea that investors seek to maximize the expected utility of wealth. Neumann and Morgenstern's methodology is now the basis in some economic models for analyzing how investors make decisions under risky conditions.

For most investors, the prospect of earning more money or achieving a higher return is preferable and constant, according to expected utility theory. No explanation required. But the marginal satisfaction that comes from earning another dollar diminishes as wealth increases, as Bernoulli explained three centuries ago. Investors' reaction to loss also changes as their wealth rises and falls. One lesson is that the pleasure of earning an extra dollar rarely equals the grief of losing a marginal buck. In addition, the relationship of pleasure and pain varies from investor to investor.

Changes in an investor's attitude to risk imply changes to asset allocation. Arnott (1995) explains that an investor's utility plays a role in determining if TAA is or isn't appropriate. The basis for the observation begins with the recognition that a bull market increases investor wealth. At the same time, as market prices increase, expected returns fall.[37] "If the long-term investors' risk tolerance does not change, they will respond to the *reduced* prospective returns by moving to a more defensive posture, all things being equal."[38]

Arnott says that these investors are "natural candidates" for TAA. As he explains, "The improved return prospects that come with a newly fallen market increase the prospective rates of return; in the absence of a change in risk tolerance, the investor should take advantage of the opportunity and buy. This is what tactical asset allocation often dictates."[39]

But TAA isn't equally appropriate for all investors, and for some it may be inappropriate. Changes in wealth have little or no impact on risk tolerance for certain investors, but shifts in wealth have a more pronounced effect on perceptions of risk for others.

For investors whose risk tolerance undergoes dramatic changes as their wealth changes, TAA may no longer be practical. Arnott explains that as risk tolerance sensitivity increases, other strategies may be more appropriate, ranging from a simple rebalancing strategy that's reactive to market events to allowing asset allocation to drift to a so-called portfolio-insurance approach, which is selling after market prices drop and buying in response to higher prices.

Investors who are ideally suited for TAA are people who are relatively insensitive to changes in wealth. Their risk tolerance, in other words, is generally stable. By focusing on the long term and assuming that prospective return varies inversely with recent market trends, such investors are likely to embrace the potential for enhanced returns via TAA.

"Tactical asset allocation potentially enhances long-run returns without increasing portfolio risk, but at a cost of lower comfort, hence lower utility, for many investors," Arnott concludes.[40] On first glance, this appears to run afoul of financial economics. Earning higher return without suffering higher risk, after all, conflicts with modern portfolio theory. But higher return without higher risk is possible if the strategy also carries lower utility. Thinking of portfolio strategy in this way

> … provides an *equilibrium* framework in which tactical asset allocation can and should improve investment returns without increasing risk. The improvement in returns can come without a corresponding increase in portfolio risk only if tactical asset allocation is an uncomfortable strategy that many investors find unacceptable. We already know this to be true. Few investors rushed to buy stocks after the disastrous 1973–74 bear market, after the 1987 stock market crash, or even after the modest Kuwait bear market in 1990.[41]

Other researchers have come to similar conclusions. Clothier (1990), for example, documents that a U.S. tactical asset allocation strategy for 1973–1988 produced substantially higher returns and comparable/lower volatility compared to U.S. stocks, U.S. bonds, or a 60/40 stock/bond combination.[42] Sharpe (1990) examines the evidence that tactical asset allocation can improve returns without increasing risk. "Does this imply that tactical strategies offer something for nothing? Not necessarily," he advises, noting

Such approaches require an investor to take on added risk at the hardest times—such as when investors are poorer than usual. In an efficient market, the willingness and ability to do so should be rewarded. The reward (added return), however, is by no means sure, and it may take years to obtain.

... a tactical asset allocation strategy would appear to be appropriate only for a relatively small minority of investors. In particular, it should appeal to those who (personally or organizationally) can take a truly long-run view. It appears to be a desirable strategy for those long-run investors who can "take the heat" when it is most uncomfortable to do so. Although the added returns may be modest, in the long run their cumulative effect may be substantial.[43]

## Lower Risk

TAA is often considered as a tool for boosting return while keeping risk at comparable levels relative to a benchmark that doesn't attempt to time markets. It also works in reverse by focusing on the risk side of the equation by lowering volatility without impairing return. In either case, the goal is an improved risk-adjusted result through TAA.

Faber (2007) shows that portfolio volatility was cut by roughly one-third with a simple tactical asset allocation strategy using five asset classes relative to a buy-and-hold portfolio of the same assets during 1972–2005.[44] The TAA model is based on an equally weighted mix of the five asset classes. Each asset class is either fully invested or in cash depending on whether the index closes the month at above or below its ten-month moving average. The determining factor is the closing price relative to the average for the trailing period. Whenever an asset class's index closes a month at a price below its ten-month moving average, the capital for the asset class is moved to cash. When the price closes the month above its moving average, the asset's equal-weighted share of the portfolio is redeployed from cash to the index.

For the thirty-three years through 2005, Faber reports this TAA strategy posted comparable returns versus a buy-and-hold strategy, each using the same five broad asset classes. TAA earned an annualized 11.9 percent for 1972–2005, slightly above the 11.6 percent for the buy-and-hold portfolio. But while the performances are similar, the TAA's risk (standard deviation) is far lower at around 6.6 versus 10.0 for the buy-and-hold strategy.

Faber observes that the buy-and-hold performance is respectable and highlights the benefit of diversification. The five-asset-class buy-and-hold portfolio's annualized return for 1972–2005 is comparable to the performance of U.S. stocks alone, based on the S&P 500, although volatility for the multi-asset-class strategy is substantially lower than equities alone. But the TAA portfolio reduces volatility quite a bit more, and without reducing return.

Faber and Richardson (2009) update the results through 2008 and reconfirm that 1) diversifying beyond equities reduces volatility with minimal, if any reduction in return relative to owning stocks in the long run; and 2) introducing a momentum-based timing model for managing multiple asset classes further diminishes overall portfolio volatility while delivering a comparable return to a buy-and-hold strategy using the same asset classes.[45]

One theory for why TAA has the capacity for generating superior risk-adjusted results is that risk premia fluctuate among the various asset classes. It's debatable if the fluctuations are evidence of market inefficiency or the market's shifting expectations and discounting assumptions about the future. Supporting the latter view, Fama and French (1989) and others have argued that expected returns are lower in times of general economic strength; during periods of economic weakness, expected returns are higher. Expanding the idea to multiple asset classes on a global basis increases the possibility of seeing an ever-shifting mix of expected risk premia through time.

Exploiting the dynamic state of expected risk premia is the basis for expecting TAA to add value to buy-and-hold and conventional rebalancing strategies. It may not always be clear how to exploit the fluctuating risk premia across asset classes on a systematic basis, although TAA as a general concept is designed to do just that. The simple moving-average model of Faber (2007) appears to be an effective system that captures the oscillating state of expected return premia. In fact, there are many applications of TAA. A few examples include are:

1. Fundamental valuation models that use dividend yield, price-earnings ratio, interest rates, and other financial factors to assess the relative attractiveness of asset classes
2. Price momentum signals, such as the one in Faber (2007)

3.  Business cycle/macroeconomic factor-based models, such as focusing on the term spread (the spread between long and short interest rates), the credit spread (the difference in rates between high-grade and low-grade corporate bonds), and various business indicators, such as factory production and employment trends

The opportunity to profit from the changing set of risk premia among asset classes is at the heart of why TAA seems to enhance risk-adjusted portfolio results in several studies. Some analysts assert that the differences in risk premia are larger across asset classes than within asset classes. That's partly a reflection of segmentation of global markets.

The so-called home bias is now a staple in the literature. French and Poterba (1991) and Tesar and Werner (1995), for example, find that investors heavily favor their respective domestic market despite the well-known benefits of international diversification. To the extent that risk premia are available globally, any preference for investing domestically creates greater arbitrage opportunities across asset classes and international markets for those willing to venture further afield.

"As a result, while inefficiencies are quickly arbitraged away within large markets, inefficiencies between markets may go unnoticed by participants for some time," Nguyen (2004) reasons. "Different regions and countries also continue to have different and independent economic drivers, such as monetary policy, fiscal policy, and investor rights.

"These differences usually lead to significant disparity in performance and pricing between markets."[46] In addition, the tendency to overlook global tactical asset allocation (GTAA) in money management versus the more widely used strategies of picking individual securities also enhances the prospective opportunities for a global focus on broad asset classes, Nguyen advises.

Other analysts have made similar claims about the potential for multi-asset-class arbitrage on a global basis. A 2003 research brief on GTAA from Goldman Sachs states that "there are strong reasons to expect market inefficiency or deviations from equilibrium levels especially *across* global capital markets, where relatively less capital chases market inefficiencies than within a given country's local market."[47]

None of this is surprising in light of what academics have uncovered since the 1980s on the evidence in favor of partial return predictability for stocks and bonds. Indeed, the predictability may even be rational in the context of fluctuating business conditions, a catalyst behind the idea that investors demand varying future rates of return depending on the moment in time. Investment opportunities aren't constant so neither are investors' requirements for return and their perceptions of risk. As the academics say, the opportunity set changes.

Merton (1973) said as much within the context of modern portfolio theory more than thirty years ago. The concept of dynamic asset allocation was largely ignored in the early 1970s, in part because the random walk theory was so widely embraced at the time. But a lot has happened in finance in the past thirty years. The ideas outlined by Merton and others have enjoyed a renewal in the wake of the growing body of literature that suggests that some of the fluctuations in the opportunity set may be partly predictable after all. The fact that investors' preferences, financial requirements, and perceptions evolve as well lays the groundwork for managing asset allocation in something more than a reactive way. In short, there's a case for tactical asset allocation to some degree.

## A Few Caveats...

TAA offers intriguing possibilities for exploiting the fact that risk premiums fluctuate, but it's not a free lunch.

There are at least three fundamental reasons why we should be cautious when assessing TAA's prospects: markets, investment skill, and the challenge of integrating TAA with long-term objectives. The caveats don't necessarily invalidate TAA, although investors should be aware of the associated risks.

The financial literature tells us that returns are partly predictable, but that means that returns are still partly unpredictable. In fact, the predictable component is usually, if not always, the minority partner with uncertainty. As a result, the potential for erroneous decisions, and therefore loss, is constantly lurking behind all attempts at second guessing the market's passive asset allocation. Remember, too, that even after controlling for investor error, TAA's benefits, all else equal, are destined to vary, perhaps dramatically.

The reason: the changing nature of market trends and how asset classes relate to one another in one period versus another.

Meanwhile, TAA holds out the potential for generating superior risk-adjusted return, but only for those investors who wield the necessary skills for accurately evaluating opportunities that arise from varying risk premia and/or designing a TAA program that generates superior results over time. Skillful management of the beta mix, in other words, is essential.

Another challenge with TAA is that it may not deliver optimal results over the long term even if it's ideally executed in the short run. This is a subtle point and it seems to contradict the empirical studies that show TAA can be productive over extended periods of time. But some academics observe a challenge in trying to maintain an "optimal" asset allocation with TAA in a strategic setting.

As Brennan et al. (1997) explain, TAA's raison d'être is adjusting the portfolio mix for building the optimal portfolio for the investment horizon immediately ahead. Conceptually, this short-term outlook may conflict with a strategic-minded investor's horizon that encompasses multiple investment periods. As a result, what appears to be an optimal TAA mix for the foreseeable future may be less than ideal, or even detrimental, over longer periods.

Consider an investor using a simple TAA system intent on optimizing the opportunities for the next twelve months ahead. At the end of that period, he revisits the asset allocation and resets it for the next period, based on current information. He repeats the procedure every twelve months. Over the course of two decades, the TAA investor has effectively managed the portfolio for twenty distinct investment horizons, each lasting twelve months. The question is whether the investment decisions that are optimal for each twelve-month period are also collectively optimal when measured over twenty years. The answer depends on the TAA program.

There are no easy solutions because investment decisions remain subjective to a large degree, particularly in the presence of different time horizons. A simple example is comparing the risk in a short-term bond versus a long-term bond. For some TAA models, the fact that interest rates change can negate the case for owning a long-term bond whose maturity extends beyond the end of the current investment horizon. That is, the possibility of capital losses at the end of the investment horizon triggered by rising interest rates may convince a TAA investor to avoid the long-term bond. By contrast, an investor with a time horizon that exceeds the long bond's maturity may view the same security as riskless, even if rates increase. Why? Because if interest rates rise, the long-term investor can purchase new long-term bonds issued at higher yields after the end of the current investment period.

Looking beyond the next investment period introduces the intertemporal hedging factor in portfolio design, as per Merton (1973). From a practical standpoint, adding a multi-period dimension to asset allocation is reasonable because it calls for hedging the possibility of negative shocks to certain asset classes. The risk of higher interest rates, for example, is considered in a multi-period investment strategy, whereas in a myopic asset allocation plan, the risk of a changing risk premia through time may be overlooked or intentionally minimized.

The challenge is ironic since TAA's basic appeal is optimizing the opportunity that flows from a state of fluctuating risk premia. But depending on how the plan is designed and managed, pursuit of portfolio optimization via TAA may heighten the risk of owning a portfolio that's suboptimal in the long run. The central challenge for investors who embrace TAA, beyond managing it skillfully, is maximizing its short-term advantages while minimizing the possibility of jeopardizing one's long-term goals.

Is this challenge fatal? Not necessarily, although investors must be aware of it. Ultimately, the question is one of how to integrate TAA into a long-term investment strategy. Recognizing the trade-off of short-term advantage at the possible risk to long-term results is essential for weighing TAA's pros and cons.

This conundrum offers yet another example for why we must remain forever suspicious of reported solutions for the investment challenge. What appears to be a free lunch is instead a decision that usually trades one risk for another. Sometimes the merits of the trade-off are obvious and perhaps even compelling, such as when we choose diversification over a more concentrated portfolio, which trades the potential for higher absolute return in exchange for greater portfolio stability and higher risk-adjusted performance.

The embedded risk and reward structure of TAA is more subtle. The potential for boosting return looks enticing, and in fact there's a persuasive case for expecting higher return with TAA compared with a conventional rebalancing strategy for managing asset allocation. But there's a cost associated with the potential for higher return. Lower utility is one. The threat of impairing long-run investment objectives may be another.

Each investor must decide if the TAA risk is manageable and ultimately worthwhile. There is no standard answer because every investor's asset allocation requires custom design and management. As such, everyone must decide on a rebalancing strategy and how or if that fundamental approach to managing asset allocation should be augmented (replaced?) with TAA.

Finance theory tells us to begin with asset allocation by choosing a plan that reflects our circumstances. The next step is deciding how to manage the asset allocation, also with our preferences in mind, which includes selecting an appropriate rebalancing system and perhaps adding a TAA element. As we discuss in the next chapter, that's a reminder that we must think strategically about how we're different from the average investor, and what that means for asset allocation.

## Chapter Notes

1. Sharpe (1987), p. 27.
2. Ibid., p. 28.
3. Ibid., pp. 28–29.
4. Bernstein (1992), p. 247.
5. Fouse (1987), p. 11.
6. Ibid., p. 11. Gray's article appeared in 1974 (Vol. 30, No. 3, FAJ).
7. Siegel et al. (2001), p. 7.
8. Ibid., p. 1.
9. Weigel (1991), p. 63.
10. Campbell and Viceira (2002), p. 6.
11. Ibid., p. 6.
12. Fama and French (1988), p. 247.
13. Fama and Schwert (1977).
14. Keim and Stambaugh (1986).
15. Campbell (1987).

16. French, Schwert, and Stambaugh (1987).

17. Kothari and Shanken (1997).

18. That's not to say that Treasuries are risk free, although historically they've come as close to that ideal as any paper investment can be. The "safety" is a direct function of the credibility and economic capacity of the United States. Although a U.S. default is possible, it's considered highly unlikely. That said, Treasuries can suffer dramatic declines in price. In addition, they're also subject to the ravages of inflation (except, of course, the inflation-indexed series of Treasuries). Treasuries, in sum, aren't free of risk, although practically speaking there's minimal risk, particularly if held till maturity.

19. William Bernstein (2002), p. 54. Bernstein goes on to explain that the nearly 1 percent difference in actual return versus forecasted return "was due to the fact that stocks had become considerably more expensive (that is, the dividend yield had fallen) during the period."

20. Arnott and von Germeten (1983), p. 33.

21. Interview with author, 2009.

22. Loomis (2001).

23. Examples include Econometrics Toolbox from MathWorks (www.mathworks.com), G@RCH from OxMetrics (oxmetrics.net), and SCA Workbench from Scientific Computing Associates Corp. (scausa.com).

24. Minsky (1992).

25. Schumpeter (1942).

26. Minsky (1992), p. 8.

27. Hamilton and Lin (1996), p. 591.

28. Engle (1993), p. 72. The paper offers an excellent overview of quantitative models for estimating volatility.

29. Marquering and Verbeek (2004), p. 407.

30. Fleming et al. (2001), p. 329.

31. Longin and Solnik (1995), p. 3.

32. Coaker (2007), pp. 53–54.

33. Chow et al. (1999), p. 67.

34. Wainscott (1990), p. 59.

35. Bernoulli (1738), p. 24.

36. The book by Neumann and Morgenstern (1944) is also highly regarded for introducing so-called game theory to economics. Game theory is a mathematics-based methodology for modeling behavior and choice in the presence of other participants who are competing for similar objectives in search of an equilibrium state, i.e., the point at which decisions and choice are stable.

37. The relationship of higher (lower) market prices and lower (higher) prospective return is based on the evidence discussed previously that risk premia vary through time and are mean reverting. As a result, high returns today imply lower returns in the future and vice versa.

38. Arnott (1995), p. 233.

39. Ibid., p. 233.

40. Ibid., p. 235.

41. Ibid., p. 235.

42. Clothier (1990), p. 45.

43. Sharpe (1990), p. 37.

44. The five asset classes: U.S. stocks (S&P 500), foreign stocks (MSCI EAFE), the ten-year Treasury note, commodities (Goldman Sachs Commodity Index), and real estate (National Association of Real Estate Investment Trusts Index).

45. See Chapter 7, Faber and Richardson (2009).

46. Nguyen (2004), p. 1.

47. Goldman Sachs (2003), p. 8.

## Chapter 8

# Customizing Asset Allocation

THE ASSET ALLOCATION choices are virtually limitless, but most of them are wrong. Finding the one that's right is the goal, of course, but the task is tougher than it sounds because the optimal asset allocation varies depending on the investor.

Everyone should design a portfolio that's tailored for their circumstances, which means there's just one asset allocation that matches each investor's expectations, objectives, and risk profile. In practice, identifying the absolute perfect mix of assets may be impossible. So it goes when trying to anticipate the morrow with imperfect information today. But at least we know where to begin: the market portfolio.

As we've discussed, the global market portfolio—holding everything in its market-value weights—is the default asset allocation. The standard finance theory tells us that this will be the optimal portfolio for the average investor for the infinite future. By definition, this investor is a composite of everyone, so it's unlikely to complement a real investor's risk/return profile. That suggests that everyone should adjust the unmanaged market portfolio to suit their specific situation. To the extent you're something other than average, your financial personality should be reflected in your asset allocation.

The standard solution is the separation theorem of Tobin (1958), which tells us to adjust the cash allocation relative to the market portfolio. Investors with a greater appetite for risk would hold a higher proportion of the market versus cash; investors with a lesser tolerance for risk hold more cash relative to the market. But all investors, Tobin advised, should hold the market portfolio, with the only concession to one's risk profile reflected in the mix of the cash allocation relative to the weight of the market portfolio.

Almost no one follows this advice, a preference that Canner et al. (1997) label an "asset allocation puzzle." One possible explanation is the recognition that investment opportunities aren't constant and so the one-period assumption of the separation theorem isn't practical for long-term investors.

That leads us back to the market portfolio as the starting point for considering the investment choices with the expectation that Mr. Market's default asset allocation will be adjusted based on personal preferences and expected opportunity and risk. But in order to build this custom portfolio and manage it dynamically, we'll need to think carefully about three basic questions:

- How much risk can you handle?
- What's your investment horizon?
- What risks are specific to you?

## Risk Tolerance

Deciding how much risk you can endure generally is the first step for designing asset allocation that's financially suited to you, as an individual investor.

A simple rule of thumb might be one of equating risk tolerance with the portfolio's equity allocation. A higher allocation in stocks translates into higher risk and therefore higher expected return. But how much is too much? Or too little? Quantifying risk tolerance in more detail is complicated, so great care is required in identifying reasonable estimates.

That's one reason why it's tempting to generalize one's capacity for tolerating risk. Rules of thumb are often used when there's no obvious way to precisely quantify how much of the usual hazards in the capital and commodity markets you can accept. One is John Bogle's so-called age-based rule for the stock/bond allocation, which recommends that the percentage in bonds should track your age. A thirty-year-old investor holds 30 percent in bonds; a sixty-year-old has a 60 percent bond allocation. As a basic principle, the notion of reducing the equity allocation as one ages is sound. But even Bogle says his advice is just a general rule and so it needs to be fine-tuned for each investor. Indeed, like all generalizations, this one glosses over the details, such as ignoring asset class valuations.[1]

In short, beware of oversimplifying what is ultimately a critical decision. It's easy to declare that you're prepared for "high" or "low" risk. But what do such labels really mean? Some investors naïvely claim they're eager to earn high rates of return for the long haul even though they aren't prepared for high volatility in the short term. Meanwhile, self-proclaimed low-risk investors may be underestimating that such a strategy may leave their future liabilities woefully underfunded in the years ahead.

Ultimately deciding your risk tolerance comes from within, but not easily. The answer lies in coming to terms with greed and fear and understanding what that means for making real-world investment decisions. But there's no clear path, no succinct plan, despite the fact that the subject has been studied extensively.

Establishing robust, reliable assessments of risk tolerance is difficult, in part because it's a subject open to interpretation. The task has even been known to overwhelm financial professionals, according to Roszkowski and Grable (2005), who report that "financial advisors are not particularly good judges of their clients' financial risk tolerance."[2]

Although the subject of risk tolerance doesn't lend itself to easy solutions, the main question is still related to the standard approach to modern portfolio theory: how much volatility can you bear relative to the return you seek? Higher return generally comes at the price of higher volatility, and so you must be confident that your answer in concept will remain relevant in practice, now and in the future.

For another perspective on risk, compare yourself with the average investor. Finance theory counsels that the average investor with an infinite time horizon will hold the market portfolio, which we're defining as a globally diversified portfolio of stocks, bonds, real estate (REITs), and commodities, weighted by their market values. For example, one measure of the market portfolio dropped roughly 26 percent in the dramatic selloff of 2008.[3] That's modestly better than U.S. stocks, which posted a 37 percent total return loss in that year. Meanwhile, intermediate Treasuries earned a 13.1 percent total return in 2008.[4] Could you tolerate the loss endured by the average investor in 2008 as implied by the market portfolio? That was an unusually painful year generally, so it represents a stress test of sorts for gauging risk.

For another perspective, Cochrane (1999b) advises that "the overall market is about 60% stocks and 40% bonds, so average levels of risk aversion, whatever they are, wind up at this value."[5] Above-average risk tolerance by that standard suggests someone who can accept an equity allocation above 60 percent, along with the volatility that it's likely to bring.

Many variables ultimately go into determining an investor's risk tolerance, of course. A few of the obvious ones include an investor's overall financial wealth, income, family circumstances, and tax situation. Meanwhile, there are a variety of tests, research papers, and other literature focused on the subject.[6] Some general findings identified in the literature over the years include, according to Hallahan et al. (2004):

- Risk tolerance generally falls with age.
- Females have a lower tolerance for risk than males.
- Education, income, and wealth are positively related with a higher tolerance for risk.
- Unmarried investors are more tolerant of risk compared with married couples.

Ultimately, the determination of risk tolerance is a personal decision. Financial planners and other advisors can offer valuable guidance. But in the end, deciding on a comfort level with risk is subjective, and only you can define your capacity for tolerating risk. Even two investors who are identical in every way are likely to have different attitudes toward investment risk.

That raises the possibility that measuring risk will always be an imprecise task that's prone to error, ambiguity, and personal preferences. Such is the nature of surveying risk, which is heavily influenced by psychological and emotional factors.

How could it be otherwise? Risk, after all, has multiple definitions. When we speak of risk, we're speaking of many things. The conventional understanding of risk for analyzing investment portfolios and comparing asset classes is return volatility, measured as annualized standard deviation. There are many other definitions of risk, of course, some of which have been examined in these pages, such as beta and

Sharpe ratio. Ambrosio (2007) identifies ten quantitative risk metrics, and that only begins to scratch the surface.

Difficult or not, a solid understanding of how you think about risk is critical for building an asset allocation strategy that fits your financial and emotional circumstances. Risk and return are intimately connected, which demands that we understand both sides of the equation, starting with an analysis of our capacity for tolerating risk in order to capture a sufficient level of return to fund our long-term financial goals.

## Investment Horizon

In contrast to determining risk tolerance, identifying your investment horizon is easy, or so it appears. The apparent simplicity, however, can be deceiving. It's one thing to declare that you're investing for twenty years. Sticking with a twenty-year investment horizon for the duration is something else. The main hazard is bailing out of your investment strategy when the inevitable bear market arrives. Bull markets can derail an investment strategy too, by inspiring investors to abandon diversification in favor of more concentrated strategies that look attractive in a period when prices generally are rising.

Fear and greed, in other words, threaten your otherwise prudent asset allocation plans. A recent survey of financial planners, for instance, reports that 77 percent of advisors say that it's difficult to convince clients to maintain their asset allocation plan when markets are trending strongly, up or down.[7] The task is all the more difficult if you've overestimated your risk tolerance.

Investors should think carefully about how long they plan on holding an investment portfolio because time horizon is a key factor in setting asset allocation. For most investors, the primary investment objective is funding retirement. A forty-year-old investor who expects to retire at sixty-five has a twenty-five-year investment horizon. The resulting asset allocation will necessarily differ from a sixty-five-year-old retiree.

Recognizing that you have decades to invest, or not, is the first issue to consider. After all, anything less than a ten-year horizon might reasonably be considered "short term." That's somewhat arbitrary, although not necessarily unreasonable. There are few ten-year periods with negative stock returns in the U.S. since 1926, but history reminds that losses aren't unknown over such time periods. The three instances of red ink over ten-years for large-cap U.S. stocks (1929–1938, 1930–1939, and 1999–2008) may or may not repeat, but since such declines have already occurred, it's best to presume that they can occur again.[8] Twenty-year rolling periods post no losses for large-cap domestic equities, although 1929–1948 comes close with a spare 3.11 percent annualized total return.[9] History is hardly a guarantee of what will or won't happen, but it does offer a guide for thinking about what's possible.

In choosing an asset allocation of stocks, bonds, and other assets, time horizon is at least as important as expectations for return, volatility, and correlation of returns among securities. But thinking about how long you'll be investing hasn't always been revered in the academic literature.

In the early interpretation of modern portfolio theory, time horizon was less important, perhaps irrelevant. That's partly a reflection of using the random walk theory for explaining the return-generating process in the capital markets. If prices move randomly, time horizon has no influence on expected return and risk. Returns that are independent from one period to another imply a stable outlook for performance, volatility, and therefore asset allocation. All things equal, one can make a case that an investor with a five-year horizon should have the same asset allocation as investors with a twenty-year horizon if returns are randomly distributed.

Under that assumption, asset allocation should be static. If the initial asset mix is optimal today, there's no reason to change it tomorrow once we assume that securities prices fluctuate randomly. That was how many financial economists viewed the world in the 1970s. But we now know that returns are partly predictable and that there are multiple factors, or betas, influencing asset prices. Asset allocation, as a result, should be partly dynamic, and each investor should build a custom portfolio to satisfy his needs and expectations.

The older, traditional interpretation of modern portfolio theory—static asset allocation and everyone holds the market portfolio—isn't necessarily wrong, but it's overly simplistic. It only offers an approximate solution, albeit one that's ideal for the average investor over the very long run. But once we consider the evidence of time-varying risk premia and other new insights in the literature, the case weakens for 1) ignoring time horizon and 2) favoring a static asset allocation that's based on the value-weighted market portfolio.

A useful way to think about this is with the example of betting on coin flips. In the real world, coin flips are random: if heads comes up, that has absolutely no influence on the next flip. The outcome is totally random. The randomness means that betting on heads for the next flip is equally risky regardless of how long you play the game. You have a 50 percent chance of being right (or wrong) if you flip the coin once or 10,000 times. Time horizon doesn't matter.

Now imagine another world where every coin flip delivers the opposite of its predecessor. A flip that gives you heads will always be followed by a flip that produces tails, and vice versa. In this world, two coin flips incur less risk than one flip since you're sure to win by betting on heads if you flip twice. But there's only a 50 percent chance of winning if you flip once. The longer run is safer than the short run, and so time horizon matters when the results of the flips aren't randomly distributed.[10]

Investment horizon is also important for asset allocation if prices aren't random. If the market isn't random, it can be shown mathematically that expected return for equities rises faster than does risk (variance of return) as investment horizon lengthens. In other words, the gap in return exceeding risk expands the further into the future we look. That suggests that we should hold more in stocks relative to, say, bonds as our anticipated holding period increases.

Still, investors need to proceed cautiously here. The opportunity for predictability shouldn't be confused with a guarantee of predictability. Depending on the time period and the investor, attempts at dynamic asset allocation may reduce or eliminate returns compared with systematically rebalancing back to a static asset allocation mix. Certainly there's ample evidence in the financial literature that reminds that most investors who try to time the market pay a price. For example, one study reports that timing decisions for equity mutual funds reduced the average return for investors by 1.56 percent annually during 1991–2004.[11]

That raises the question of how much predictability to assume in crafting asset allocation. Alas, there are no obvious answers other than to err on the side of caution. Yes, there are many studies showing that dividends, for instance, harbor some information about future returns, but the research is still less than definitive.

Consider that a study of the S&P 500 and its predecessor index for 1871–1997 shows that the dividend-to-price ratio (D/P) "shows a strong tendency … to predict future price changes," as suggested by the R-squared of 64 percent in the relationship between D/P and subsequent year change in the stock market price.[12]

If D/P was a sure thing for predicting future return, the R-squared would be 100 percent. Alternatively, if D/P is completely worthless for forecasting return, the R-squared would be zero. The fact that the authors measure it as 64 percent implies that there's a relationship between D/P and future performance, a statistically robust relationship, in fact. But 64 percent isn't 100 percent, and so there's plenty of room for times when D/P stumbles as a predictive variable. Perhaps D/P's forecast will take longer than usual to arrive; or maybe the forecast will be completely wrong the next time. In short, the 64 percent R-squared suggests there's risk in predicting equity returns. There's less risk—perhaps a lot less risk than a random walk view of the world implies. But the residual risk is still a real and present danger and so investors must act accordingly when factoring in time horizon for making asset allocation decisions.

Barberis (2000) calculates how return predictability affects asset allocation in the context of time horizon. He does so by studying the expected return information generated by a simple dividend-yield model. Specifically, he analyzes horizon effects on the optimal allocation of stocks for holding periods up to ten years using different assumptions about 1) the predictability of return based on dividend yield and 2) parameter uncertainty, or the confidence (or lack thereof) about the model's forecast.[13]

For example, assuming that returns are unpredictable (normally distributed, à la the random walk model) and the investor is confident about the forecast, the allocation to equities is constant regardless of investment horizon.

By contrast, imagine that returns are predictable using the dividend yield, and an investor is confident about the model's prediction. In this case, the equity weight in the portfolio rises as investment horizon lengthens, from roughly 40 percent with a one-year horizon to nearly 100 percent at a ten-year horizon. But after introducing parameter uncertainty into this setting—i.e., a degree of doubt about the dividend-yield model's predictions—the allocation to stocks suffers a bit. Even if dividend yield holds value for estimating future returns (returns aren't randomly distributed), the allocation to stocks reaches a roughly 60 percent ceiling and then modestly falls for investment horizons beyond five years if we're unsure about the prediction.

The worst-case scenario for equity allocations arrives under the assumption that returns are randomly distributed and there's uncertainty about the model's forecast. In this case, the longer the holding period, the lower the portfolio's weight in stocks.

"Our analysis shows that sensible portfolio allocations for short- and long-horizon investors can be very different in the context of predictable returns," Barberis concludes. "Time variation in expected returns induces mean-reversion in returns, slowing the growth of conditional variances of long-horizon returns. This makes equities appear less risky at long horizons, and hence more attractive to the investor."[14]

Yet Barberis also inspires erring on the side of caution with equity allocations. Asset prices aren't subject to a pure random walk but neither are they completely predictable. Nor can we be sure of any model's predictions. Risk, as always, is omnipresent. That's the basis for expecting a risk premium in the first place and for remaining cautious about the details and timing of return projections. Predicting, as the old saw goes, is difficult, especially about the future.

How cautious should you be when making assumptions about return predictability and the implications for adjusting asset allocation? Your general tolerance for risk, as discussed above, is one factor that will influence your faith in a model's forecasts. Another is your view of the model that generates the forecast. For simplicity, Barberis uses only dividend yield for predicting return. In the real world, dynamic asset allocation should draw on a broader range of variables beyond yield. In theory, a more robust model should be more reliable, assuming it's designed intelligently. Even so, there's always a degree of uncertainty about predictions, although the uncertainty varies depending on the model dispensing the forecasts.

## Distinguishing Your Risks

After determining your general risk tolerance and investment horizon, and considering how this information influences your investment decisions, it's time to figure out how you compare with the average investor. The answer will impact your initial asset allocation design plan.

Designing and managing asset allocation that's customized to your circumstances requires identifying the major risks that are relevant to you as an investor. In other words, you need to figure out why you should design a portfolio that deviates from the market's asset allocation. This is really a process of deciding which risk factors to emphasize and which ones to minimize or sidestep altogether and how that compares with the market's asset allocation.

This approach to risk analysis and management is quite different from the one suggested by the conventional interpretation of modern portfolio theory. In MPT's standard framework, everyone wants to minimize market risk (volatility) for a given level of return. In this setup, investors care only about return and portfolio volatility. In the old way of thinking, the market factor—the market beta—is the primary source of risk, and it dominates the task of designing and managing asset allocation. The basic choice for investors under the classic MPT model is choosing the degree of exposure to the market beta by adjusting the portfolio's cash allocation. This approach isn't necessarily wrong, at least not fatally so. But financial economists now recognize that portfolio design should be more nuanced in the wake of a deeper understanding of the market's return-generating process. In other words, a variety of betas drive return instead of just one under the earlier interpretation of MPT. The challenge is deciding which betas are relevant for your particular financial situation.

Thinking of portfolio strategy in terms of multi-factor pricing begins with Merton (1971, 1973), who challenged the old view that expected return is stable and that the market beta is the lone driver of risk premia. Merton's theory suggested a more dynamic approach to portfolio theory by offering a model that embraced the idea that investors are concerned about specific risks beyond the market generally. In turn, that inspires a dynamic asset allocation process for building and managing optimal portfolios.

The world wasn't ready for dynamic portfolio theory in the early 1970s, a time when the random walk hypothesis and CAPM's one-beta view were widely accepted as the explanations for market behavior and the pricing of risk. The notion that returns might be partially predictable seemed unlikely in those days. The early view of MPT assumed constancy in the future, so building the optimal portfolio was a one-time event that required little adjustment through time. Under those assumptions, there was little incentive for designing portfolios that deviated from the market's asset allocation or dynamically managing the asset mix. No wonder, then, that Merton's update on CAPM languished.

Today, with the benefit of several decades of additional financial research, it's clear that investment opportunities and risk are in constant flux and that multiple betas influence portfolio results. That's given new life to Merton's dynamic, multi-period model, which lays the foundation for much of the twenty-first century's state-of-the-art thinking on asset allocation. References to Merton (1973) are now common in financial economics. The model's main contribution for thinking about portfolio design is formally recognizing that there's more than one risk factor to consider. The market beta that governed the early thinking in modern portfolio theory is still relevant, and it remains part of the solution. But it's no longer the only source of risk to consider.

Everyone should still hold the market portfolio, but it should be augmented by considering other risks that are relevant. The question is: what risks are important to you?

Everyone has their own private menu of assumptions, expectations, fears, goals, and financial situation. It's obvious, then, that there are no generic solutions and so each investor has to carefully consider which risks are germane. The results inevitably will vary. What's relevant for one investor may be less so, if not extraneous, for another.

As a simple example, consider interest rate risk and two investors. One is young, twenty-five years old, and just starting out in a promising career with an equity-heavy asset allocation. The second investor is sixty-five, newly retired, and relying on income generated by a short-term government bond portfolio. Each is likely to have a different view of the investment implications that accompany a state of falling interest rates. Economic history suggests that lower rates promote economic growth, which will benefit investors who depend on labor income, such as our twenty-five-year-old worker. Economic growth is also likely to enhance equity returns. Meanwhile, a retired investor who depends on bond income will suffer a lower payout stream when rates fall. That gives the retiree an incentive to hedge the risk of a future decline in interest rates. The twenty-five-year-old investor, by contrast, is likely to benefit from lower rates, so lower rates pose no risk.

As another example, imagine an executive at a large oil company. Her career is closely tied to the fortunes of the energy business. As the price of oil waxes and wanes, so too go her career prospects, at least in theory. Recognizing the risk, the executive might favor owning a customized version of the market portfolio that reduces, if not eliminates, the energy beta. One option is building an equity portfolio that avoids energy stocks.

In fact, there are an infinite number of portfolio combinations. The challenge is finding the mix that's right for you, and then managing the chosen asset allocation dynamically, which we'll discuss in more detail in the next chapter.

Meanwhile, let's review one more example of how modern portfolio theory's evolution alters the standard asset allocation framework. As we've discussed, each investor should design a portfolio that reflects his particular risk profile. For simplicity, here's a look at what happens when we add one extra beta to the conventional market portfolio. In this instance, the new goal is what's known as multi-factor efficiency.[15]

For most people, the main risk beyond the standard market beta is related to their job—losing it. We can summarize this risk as recession risk. When the business cycle enters a period of contraction, the odds of job loss rise. The stock market usually suffers in such periods, in part because a shrinking labor pool (or the threat of such) reduces consumer spending, which trims corporate earnings as the public pares nondiscretionary purchases such as buying new cars and taking expensive vacations. Because labor income represents a vital, in many cases dominant, portion of household income for most people, the loss of one's job, or the fear of losing it, casts a long shadow on expectations about return and risk.

The fact that stocks tend to fall sharply during recessions is exacerbated by the higher risk of job loss in those periods. To some extent, the market beta and the recession beta are closely linked. But while the financial literature suggests that some of the equity premium is a payoff for bearing recession risk, most investors with a job would rather give up a portion of return in exchange for a smoother ride in their portfolio during periods of economic contraction.

If we consider recession risk as a distinct beta that's also a contributing source of risk premia, building the optimal portfolio now incorporates three variables: return and volatility, as identified in the standard version of MPT, plus a recession factor. The investment decision then becomes one of optimizing all three to satisfy the investor's goals. Investors still want portfolios that maximize expected return at a given level of risk, as per the standard approach to MPT. But that objective is now pursued in context with simultaneously minimizing recession risk. As Cochrane (1999b) explains, under this expanded set of conditions for this example, investors focus on three portfolio attributes:

1.  they want higher average returns
2.  they want lower standard deviations or overall risk
3.  they are willing to accept a portfolio with a little lower mean return or a little higher standard deviation of return if the portfolio does not do poorly in recessions[16]

Satisfying all three creates a portfolio that's known as multi-factor efficient. Keep in mind that different investors will choose different optimal mixes. For those who are sufficiently wealthy and derive most or all of their current income from savings and non-labor income, the recession beta may pose little if any threat. By contrast, investors who rely primarily on paychecks will perceive a greater risk from recession. The larger point is that different investors will choose different optimal portfolios. The idea that everyone holds the same market portfolio is no longer valid.

Merton (1973) anticipates this multi-dimensional, customized portfolio analysis. In his intertemporal CAPM, investors are concerned with hedging the so-called state variables while maximizing expected return and minimizing volatility. For most investors, the future risk of recession seems to generalize one crucial state variable. In that case, the recession beta is a principal source of risk premia, along with general volatility. Just as investors anticipate earning a higher return for assuming higher levels of volatility in the portfolio, they also expect higher returns in exchange for greater exposure to recession risk.

If most investors are eager to hedge the fallout of recession, there will be a risk premium associated with this beta. That suggests that those assets that are likely to be hurt more in a recession will generate higher returns generally. In fact, the Fama-French 3-factor model is considered a reasonable, albeit indirect proxy for recession risk. Portfolios that are more sensitive to small value stocks (small-cap shares with prices that are low relative to book value) appear to explain the additional returns that aren't explained by a market-cap-weighted portfolio of stocks. This extra risk premium appears to be compensation for holding investments that are subject to higher risks associated with economic cycles.[17]

In that case, aggressive investors should not only hold less cash and more of the market portfolio, they should also own a higher-than-average weight in small-cap-value stocks. Meanwhile, conservative investors should hold more cash and a below-market-weight allocation to small-cap value equities.[18]

In a world of multiple betas, investors must figure out which risks they want to hedge, or not, and by how much. This collapses to an initial decision of how to modify the standard market-value-weighted market portfolio based on your risk profile and time horizon.

For most investors, the task begins with a judgment of how to weight the recession beta in the portfolio. Additional customizing based on personal circumstances can enhance the strategic mix. For some investors, inflation hedging may be a priority, for instance. For others, reinvestment risk may be crucial. After identifying the risks that matter, the investor will build and manage a portfolio that satisfies his risk profile.

Each investor ends up in a different financial destination, but everyone should begin their financial journey at the same location: the standard market portfolio that holds all the major asset classes in their value-weighted mix. This is everyone's benchmark because ultimately this is the portfolio chassis that everyone will be customizing. It's also the classic equilibrium portfolio that everyone can hold without affecting price. In fact, the value-weighted market portfolio is what everyone holds in the aggregate. As such, it's a natural and neutral benchmark, and one that presents a passive asset allocation of the available choices.

If you're average, you'll hold the market portfolio as outlined in the standard version of the modern portfolio theory. If not, you'll adjust the market portfolio to reflect the risks that are important for you. It's possible that some investors will have a risk profile that's close to average. In that case, holding something approximating the market portfolio may still make sense.

But most investors aren't average, a recognition that should be reflected in the asset allocation to some extent. Keep in mind, however, that there are limits to hedging risks and seeking to take advantage of predictability beyond owning the market beta of the classic modern portfolio theory. For example, if too many investors decide to exploit the recession beta by owning small-cap-value stocks in excess of the market-cap weight, the prospective risk premium will evaporate.

Therein lies the danger of moving too far away from a passive asset allocation implied by CAPM. The expected risk premiums for some betas may look enticing based on the past, but there's no guarantee that they won't diminish or vanish completely in the future, either for long periods of time or perhaps permanently.

Yes, the excess return associated with small-cap-value stocks through history appears to endure, but not consistently. In the 1990s, notably, the small-cap-value premium seemed to be in hibernation.[19] With the benefit of hindsight, investors would have done better to overweight large-cap-growth stocks at the time, which handily beat small-cap value for the decade. Small value has since returned to form and taken the lead in the twenty-first century through the end of 2008. Is that an anomaly? Perhaps not, considering that small-value stocks also have posted superior returns since 1928. Nonetheless, there may again be periods when small-cap value trails.

The caveat isn't surprising. Cochrane (1999b) observes that if dividend yield and other fundamental metrics do in fact forecast return, that's "*because* the average investor is unwilling to follow the value and market-timing strategies." As he explains,

If everyone tries to time the market or buy more value stocks, the premiums from these strategies will disappear and the CAPM, random walk view of the market will reemerge. Market-timing can only work if it involves buying stocks when nobody else wants them and selling them when everybody else wants them. Value and small-cap anomalies can only work if the average investor is leery about buying financially distressed and illiquid stocks. Portfolio advice to follow these strategies *must* fall on deaf ears for the average investor, and a large class of investors must want to head in exactly the other direction. If not, the premium from these strategies will not persist.[20]

That's one reason why we should be cautious about completely abandoning the old version of MPT. Over time, it's quite possible if not likely that beating the market portfolio will remain difficult as a long-term proposition, even in the wake of all the new research suggesting otherwise. While there's a rational case for adjusting the market portfolio to suit our needs and take advantage of apparent opportunities, we should think long and hard before deviating too far from this benchmark. To the extent you do so, paying close attention to how much you pay for risk is critical, as the next chapter explains.

## *Chapter Notes*

1. See Chapter 3 in Bogle (2000).

2. Roszkowski and Grable (2005), p. 43.

3. Based on the Global Market Index, published by The Beta Investment Report (BetaInvestment.com).

4. *Ibbotson* (2009), p. 37.

5. Cochrane (1999b), p. 73.

6. A sampling of recent literature on measuring risk tolerance includes Grable (2008) and Yook and Everett (2003).

7. Alliance Bernstein Investments (2005), p. 2.

8. *Ibbotson* (2009), pp. 44–45.

9. Ibid., pp. 46–47.

10. The coin flipping example is from Cochrane (1999b), p. 63.

11. Friesen and Sapp (2007).

12. Campbell and Shiller (1998), p. 13. The paper advises in 1998 that dividend "ratios are extraordinarily bearish," a warning that was followed by a severe bear market two years later.

13. The portfolios analyzed make an assumption about investor risk aversion and employ a buy-and-hold strategy in order to isolate the horizon effects. Parameter uncertainty refers to doubt about the model's forecast. That's distinct from whether returns are predictable.

14. Barberis (2000), p. 261.

15. The following example of so-called multi-factor efficiency is inspired by Cochrane (1999b, p. 62), who points out that the underlying theory is based on Merton (1969, 1971, 1973) and the analysis of Fama (1996).

16. Cochrane (1999b), p. 62.

17. See Fama and French (1996) for a discussion of the theory behind this view.

18. In practice, underweighting small-cap-value stocks may have little effect in a broad equity portfolio weighted by market cap since small cap value typically constitutes a fraction of overall stock market capitalization. For example, small-cap-value stocks represented 7.3% of total U.S. equity capitalization on July 2, 2009, according to data from Standard & Poor's.

19. Some market observers say that the fading of the small-cap-value premium in the 1990s was due to the arrival of the Fama and French research that formally identified the risk premium linked to these stocks. In effect, the secret was out and the market availed itself of the risk factor's higher return. If so, it's not clear why small-cap-value stocks posted a premium again in the 2000s through 2008. Perhaps the explanation is that small-cap-value risk is robust through time, although not necessarily in the short run.

20. Cochrane (1999b), p. 70.

## Chapter 9

# Equilibrium, Economics, and Estimates

FINANCE THEORY IS COMPLICATED, but the first question for asset allocation is simple: should you own the market portfolio?

Yes, if you're comfortable with the long-term risk appetite of the average investor. If not, you can adjust the market portfolio to satisfy your risk profile and investment objective, which is what most investors will do and probably should do, although generic solutions here are elusive.

As the previous chapter explains, maintaining a custom asset allocation requires analyzing your general tolerance for risk, considering your investment horizon and identifying the betas that are important to you. This is what the new finance tells us to do, but beware: once you opt for something other than the market portfolio, you'll have to work harder. Unlike owning a passive allocation to the major asset classes, a customized strategy doesn't manage itself. Keep in mind, too, that there's no guarantee that the additional effort of designing and managing a personalized strategy will pay off relative to owning the market portfolio. The critical variables: your ability to analyze markets and make timely adjustments to asset allocation. Quite often these variables equate with adopting a contrarian outlook of some degree, which means that dynamically managing asset allocation will be challenging.

That's a price worth paying if the results are satisfying. But pursuing a different set of risk and return goals from what the market offers introduces an additional layer of uncertainty because it requires making forecasts and analyzing market conditions, which increases the possibility of error. Even a flawless asset allocation that matches your personal profile and optimizes prospective opportunities as they currently exist will need tending to keep the market's volatility from throwing your strategic plans asunder. This is neither easy nor intuitive, but that's no surprise. The rationale for holding a portfolio that's different than the market mix arises from the expectation that you'll earn superior risk-adjusted returns or satisfy a particular risk demand that won't be fulfilled by holding the market portfolio.[1] Either way, no one should expect to earn premium results at no extra cost.

If you decide to embrace a custom asset allocation, the basic option for maintenance is rebalancing. After picking the strategic weights for each asset class, a rebalancing regimen keeps the initial asset allocation intact.

A simple 60 percent stock/40 percent bond allocation, for instance, is easily maintained with conventional rebalancing, which shuns forecasting in favor of reacting to market trends by reinstalling the previous asset allocation. In this example, we can think of this 60/40 mix as the strategic asset allocation.[2] Under the old finance, these strategic weights are static as they relates to market forecasts. On the other hand, the asset mix can and should change for personal reasons. As the investor ages, for instance, the equity allocation might be lowered and the bond allocation raised. But there's no allowance in the old finance for changing the strategic asset allocation based on market forecasts. If market behavior is a random walk, as it is under an older reading of modern portfolio theory (MPT), and this assumption informs the initial portfolio design, the asset allocation remains unchanged. Or so the old finance advises.

In an updated view of MPT, changes to the investor's personal situation are still catalysts for modifying the asset mix. But the new finance also allows for revisions to the strategic portfolio mix for market reasons too.

MPT's twenty-first century incarnation calls for dynamic asset allocation, which we're defining as actively managing the strategic mix of assets for a long-term horizon. The rationale for dynamic asset allocation rests on four basic ideas drawn from the insights offered in the financial literature published since the 1980s. One is that economic and financial market cycles prevail. Two, there are additional, albeit fluctuating risk premia associated with these cycles, and the fluctuations impact expectations and strategic assumptions.

Three, expected risk premia are partly predictable, which invites investors to respond by changing the asset allocation. Four, optimal portfolio strategies will vary based on investment horizon.

What happens to tactical asset allocation (TAA) in all of this? The TAA distinction is no longer relevant because all prospective-oriented portfolio adjustments become folded into a strategic-minded application of dynamic asset allocation. Recall from Chapter 7 that TAA is a supplement or perhaps an alternative to rebalancing, which is a reactionary process that returns an asset allocation to its previous setting. As such, rebalancing shuns forecasts. TAA, by contrast, alters the asset mix within the strategic asset allocation as an effort at enhancing portfolio results for the next investment period. Formally recognizing TAA is appropriate only under a static definition of strategic asset allocation framework for a one-period investment horizon. Once we embrace the dynamic management of asset allocation, much of what's considered TAA becomes integrated into the strategic decision-making process for a multiple-period horizon that serves a long-term investor. We can exploit the TAA-related research in dynamically managing strategic asset allocation, but we needn't officially distinguish tactical from strategic decisions in the new finance.

## Start with Equilibrium

Before we can begin making dynamic judgments about strategic asset allocation, we need a neutral reference point for assessing the markets and incorporating our views about the future into the portfolio. In short, we need an estimate of equilibrium risk premiums for individual asset classes and the portfolio overall. From this foundation, we can amend the asset allocation based on our risk preferences and expectations.

Equilibrium risk premiums are returns over the risk-free rate (defined here and throughout as the three-month Treasury bill return) when supply equals demand. If the market is efficient, or reasonably so in the long run, equilibrium-based projections of risk premia are an unbiased (or at least a minimally biased) platform for considering the future and how the estimates intersect with our forecasts. The underlying theory of equilibrium risk premia is informed by the capital asset pricing model, which anticipates that the market will continually reprice assets until demand matches supply. Even if markets aren't in constant balance and prices sometimes move away from equilibrium, the deviations represent opportunity, advise Litterman and Black (1991) and Litterman (2003). Imbalances, in other words, are likely to be temporary. As Litterman explains,

> We need not assume that markets are always in equilibrium to find an equilibrium approach useful. Rather, we view the world as a complex, highly random system in which there is a constant barrage of new data and shocks to existing valuations that as often as not knock the system away from equilibrium. However, although we anticipate that these shocks constantly create deviations from equilibrium in financial markets, and we recognize that frictions prevent those deviations from disappearing immediately, we also assume that these deviations represent opportunities.[3]

To keep the following illustration manageable, we'll limit our example of calculating equilibrium risk premia to three asset classes. We'll also simplify the discussion of the analytical process. In practice, we can use any number of asset classes in search of a robust forecast of the market portfolio's equilibrium risk premium. The academic literature suggests including as many asset classes as is reasonable for creating a robust proxy of the market portfolio. In demonstrating the basic process of estimating risk premia, however, we consider only U.S. stocks, intermediate U.S. government bonds, and foreign equities in developed markets in our cursory review of the methodology.

Estimating the equilibrium risk premium from Equation 1 is based on Brinson (1995) and defined as

$$\text{Sharpe ratio} \times \sigma_i \times \rho_{im} \qquad (1)$$

with the variables defined as

Sharpe ratio = the price of risk, defined as the market's excess return over the risk-free rate divided by the market's annualized volatility (standard deviation of return)
$\sigma_i$ = standard deviation of asset $i$
$\rho_{im}$ = correlation of asset $i$ with portfolio $m$

The immediate goal is generating a forward-looking estimate of the equilibrium risk premia. That requires judgment about the future. How should we proceed? One option is using the unadjusted historical record as an approximation of expected return premia. But this approach in isolation is suspect because recent past returns are often volatile and so they may be misleading as a long-run prediction. That inspires using longer periods of history as a forecast, although that introduces complications too. For instance, using the past one hundred years of equity returns is an implicit assumption that the investor's time horizon is of similar length, which, of course, is wrong. In addition, it's not always clear which historical period is the most relevant for the period ahead. That presents another challenge since even long, distinctive stretches of market history can vary substantially from one another in terms of reported risk and return. Overall, we should be suspicious of exclusively relying on any one past investment period, no matter how long or short, for estimating the future.[4]

We can't ignore history, but neither should we blindly accept it at face value. Instead, we need to integrate the lessons in the historical record with an informed estimate of the future. Equation 1 is a good start by inferring the risk premia indirectly from three variables: the price of risk (Sharpe ratio), the volatility of assets, and correlations of each asset class with the overall portfolio.

As an example of why extrapolating the past alone as an estimate of the future can be precarious, consider the annualized total return premiums earned for the ten years through the end of 2008 (returns calculated after subtracting the risk-free rate, defined as the three-month Treasury bill).

U.S. Stocks: –4.5%
Foreign Developed Stocks: –1.9
Intermediate U.S. Government Bonds: 2.9%[5]

Note that the equity risk premia for domestic and foreign equity markets above are negative. Yes, that's the historical record for the decade, but there's little reason to expect that stock markets will retreat as a general proposition in considering the long-run future. More generally, we should be cautious about using these raw historical numbers as estimates for prospective risk premia since the ten-year period through 2008 reflects a particular set of economic and financial conditions that are unlikely to repeat. Indeed, the decade through 2008 witnessed, among other things, a sharp drop in interest rates and inflation along with two sets of unusually potent bull and bear markets. By the close of 2008, in the wake of the year's financial crisis, the trailing ten-year performance for equities suddenly paled relative to its long-term record. Extrapolating recent history, then, looks ill-advised for estimating risk premia since the recent past was unusually chaotic.

The question is how to generate a more realistic outlook. The answer is multifaceted and so a comprehensive treatment is beyond the agenda here. But as a simplified example of the process, we can begin by applying some of the lessons suggested in the financial literature. For instance, we're told that dividend yield is one variable that offers clues about future return. On that basis, consider that the trailing twelve-month dividend yield for U.S. stocks at 2008's close was 3.2%. We also know that the nominal long-run rate of growth in dividends has been roughly 5.9% a year for the six decades through 2008 for U.S. stocks.[6] The Gordon equation estimates the long-run stock market return as the sum of the current dividend yield and the long-run dividend growth rate.[7] Using 2008's closing yield of 3.2% and a dividend growth rate of 5.9% implies a prospective equity return of 9.1%—a world above the modest loss for the ten years through 2008. Meanwhile, foreign developed equities at 2008's close posted a trailing twelve-month yield of 5.2% and the ten-year Treasury note ended the year at a 2.3% yield.[8]

We can also look to volatility trends in late 2008 for additional support in thinking that future equity returns look encouraging relative to the discouraging record for 1999–2008. As the academic literature shows, volatility tends to cycle through time, typically with high points arriving in bear markets. The fact that equity market volatility around the world surged to highs unseen in decades in 2008 implies lower future volatility. Because lesser volatility tends to be associated with relatively higher returns versus the previous period, we have another variable that hints at prospective equity returns that will compare favorably with the ten years through 2008.

For additional perspective, let's now calculate the expected equilibrium risk premiums as per Equation 1. We begin with Sharpe ratios for each of the three assets in our portfolio example. As a starting point, consider that annualized equity total returns for 1970–2008 are 9.5% for U.S. stocks and 9.7% for foreign developed-market stocks.[9]

The historical performance is comparable to what the Gordon equation implies as of 2008's close. But let's be cautious and assume that dividends will grow more slowly in the future compared with the past, rising by just 2% annually in the years ahead versus the 5%-plus reported for the postwar decades. Adding our assumption of 2% dividend growth to the 2008 year-end yields in domestic equities (3.2%) and overseas markets (5.2%) dispenses annualized total-return projections of 5.2% for U.S. stocks and 7.2% for foreign stocks.

We needn't rely on the past for thinking about government bonds since we know with a high degree of confidence that the current yield will become the total return if the security is held to maturity. As such, the 2.3 percent yield for the ten-year Treasury note at 2008's close is also the annualized return forecast for intermediate government bonds.

Next, we need to subtract a risk-free rate from the nominal returns to calculate a Sharpe ratio. At the end of 2008, short rates were extraordinarily low. The three-month Treasury bill was just above zero, closing the year at 0.1 percent.[10] That compares with a 3.7 percent annualized total return for three-month T-bills in the modern era (1926–2008).[11] We know, too, that the low rates at the end of 2008 were the direct result of the Federal Reserve's extraordinary monetary stimulus efforts aimed at softening the effects of the recession and the financial crisis. Since short rates can't drop much lower, and a future economic recovery will eventually raise the demand for credit, short rates are likely to be higher in the years ahead. Let's use the long-run (1926–2008) inflation rate of 3.0 percent as an estimate of the risk-free rate.[12]

Taking those assumptions and then subtracting an expected risk free rate of 3.0 percent produces excess-return forecasts:

U.S. Stocks: 2.2%
Foreign Developed Stocks: 4.2%
Intermediate U.S. Government Bonds: –0.7%

To compute Sharpe ratios, we need to divide the excess returns by a volatility forecast. Note that standard deviations rose sharply in 2008 amid the dramatic selling that consumed the markets for most of the year. That compares with relatively low volatility for equity returns during 2004–2007, a period of generally rising asset prices. During those four years, annualized monthly standard deviations of large-cap U.S. stocks in each calendar year ranged from roughly 6.5 to a bit over 10 before jumping to more than 14 for 2008. But since volatility cycles, the historical record suggests that volatility will fall from 2008's lofty level. Even so, let's assume that the future will be more volatile than the recent past suggests and project that domestic equity returns will remain at a relatively high standard deviation of 12 on a calendar year basis. Foreign equities tend to exhibit even higher volatility from a U.S.-dollar-investor perspective and so we assume a standard deviation of 18, or slightly above the reported figure of around 17 for 1998–2008.[13]

As for bonds, volatility for intermediate government securities has fallen in recent years, in part because interest rates have dropped to record lows. Because interest rates can't fall much further, if at all, we're suspicious of the recent lull in fixed-income volatility. For 1999–2008, intermediate Treasuries posted an annualized standard deviation of 5. Yet the 8.8 volatility of the 1980s looks more reasonable going forward. Why? Interest rates were rising in the 1980s, in part because the Federal Reserve tightened monetary policy in the early part of that decade to fight inflation. Although the inflation outlook at the end of 2008 was quite low and bordering on deflation, one could reason that higher rates were coming as the economy rebounds in the ensuing years. In turn, the trend would likely elevate inflation to something approaching historically average levels. The forecast suggests raising the volatility estimate for bonds above its record in the past decade and so we estimate a volatility of 7 for intermediate government bonds, or modestly higher from the reported 5 for the asset class during 1999–2008.[14]

Summarizing, our volatility estimates are:

U.S. Stocks: 12
Foreign Developed Stocks: 18
Intermediate U.S. Government Bonds: 7

With the resulting Sharpe ratios:

U.S. Stocks: 0.18
Foreign Developed Stocks: 0.23
Intermediate U.S. Government Bonds: –0.10

In addition to forecasts of Sharpe ratios and volatility, the third input required for calculating Equation 1 is correlation. Let's begin by looking at ten-year correlations through 2008 for each of the three asset classes relative to a market-cap weighted portfolio of the trio, as determined by market values on December 31, 1998. The resulting correlations for 1999–2008 are 0.97 for U.S. stocks, 0.96 for foreign developed stocks, and –0.29 for intermediate government bonds.[15] Correlations tend to rise during severe periods of selling and so the reported numbers are somewhat skewed to the high side for equities in the wake of 2008's dramatic losses. Meanwhile, because of the rush to the safe harbor of Treasuries in 2008, the normally low correlations for bonds are somewhat exaggerated as a modestly negative reading. Anticipating a more conventional relationship for correlations in the years ahead, we forecast slightly lower correlations for equities and slightly higher correlations for government bonds, resulting in correlation estimates:

U.S. Stocks: 0.9
Foreign Developed Stocks: 0.9
Intermediate U.S. Government Bonds: 0.2

With all the necessary estimates in hand, we now calculate the implied equilibrium risk premiums for each asset class as per Equation 1:

U.S. Stocks: 1.9%
Foreign Developed Stocks: 3.7%
Intermediate U.S. Government Bonds: –0.1%

In order to compute the equilibrium risk premium forecast for the entire portfolio, we multiply the individual predictions above by their respective market-cap share of the total portfolio. The relevant asset allocation numbers as of 2008's close:[16]

U.S. Stocks: 42%
Foreign Developed Stocks: 46%
Intermediate U.S. Government Bonds: 12%

Using a passive asset allocation based on the respective market caps as of 2008's close, the projected equilibrium risk premium for the portfolio is 2.5 percent. Remember, this is a risk premium forecast and so by definition it excludes an estimate of the risk-free rate. As such, the expected equilibrium risk premium of 2.5 percent for the portfolio translates into an expected *total* return of 5.5 percent after adding a forward-looking 3.0 percent risk-free rate, for instance.

Now that we have equilibrium estimates of risk premiums for each asset class, what do they imply? One option is to use portfolio optimization software to analyze the results and determine the optimal asset mix. But this approach faces challenges. One hazard is that the standard mean-variance optimization analysis of Markowitz (1952, 1959) is sensitive to return forecasts. Small changes in return expectations can radically alter the recommended asset allocation. For instance, imagine two assets that are similar except that one has a modestly higher expected return. In that case, optimizers may allocate everything to the asset with the higher return and avoid the other asset. The lesson is that it's dangerous to blindly accept recommendations from optimization software. In addition, the sensitivity of optimization makes it hard for investors to incorporate their views into conventional optimization software without modifications, such as setting maximum and minimum levels for asset weights. These hazards don't invalidate optimization software, although the challenges remind that investors should be aware of the pitfalls of computer-based asset allocation decisions.

Whether you're using optimization software or using another methodology, the goal is designing an asset allocation that's optimal for the future, not the past. Historical data, then, only brings you so far, no matter how deeply you analyze the numbers. At some point in crafting an asset allocation, you'll need to make choices about what's likely to unfold in the future. Those forecasts needn't be bold departures from what equilibrium implies, nor must you have a strong opinion about every asset class at all times. But unless you're willing to accept the market portfolio, some level of predicting is necessary.

It's also worth reminding that calculating Equation 1 makes a number of assumptions, so changing projections necessarily alters the risk premia forecasts. Different investors will come to different conclusions about the future. Meanwhile, what seems reasonable today may look unrealistic tomorrow. We should also assume that our forecasts, no matter how thoroughly researched, will be less than perfect. That inspires thinking about the real-world implications if we're expecting, say, a 2.5 percent risk premium for the portfolio and end up with 1.0 percent or even a small loss. If that's unacceptable, perhaps it's time to go back to the drawing board and reassess expectations and risk tolerance.

In addition, we've simplified the process discussed above for illustration purposes. An actual projection of risk premia, by contrast, should incorporate additional market variables and asset classes into the analysis beyond the ones cited. That's a reminder that we need informed research about what the future may bring. As the old saying goes, garbage in, garbage out.

Otherwise, our forward-looking equilibrium risk premia reflects a neutral view of the future. A long-term investor with no particular market outlook should consider the equilibrium projections as a basis for a portfolio strategy. Alternatively, an investor with definite expectations about one or more of the asset classes would integrate her views into the asset allocation by altering the neutral weights to reflect the outlook.

For instance, let's say that an investor is quite a bit more bullish on U.S. stocks for the next three to five years compared with the assumption in the long-run equilibrium risk premium forecast. Adapting that view into the asset allocation in the example above translates into raising the U.S. equity weight over the equilibrium weight of 42 percent of the total portfolio; a more bearish perspective calls for a lower-than-average 42 percent weight.

Estimates of equilibrium risk premia provide investors with a reference point for adjusting the asset allocation, if at all. Expecting that future returns will deviate from the implied equilibrium predictions in the short-to-medium term suggests changing the passive market-cap asset allocation. How should we examine the prospects for deviations from equilibrium? The first step is developing some perspective on a key driver of time-varying risk premia: the economic cycle. In short, we should attempt to answer the question: where are we in terms of the economic cycle? If the risk of recession appears high, we're going to think differently about prospective risk premia than if we perceive economic growth to be the more likely scenario.

## In Search of Economic Context

Formally modeling the business cycle and analyzing its relationship with securities pricing and investment returns is a relatively new discipline in asset management, but the underlying concept is ancient. In what may be the oldest recorded macroeconomic forecast, the Book of Genesis says of cyclical fluctuations:

> Behold, there come seven years of great plenty throughout all the land of Egypt:
> And there shall arise after them seven years of famine; and all the plenty shall be forgotten in the land of Egypt... [17]

The modern age of economic research focused on business cycles began in the 1920s, according to Achuthan and Banerji (2004). In that decade, economist Wesley Mitchell, who helped found the National Bureau of Economic Research (NBER), wrote a proper definition of cyclical fluctuations in the economy that "provided researchers with the first map of the territory they had set out to explore."[18] In the following years, researchers at NBER pioneered the study of business cycles, which fostered the development of leading indicators, or measures of economic and financial activity that are thought to offer clues about the future. An NBER research bulletin from 1938 introduces the first list of leading indicators, explaining, "What we have to offer is a digest of past experience, which we take to be on the whole the best teacher of what to expect in the near future."[19]

Formal models that use leading indicators for estimating risk premia date to the 1960s and 1970s.[20] Heathcotte and Apilado (1974) are credited by some with publishing the first empirical study on predicting stock prices by way of leading indicators.

Today, the academic literature offers a broad array of evidence that links excess returns and macroeconomic trends. A recent example is Faugere and Van Erlach (2009), who demonstrate that the equity premium is closely related to business cycle risk. A number of studies have made similar observations since the 1980s, including

Cochrane (1991) and Shawky and Peng (1995). Schwert (1990) studies a century of data through 1988 and finds a "strong positive relation between real stock returns and future production growth rates,"[21] a result that echoes Fama (1990). Brocato and Steed (1998) show the value of adjusting asset allocation based on changes in the business cycle. Meanwhile, Jensen and Mercer (2003) present evidence that monetary policy, which influences the timing of the business cycle, conveys useful information for adjusting asset allocation.

Searching for a more granular linkage, Lettau and Ludvigson (2001a) identify a connection between general consumption, wealth levels, and equity returns, reporting that "fluctuations in the' consumption–wealth ratio are strong predictors of both real stock returns and excess returns over a Treasury bill rate."[22] The logic is that when investors anticipate higher returns, they're inclined to consume more, in which case a higher level of consumption implies higher expected returns.

Campbell and Diebold (2009) also advise that' expectations about business conditions offer clues about excess returns. During periods of weak business conditions, the outlook for excess return is relatively high, and vice versa.

Meanwhile, a new generation of studies began appearing in the late-1980s and early 1990s that found that the inversion of the Treasury yield curve (short rates above long rates) was a sign of an approaching recession. Normally, the yield curve is upward sloping, meaning that longer maturities command higher yields. This is the normal state for the bond market. Economic logic suggests that longer holding periods incur higher risk, so investors should be compensated with higher yields. When this relationship in the term structure of interest rates changes so that short rates are above long rates, the shift implies a related change in economic expectations.

Estrella and Hardouvelis (1991) show that the curve tends to be downward sloping (short yields above long yields) near or during the onset of a cyclical downturn. During recessions, the curve is upward sloping (short yields below long yields). That gives more weight to Fama and French (1989), who observe that the equity risk premium moves countercyclically with the business cycle so that expected returns are relatively high in recessions compared with forecasts during economic expansions.

Dahlquist and Harvey (2001) find that the yield curve inverted ahead of each of the five U.S. recessions from 1969 through 2001. Updating the report shows that that the recession that began in late-2007 was also foreshadowed by a rise of short rates above long rates.

A number of subsequent studies detect a relationship between the shape of the yield curve and the economic cycle. Summarizing the literature, Rosenberg and Maurer (2008) report: "Since the 1970s, an inverted yield curve has been a reliable signal of an imminent recession. One interpretation of this signal is that it reflects market expectations that current monetary policy is tighter than it will be in the future, owing to an upcoming deterioration in the economic outlook."[23]

## Strategic Implications of the Economic Cycle

Macroeconomic risk doesn't explain everything, but it describes a lot, and so all investors should consider this factor in the context of how it affects risk premia. No one's likely to predict the ebb and flow of the economic trends with a high degree of certainty, but developing a general sense of where we are in the cycle can be productive for thinking about the prospects for the major asset classes.

The fact that the business cycle endures offers a general statement for why risk premia change. Thirty-three recessions have been recorded in the U.S. since 1857, reports NBER, the institution that dates business cycles. No one will be surprised to learn that the stock market tends to suffer during economic contractions and thrive in times of general prosperity. The immediate explanation is that earnings suffer in recessions, and the suffering is passed on to investors by way of lower equity prices.

There's still a fair amount of debate in the dismal science on the details of why excess returns should fluctuate with the business cycle and why those excess returns appear to be partly predictable based on macroeconomic factors. For some, the answer is that the capital markets are inefficient. The alternative view is that risk premia vary through time, and rational investors adjust their expectations based on the ever-shifting state of current conditions. The market, in other words, applies different discount rates as economic and financial trends proceed. In either case, the empirical evidence suggests that investors should monitor macroeconomic fluctuations for clues about expected risk premia.

The standard interpretation of modern portfolio theory advises that consistent outperformance of the market portfolio is impossible without assuming additional risk. Yet a number of studies over the years have shown that the workhorse of MPT, the capital asset pricing model, doesn't capture the full spectrum of risks that determine prices. Various studies over the years have identified so-called risk anomalies that appear to violate MPT's central tenet. Small-cap stocks, for example, have been identified as offering higher returns than a strict reading of CAPM allows.

Two decades of additional research, however, suggest that a fair amount of the anomalies aren't risk factors per se; instead, they're surrogates for other betas driving the market portfolio— betas that are identified only through a more granular reading of market behavior than is possible with CAPM. One of the basic factors that determine prices is what some have labeled the recession beta. Among the more convincing theories that explain the phenomenon is the Fama-French (FF) 3-factor model, which posits that the small-cap-value premium is a proxy for what we'll call the recession beta.

Recall that the FF model says that small-cap, and value equity factors go a long way in resolving the shortcomings of the conventional CAPM. On its own, CAPM doesn't completely explain risk and return. In particular, small companies trading at low prices relative to book value earn higher returns over time than the CAPM predicts. It's not necessarily fatal for CAPM, which does a pretty good job of explaining risk and return over time. But the FF model offers a compelling resolution that enhances the securities pricing story.

The idea that an asset pricing model requires more than one factor isn't surprising in light of Merton (1971, 1973).[24] In fact, we should expect no less. Merton theorizes that state variables, or additional betas, must be identified to fully explain the relationship between risk and return in the capital markets. In his papers, he lays out a framework that states that "in equilibrium, investors are compensated in terms of expected return, for bearing (systematic) risk, and for bearing the risk of unfavorable … shifts in the investment opportunity set …."[25] Merton uses interest rates as one example of a shifting opportunity set, and for at least two reasons: they fluctuate and they're an important financial variable.

Another example, and perhaps the most important one that's common for most investors, is what we label the recession beta. The average investor will have no trouble identifying the risk of an economic slump as a critical factor for asset pricing and asset allocation. Isolating the recession beta directly is problematic in an investment context, however, since you can't buy or sell the economy, at least not directly. But you can use proxies that replicate some degree of the recession beta. Interest rates are one proxy; small-cap value stocks appear to be another.

The FF model shows that adding the small cap and value factors to the market portfolio explains 95 percent of the variability in stock returns. That's in contrast to 70 percent with the one-factor CAPM. Fama and French (1993) extend the model to include two fixed-income factors: term risk (the premium associated with longer versus shorter bond maturities) and default risk (the premium linked with corporate bonds over government bonds).

For most investors, the market portfolio plus the four factors identified in the FF model offer a rich palette for customizing portfolios in line with the implications of Merton (1973). Some investors may wish to go further by considering, say, career risk for adjusting the investment portfolio. An investor who works on Wall Street, for instance, might consider reducing the portfolio's sensitivity to negative shocks directly affecting the financial sector because her job is already closely linked with the economic cycle. Meanwhile, a tenured professor with a guaranteed income for life may want to hold a higher-than-average equity allocation because his career prospects resemble the income stream of a bond.

In any case, the five-factor paradigm is a prudent way to begin thinking about asset allocation. The assumption is that the so-called anomalies that have created difficulty for CAPM in explaining equity returns are resolved in the FF model. In addition, the small-cap and value factors identified in Fama and French (1992, 1993) "suggest that it is an equilibrium pricing model, a three-factor version of Merton's (1973) intertemporal CAPM (ICAPM) or Ross's (1976) arbitrage pricing theory (APT)."[26]

That opens the door for seeing the small-cap-value factor as a proxy for a state variable of significance for the average investor.

The rationale is that the low valuations routinely assigned to these companies suggest that they're already suffering from a business standpoint. The catalysts for the vulnerability vary, depending on the company. It may be poor sales at one versus a deteriorating balance sheet at another. Chan and Chen (1991) report that small companies tend to have high financial leverage and cash-flow problems, which heighten susceptibility during periods of macroeconomic distress.

Small-cap-value stocks are on the defensive generally. That's true for value stocks overall, but the challenge is compounded for smaller firms, which are less able to weather tough times compared with large corporations. The outlook for small-cap-value firms is all the more uncertain when the economy's shrinking. No wonder that tolerance for holding the most vulnerable companies is likely to wane during a recession.

The penchant for sidestepping small-cap-value shares in times of distress lays the groundwork for thinking of the value and size premia as special risk factors for explaining equity returns à la the three-factor model of Fama and French. A number of studies in recent years suggest as much. Liew and Vassalou (2000), for example, present evidence that the small-cap-value premium forecasts economic growth in the developed world. This implies that these stocks capture some degree of business cycle risk.

A similar linkage is established in Vassalou (2003), who constructs "mimicking portfolios" that are thought to predict changes in the U.S. GDP. These mimicking portfolios include several variables that have been identified in the literature as useful for predicting economic cycles, including the term premium (the return difference between a thirty-year government bond and a thirty-day Treasury bill); the default premium (the difference in return between long-term corporate bonds and long-term government bonds); and a measure of the deviations in the common trend between consumption, asset wealth, and labor income à la Lettau and Ludvigson (2001a). This "news" on future changes in the GDP trend explains U.S. equity returns about as well as does the small-cap-value factor, Vassalou (2003) reports.

As financial economists continue studying this relationship between economic cycles, risk premia, and small-cap-value stocks, the argument strengthens that 1) expected returns are somewhat predictable in connection with analysis of the business cycle; and

2) small-cap-value stocks generate higher average returns than large-company stocks.

Yogo (2006) finds that returns on small stocks and value stocks are "more procyclical" relative to large stocks, a distinction that explains small-cap-value's higher average performance. He observes that the covariance of returns for these stocks with durable goods consumption is higher at the bottom of business cycles than at the peaks. Linking household consumption trends with equity premiums, Yogo concludes that small stocks and value stocks earn relatively meager returns during recessions. In sum, there appears to be a risk premium specific to small-cap-value stocks. It fluctuates through time, and it's associated with the business cycle. As a result, the premium is evident only over a full business cycle or more.

This is yet another study that suggests that small-cap-value risk is a proxy for the recession beta. Not a direct proxy, necessarily, but one that's sufficiently close so that investors can equate the two for designing and managing asset allocation. Small-value equities offer a higher expected return as compensation for bearing the extra risk. If you're willing and able to endure higher equity risk by owning more small-cap-value than the average investor, your expected return is higher.

In the short term, however, small-cap-value can and does underperform, in part because of the economic cycle. As Yogo (2006) and other researchers suggest, the prospective return on small-cap value changes. In turn, strategic-minded investors may want to adjust the small-cap-value weight accordingly by keeping an eye on economic cycles.

## Historical Clues

Small-cap-value stocks are among the most economically sensitive of securities, although economic cycles influence all asset classes, albeit in varying degrees and perhaps on different time schedules. But before making judgments about whether it's timely to modify the market-cap weight for a given asset class, investors should establish a strong view relative to the implied risk premia computed from Equation 1. To do that we must take a closer look at how the various asset classes process risk and return. That's a complex subject with a broad and deep library of research, yet we can still highlight some of the basic principles with a few real-world examples drawn from recent history.

Let's begin by comparing the 2000–2002 bear market and the 2008 market collapse. Asset allocation's stabilizing powers were stronger in the earlier period, in part because of REITs. Stocks took a beating in 2000–2002, but the losses were offset by gains in real estate securities. That contrasts with 2008, a year when both stocks and REITs suffered. Why did the diversification benefits tied to REITs work well in 2000–2002 only to evaporate in 2008?

Valuation may be one reason. When the U.S. stock market peaked in March 2000, the trailing twelve-month yield for equity REITs was 8.3 percent, or well above the benchmark ten-year Treasury note's 6.3 percent.[27] In other words, REITs offered a 200-basis-point yield premium over the safe haven of Treasuries. Fast-forward to the next peak in U.S. stocks: October 2007. The REIT yield that month was 4.2 percent, or thirty basis points below the ten-year note's 4.5 percent. The case for REITs, then, was quite a bit weaker in 2008 versus 2000.

We shouldn't be so naïve as to think that yield spread alone dictates the future. But neither can we ignore the fact that investors were being paid a premium to hold REITs in March 2000—a premium that evaporated by October 2007 relative to the benchmark ten-year note.

Let's recognize that yield is a key allure of holding REITs, which must pay out 90 percent of their income as dividends to shareholders. It's reasonable, then, to wonder if the asset class was attractive when a risk-free Treasury offered a superior payout in late-2007. REITs generally offer a higher yield compared with the ten-year Treasury, but not always. Why take the extra risk of holding REITs if a risk-free Treasury offers a superior yield?

Of course, one could have made the argument in October 2007, as some did, that the anticipated capital gains for REITs in the years ahead would more than compensate for the relatively sparse yield. But that forecast at the time was suspicious for a number of reasons. One was that from the vantage of 2007, REITs had enjoyed an extraordinary long bull market, starting in 2000. The combination of a low yield and a lengthy period of gains raised doubts about the expected return for REITs in late 2007. Did that offer a clear signal that investors should suddenly avoid REITs completely? No, since no one at the time was fully confident of the future. Nonetheless, the valuations in late 2007 implied pulling back on REITs, which were sitting on strong gains from previous years.

Valuation may have also played a role in triggering the 2000–2002 bear market in equities. A number of analysts were warning in the late 1990s that the U.S. stock market was overvalued and therefore due for a correction. One of the catalysts behind the forecast was the unusually low dividend yield. As Figure 7.1 in Chapter 7 shows, the trailing twelve-month dividend yield for U.S. stocks fell to a post–World War II low of just over 1 percent. Other accounting-based metrics, such as price-to-earnings ratio, were also suggesting that the stock market was richly valued in the late 1990s.

With the benefit of hindsight, we now know that paring back on the equity allocation was a sensible decision. At the time, however, there was some doubt. A new era, the bulls advised, had arrived and so investors were told to ignore fundamental valuation. One of the more ill-timed examples was the book *Dow 36,000: The New Strategy for Profiting from the Coming Rise in the Stock Market*, which argued that investors had begun recognizing that stocks are safer in the long run than a short-run analysis implies. As a result, the equity risk premium was declining, perhaps permanently so, the book argued. The reason: investors were slowly giving equities a permanently higher valuation compared with history. The cautionary message espoused in conventional valuation tools, such as the falling dividend yield, had therefore become irrelevant, the book suggested.

It was a tempting argument when *Dow 36,000* was published in 1999. The U.S. stock market was flush that year from its recent gains. The 28.6 percent annualized total return for 1995–1999 is the highest for a five-year holding period for large-cap domestic equities in the modern era.[28] And for a time, it was easy to think that the good times would continue indefinitely. The warning signs embedded in traditional valuation metrics appeared to have little significance as the 1990s unfolded. By 1999, the stock market's dividend yield had been declining for a decade. It was also a period when technology stocks were popular, driven in part by a widespread belief that a new digital age had killed the old investing rules.

In the end, gravity prevailed and stocks lost roughly half their value in the bear market of 2000–2002. But for several years ahead of the correction, investors who relied solely on conventional valuation metrics for forecasting equity return were penalized. Among the lessons: there are no silver bullets for assessing prospective return and risk, at least in the short term. Eventually, every tool for weighing the future fails at one time or another as a timely signal of the future.

History, in fact, is quite clear on this point. In 1958, for example, the stock market's dividend yield fell below the ten-year Treasury note yield for the first time. The unprecedented event prompted claims that the stock market was overvalued and due for a fall. The reasoning was that stocks harbored more risk than bonds and so equities should offer compensation in the form of a yield premium versus investment grade bonds. It was a reasonable assumption since the rule had always prevailed—until 1958. Some strategists that year asserted that the lower equity yield was a warning that stocks were headed for a sharp downturn, but the advice was dead wrong. Stocks rallied in the years ahead, and the equity market dividend yield remained below the ten-year's yield for the next fifty years—until 2008, when the pre-1958 relationship was reestablished.

The point is that any one variable, no matter how compelling its message, no matter how established its pedigree, is potentially fallible as a timely signal. No exceptions. What's a strategic-minded investor to do?

First, analyze a variety of market metrics and use a mix of gauges with different designs and assumptions. Accounting-based measures are useful, but a deeper understanding of internal market dynamics requires a broader survey. In addition to dividend yield and price-to-earnings ratio, for instance, watch trends in correlation, return volatility, and price momentum among the asset classes. Review recent returns over trailing three-, five-, and ten-year periods within the context of a longer-run view of history. If the asset class has generated above-average returns, that may be a sign that the market is overextended. The same is true if recent returns are spare or negative relative to history. And compare yield spreads across asset classes, as in the example above with REITs versus the ten-year Treasury note. More generally, study the history of the major asset classes and how they compare to one another through time. Develop perspective about the economic cycle too. As a starting point, consider the yield curve as it relates to the expected economic trend.

A bit of common sense never hurts either. In the bull market of 2003–2007, all the major asset classes posted gains. The extent of the buying was such that virtually any asset allocation for that five-year stretch would have delivered a strong return. It was, to put it simply, hard to lose money during those years. Genius, as the saying goes, is a bull market.

What's striking in the five years through the end of 2007 is the fact that everything boasts a gain: stocks, bonds, real estate, and commodities. Most of the returns are above-average relative to the historical record. U.S. stocks, for example, advanced by an annual 12.8 percent in the five years through the end of 2007—comfortably above the roughly 8 percent to 10 percent annualized total return that constitutes the long-run record, according to *Ibbotson* (2009).[29] Foreign stocks performed even better. REITs and commodities also enjoyed an impressive run. As a risk manager recalls in mid-2008,

> In January 2007 the world looked almost riskless. At the beginning of that year I gathered my team for an off-site meeting to identify our top five risks for the coming 12 months. We were paid to think about the downsides but it was hard to see where the problems would come from. Four years of falling credit spreads, low interest rates, virtually no defaults in our loan portfolio and historically low volatility levels: it was the most benign risk environment we had seen in 20 years.[30]

Even if you knew nothing of valuations, a reasoned look at the trailing returns for the major asset classes as 2007 unfolded suggested caution was in order because history shows that cycles endure. If you've earned extraordinary returns in broad asset classes over a multiple-year period, the history of the capital markets suggests that it's time to begin paring risk exposures in those areas that have performed the best. In fact, a simple rebalancing program using only past returns as inputs would have done just that in 2007. Using trailing returns alone would have taken money out of foreign stocks, REITs, and commodities and redeployed it to bonds and cash. That alone wouldn't have spared a multi-asset-class portfolio from the pain of late 2008, but rebalancing would have mitigated the losses, perhaps dramatically so, depending on the details of the rebalancing system and the breadth of the asset classes held.

But even that simple act was a difficult decision for the crowd. The fact that bull markets seemed to be everywhere in 2007 implied that assets were priced for perfection and that more of the same was coming. The history of financial markets teaches no such thing, although learning this lesson and applying it to real-time money management is difficult if not impossible for many investors. Why? Largely because the allure of the consensus is difficult to resist. Fear and greed, to cite the ancient explanation, are always nipping at our heels.

No one had the foresight to see the full scope of the market collapse that arrived in late 2008. But while the depth and breadth of the selling surprised almost everyone, it shouldn't have been a shock to learn that most of the asset classes succumbed to the fear that ran through the world's markets in the final months of 2008. If everything can go up simultaneously for several years at a clip, the reverse is surely possible, perhaps even probable, particularly after such a strong, multi-year run of buying.

The lesson is that cycles prevail, valuations change, and so too should asset allocations. Financial economists have spent the last thirty-plus years documenting the case for dynamically managing asset allocation to some extent as a tool for exploiting the fluctuations as well as defending the portfolio. The basic rule: favor asset classes that are paying you to assume an above-average helping of risk while pulling back in areas that seem to be priced only for perfection.

Success in designing and managing asset allocation is often a job of playing the contrarian by emphasizing asset classes that the crowd rejects and turning cautious on markets that have done well. Granted, no one can be sure of the future, which means that you should change the asset allocation slowly, over time. In some cases, it may be difficult if not impossible to form a judgment one way or the other for one or more asset classes. In those instances, the market-cap weight is the default until more compelling analysis arrives.

That said, our confidence levels can and do change, ebbing and flowing along with shifting market conditions. Expected return is often higher directly after a sharp market decline, for instance. We're still not sure of the future in the wake of a dramatic fall in prices, but we may have more confidence about prospective risk premiums than we did prior to large market moves. The same is true after a long bull market: we don't know for sure if expected return has receded after big gains. But the financial literature suggests that we should modestly integrate our informed guesses about the future into our asset allocation.

We're not talking here of sudden, dramatic changes or all-or-nothing weights for asset classes. Rather, asset allocation should evolve through time, within the parameters we've set for our strategic mix. But the ever-present risk of misjudging the future keeps us humble. Asset allocation shifts would be quick and dramatic only if you were highly confident of what's coming.

We can enhance our confidence in discounting the future by maintaining an informed perspective on the past. For all the drama in 2008, the spectacular selling wasn't unprecedented. The S&P 500's steep 37 percent loss for 2008 still falls short of the 43 percent decline of 1931. And 2008's reversal isn't all that higher than the steep losses of 1937 or 1974.[31]

And if we review 2008's stock market results from a volatility perspective, the full year looks more or less average in historical terms. Large-company stocks' annualized monthly standard deviation in 2008 was elevated versus the 2004–2006 period, but 2008's volatility looks unexceptional compared with the range of annual volatility in the previous decades.[32]

For those who were surprised by 2008's volatility, it's reasonable to ask: why? Were you unfamiliar with the historical record? If not, did you assume that big losses were no longer likely, or even possible? What was the rationale for that sunny outlook? For most investors who expected a smooth ride, the reasoning came from extrapolating what had just passed. But it was a misinformed reading of the historical record, which is to say a review that looked only at recent history.

The possibility of double-digit losses in a short time is perennial in the capital and commodity markets. If you're unwilling to accept such declines, you should own more short-term Treasury bonds or cash. If you didn't but wished otherwise after the fact, perhaps you misread your risk tolerance.

As for the complaint that asset allocation failed in 2008, that's false. Owning multiple asset classes eased the losses compared with holding, say, U.S. stocks alone. The reason: long-term investment grade corporate bonds and U.S. Treasuries posted gains in 2008. If nothing else, the year's otherwise steep losses remind that investors should think twice before completely abandoning the market-inspired asset allocation, a.k.a., owning a broad spectrum of asset classes. It was tempting to ignore bonds in the 2002–2007 run, but second-guessing markets is inherently risky and so we must proceed cautiously. Our confidence about the future is always limited and so we must beware of making extreme asset allocation choices. Adjusting the market portfolio to suit your risk profile is prudent, but the degree of adjustment must be proportional to one's confidence in the predictions that inspire moving away from the market's asset allocation.

Consider that one measure of a passive asset allocation of the global market portfolio lost 26 percent in 2008.[33] That's a big loss, although it's quite a bit better than the 37 percent drop for U.S. stocks. Would a simple rebalancing strategy have further pared a multi-asset-class portfolio's loss in 2008? Possibly.

Meanwhile, let's also recognize that asset allocation's worth should be measured over a full business cycle or two. The rationale for holding a wide array of assets has limited appeal as a strategy for optimizing results in the short run. Asset allocation isn't a tool for speculation in a given year, when almost anything's possible, especially during a global financial crisis. While there was a shortage of safe havens in 2008, the sea of red ink gives way to a broader distribution of returns for longer periods.

U.S. stocks were still suffering a small loss for the decade through the first half of 2009, and foreign developed-market stocks were up slightly. But everything else posted gains. No wonder, then, that a passive asset allocation among the major asset classes delivered a bit more than a 3 percent annualized total return for the ten years through June 2009.[34]

Might a savvy investor have earned more for those ten years by dynamically managing the same set of assets? Perhaps, although success required contrarian decisions over the years, such as pulling back on equities and boosting the bond and cash allocations in 2006 and 2007.

Beating the market portfolio will always be hard because it often requires investment choices that are in conflict with conventional wisdom. If it were otherwise, everyone would be making contrarian decisions and the associated risk premium connected with thinking independently would disappear.

Risk, it seems, is our friend *and* foe. With a bit of common sense, an understanding of market history and an informed strategy for discounting the future and using the information to adjust asset allocation, we can increase the odds that risk will work to our benefit. But that requires not only skill but eternal vigilance. Success in risk management can unravel quickly when our attention is diverted and emotion is allowed to rule the day. Perhaps that's one more reason to consider Mr. Market's global portfolio, which comes fully enabled with a self-sustaining risk management plan and foolproof defense against emotional distraction. It won't be the best-performing strategy, but neither is it likely to be the worst.

A middling result may not appeal in concept, but compared with real-world results, the average can look pretty good. All the more so if we have a high degree confidence of earning average returns via the market portfolio. That doesn't mean we should abandon the idea of customizing asset allocation and managing it dynamically. But neither should we delude ourselves into thinking that above-average results are sure to come easily, if at all. Whether we hold the market portfolio or something else, return and risk are still tightly linked.

## Chapter Notes

1. One example of an alternative goal for a custom asset allocation that's not exclusively focused on superior risk-adjusted returns is building a portfolio that appears to be a better match for the stated liabilities. A simple illustration: You plan on retiring in twenty years and estimate that your portfolio must earn a minimum of 5 percent. If you buy a twenty-year Treasury bond yielding 5 percent (let's assume the rate's available), you've funded your liability, assuming no inflation. Even if you expect that this Treasury portfolio will trail the market portfolio over the next twenty years, the choice of buying a government bond may still be considered superior in the sense that it solves your investment challenge with a high degree of confidence. The "cost" for the high confidence? The possibility, if not the likelihood, of earning less than the market portfolio.

2. Under a strict reading of the old finance, the strategic asset allocation is static and derived from a combination of the market portfolio and cash. The ratio of the two is adjusted through time to incorporate changes in the investor's personal situation—i.e., a change in career, a shift in risk expectation because of aging, etc. A more flexible reading of the old finance might allow for adjusting the market portfolio initially. For example, an investor with a relatively longer horizon may want to own more stocks than an otherwise identical investor with a shorter horizon. In any case,

once the strategic asset allocation is chosen in the old finance paradigm, the mix is static as it relates to market conditions.

3. Litterman (2003), p. 3.

4. There are a number of sophisticated statistical tools for generating relatively robust forecasts based on historical data. So-called Monte Carlo simulations are one example. Stochastic modeling software generally is now abundant, easy to use, affordable, and in the minds of many financial consultants, essential for assessing the odds that a given forecast will deliver as promised. But while these applications are useful, they're not infallible, so they're best used in concert with other forecasting techniques.

5. Author's calculations based on data from *Ibbotson* (2009), pp. 45 and 173.

6. Based on analysis of data from Robert Shiller, www.econ.yale.edu/~shiller.

7. See Gordon (1962).

8. Foreign equity yield is based on Standard & Poor's Global BMI Developed ex-US Index (www.sp-indexdata.com) and ten-year note yield from the U.S. Treasury (www.ustreas.gov).

9. *Ibbotson* (2009), p. 173.

10. Based on data from www.ustreas.gov.

11. *Ibbotson* (2009), p. 32.

12. Ibid., p. 32.

13. Ibid., p. 173.

14. Ibid., p. 95.

15. Correlations of monthly total returns are based on Russell 3000, MSCI EAFE and Barcap Intermediate Government indices using data from Morningstar Principia. Correlation readings range from 1.0 (perfect positive correlation) to 0.0 (no correlation) to −1.0 (perfect negative correlation).

16. Based on market values for Standard & Poor's Global BMI U.S. and Developed ex–U.S. stock market indices and the U.S. component of Citigroup World Government Bond Index.

17. 41 Genesis, 29–30, King James Bible.

18. Achuthan and Banerji (2004), p. 23. More generally, the authors offer an excellent primer of the business cycle and the analytical techniques for measuring and anticipating turning points.

19. Mitchell and Burns (1938), p. 1.

20. See, for instance, Latane and Tuttle (1970), pp. 293–302.

21. Schwert (1990), p. 1256.

22. Lettau and Ludvigson (2001a), p. 815.

23. Rosenberg and Maurer (2008), p. 9.

24. The arbitrage pricing theory of Ross (1976) also allows for multiple betas. But unlike the intertemporal CAPM of Merton (1973), APT is a one-period model and so it doesn't allow for a shifting opportunity set through time, as does ICAPM.

25. Merton (1973), p. 882.

26. Fama and French (1996), p. 57.

27. REIT yield based on FTSE NAREIT U.S. Equity Real Estate Index. Treasury yield is the monthly average, as reported by the Federal Reserve Board of St. Louis.

28. *Ibbotson* (2009), pp. 42–43.

29. Ibid., p. 43.

30. "Confessions of a risk manager," *The Economist*, August 7, 2008.

31. *Ibbotson* (2009), pp. 36–37.

32. Ibid., p. 98.

33. Based on the Global Market Index, compiled and calculated by The Beta Investment Report (BetaInvestment.com).

34. Ibid.

## Chapter 10

# What Have We Learned After Fifty Years?

IN THE FABLE of the blind men and the elephant, the group tries to understand and explain the animal through the sense of touch. The effort is doomed, of course, because each man touches a different part without recognizing that it's just one piece of a larger creature. In the end, no one fully comprehends the elephant, although everyone thinks they've solved the mystery. To one man, the animal is a leathery wall; to another, a fat, long snake; and so on.

Investors face a similar challenge in trying to overcome limited knowledge and decode the market's obscure rules for pricing securities. We have some information for judging how the system works, thanks to decades of economic research and careful analysis of real-world track records. But it's an incomplete knowledge and it falls far short of a full explanation. That leaves us to generalize the internal workings of a complex organism using imperfect information based on what we can discern from looking at the past. No wonder, then, that investment results are volatile at times and often less than satisfactory. How could it be otherwise when we're effectively playing chess with only a partial understanding of the rules while our opponent—a grandmaster—knows all?

In some respects, the market's a black box. There are almost certainly a set of laws that govern how the market prices securities, but we understand only a fraction of those rules and perhaps poorly. As investors, we're the blind men with our hands on the proverbial elephant. Does that suffice to make informed decisions about asset allocation? Perhaps, although the curse of investing is that we're always unsure if we're making the right decision.

Our limited understanding of the system inspires portfolio diversification and avoiding extreme bets relative to the market's asset allocation. As Charlie Ellis advises, investing has become a loser's game, which means that enhancing the odds of winning requires a strategy that excels primarily by not losing.[1] That's an increasingly wise approach as the market becomes ever more competitive, thanks to a growing array of institutional players, hedge funds, and other entities armed to the teeth with analytical power and deep pockets. This evolution in the marketplace suggests that investors are better served by focusing on avoiding setbacks rather than striving to beat the market. Simple statistics tells us why. Losses have a bigger effect on portfolio results compared to gains. Reversing a 10 percent decline requires an 11 percent rise just to break even.

Ellis looks to the game of tennis as an illustration of the underlying dynamic, citing research by Dr. Simon Ramo, who analyzed the sport's finer points in the late 1970s. "Professional tennis is a winner's game: the outcome is determined by the actions of the winner," Ellis explains. "Amateur tennis is a loser's game: the outcome is determined by the actions of a loser—who defeats himself."[2]

The lesson: making fewer errors, a.k.a. risk management, is the first order of business for investing, and that begins with diversification within and across asset classes. The challenge is figuring out how to optimize the portfolio mix. A definitive solution remains elusive, and probably always will, but we've learned enough over the past half century to give ourselves a fighting chance of earning respectable results in the long run.

## Start at the Beginning

All investors should begin by considering the market portfolio. The average investor holds this portfolio through time. The basic choice for any one investor is how to change the market's asset allocation. The case for some degree of divergence from the market is a function of the fact that we all have finite time horizons and specific risk preferences. If we're investing for, say, ten years, the risk tied to the market's asset allocation, which is optimal for the very long term, is inappropriate and so customizing the asset mix is in order.

If we decide to rebuild the market portfolio to match our liabilities and preferences, we must also consider how to manage the asset allocation. For some, perhaps most investors, a simple rebalancing system that reacts to market changes will suffice. The alternative is dynamically managing a portion of the portfolio through time based on market forecasts. Financial economics tells us that expected risk premiums are partly predictable for medium-to-long-term horizons. That implies that our strategic asset allocation should be partly fluid based on the current expectations for risk premia.

If price fluctuations are purely random, the optimal asset allocation should be fixed. Assuming you've identified the best mix of assets, there would be no reason to change the asset allocation if the random walk theory is fully accurate all of the time. But price changes aren't completely random, which opens the door for some degree of predictability and, by extension, dynamic portfolio management.

Embracing a degree of dynamic asset allocation doesn't replace rebalancing, or at least it doesn't have to. For instance, consider a simple 60/40 stock/bond asset allocation that's rebalanced whenever the mix changes by five percentage points or more. Using a straight rebalancing system, when the mix moved to 65/35, the stock/bond weights would be returned to 60/40.

But now imagine an investor who also seeks to inject a degree of dynamic asset allocation into this conventional rebalancing regime. For instance, assume again that the original asset allocation drifts to 65/35. At that point, the investor has turned relatively bullish on bonds compared to when he initially set the 60/40 asset allocation. Assume also that his expectation for equities is unchanged. As such, instead of rebalancing back to 60/40, he instead opts for a 57/43 split. Why? The modestly higher weight in bonds versus the result dictated by a straight rebalancing decision is a reflection of his forecast that fixed-income's return outlook has improved. If he is supremely confident in his prediction, perhaps he opts for an even higher weighting in bonds.

Some economists, and many investors, believe that predictability is a sign of market inefficiency, but there's an alternative and arguably more satisfying view. Market prices are equilibrium prices and so they reflect the collective effort of investors to put a price on expected risk. If the market reflects all known information at each point in time, the best forecast relies on current knowledge, which is factored into market prices. As new information arrives, the market reassesses the future, and equilibrium prices adjust.

Sometimes the price adjustments are modest, but not always. If the latest news is dramatically different from what was previously known, market prices may undergo large shifts. Let's say new information arrives, and it threatens corporate cash flows. In response, investors become more risk averse and they discount the market's expected return at a higher rate. That translates into a lower present value for equities. In other words, prices drop. In that case, the anticipated medium-to-long-run equity return probably increased. That doesn't mean that higher returns are guaranteed, although that's possible, perhaps even likely. Yet we can't forget that the expected return has risen to compensate investors for the newly anticipated jump in risk.

The process also works in reverse. If there's new information that provides a higher degree of confidence about future cash flow growth, stock prices are likely to rise, which implies that expected returns are now lower. There's still no guarantee that lesser performance is coming, but the market factors in the new information and reprices securities accordingly.

Expected return that fluctuates, it seems, can be rational. No less, then, is true for changing asset allocation. As our market-informed outlook for risk and return evolves, some of the changes should translate into a new asset mix. But how much change is too much? Or too little?

Financial economists are working on finding answers to the challenge of identifying optimal asset allocation adjustments in a world where expected risk premia fluctuate. This is far more challenging than finding the optimal asset allocation in a random walk world. If prices change randomly, once we estimate the asset mix that offers the best combination of reward for a given level of risk, the prescription will hold constant through time for a long-term investor, all else equal.

But investing is more complicated with the new finance. Expected returns aren't always randomly distributed in the short and medium terms and so our analysis of what constitutes the optimal asset allocation changes depending on when we crunch the numbers. Today's optimal mix may look less-than-optimal tomorrow, as you might guess in a world where expected returns are constantly in flux.

In addition, the old finance optimized asset allocation for one investment period ahead. Investors in the real world have multi-period investment horizons, so the additional risk that accompanies investing through time—changing interest rates, for instance—must be considered when designing and managing portfolios. Assuming a constant yield for the ten-year Treasury note, as one example, is asking for trouble if you have a medium or long-term investment horizon.

Dynamic portfolio theory considers a world of fluctuating expected returns and other factors in a multiple-investment-period setting. The goal is one of continually identifying the optimal asset allocation. The work is still in its infancy although the research is expanding rapidly.[3] In the old finance, the market portfolio was deemed the optimal portfolio; in the updated version of MPT, the optimal portfolio keeps changing. On paper, investors should continually alter asset allocation to maintain an optimal portfolio. In practice, investors are likely to be more cautious due to real-world frictions—trading costs, taxes, and the inevitability of error when estimating return and risk.

These frictions encourage staying close to the market portfolio as a general rule. To the extent we deviate from the benchmark, the second guessing should be inspired by 1) analyzing risk factors that look economically durable through time and 2) considering how signals from those factors interact with our risk tolerance, investment horizon, and personal financial situation. And if we're also inclined to manage the resulting asset allocation dynamically, the research tells us to favor periods when the signals appear particularly timely for enhancing the risk-adjusted expected return premium.

The new finance motivates thinking that we can enhance the market portfolio's risk-adjusted return, although there's never a shortage of reasons to remind us that success won't come easy. Consider the cautionary message from Welch and Goyal (2008), who review a range of variables that have been identified in the literature as useful for predicting the equity risk premium. Examples include dividends, earnings, return variance (volatility), book value, inflation, long-term government bond yields, and other metrics. Despite in-sample results in earlier studies that suggest predictability, running a new series of out-of-sample tests (using different time periods than those originally studied) on these measures reveals poor results. The implication, once again: beating the market is hard.

On the other hand, the failure of any one variable to consistently forecast return in Welch and Goyal's study isn't an open-and-shut verdict. If predictability exists, we shouldn't expect that the required analysis will be accessible simply by looking at one factor, or that a lone financial measure will remain forever functional, each and every day, for predicting market returns. If it was that easy, a strategy's success would fall victim to its own popularity.

Nor should we dismiss return predictability based on simple statistical tests alone. Cochrane (2008b) points out that it's no surprise to find that dividend-yield-based forecasts are weak predictors when the results are evaluated out-of-sample using straightforward regression analysis. It's true that such tests suggest caution for expecting dividend yield to continually generate excess return in the short run. But rejecting forecastability generally on this basis is premature. Cochrane's defense of return predictability via dividends is complex, although he summarizes his justification this way:

> If returns really are *not* forecastable, then dividend growth must *be* forecastable in order to generate the observed variation in dividend-price ratios. We should see that forecastability. Yet, even looking 25 years out, there is not a shred of evidence that high market price-dividend ratios are associated with higher subsequent dividend growth.[4]

The absence of dividend-growth forecastability lays the groundwork for why Cochrane and others argue that dividends offer some degree of information about future returns.

Cochrane offered a more accessible explanation in an op-ed piece for *The Wall Street Journal* in late 2008, right about the time when the outlook for the economy and the market was unusually bleak:

> In a recession, or following losses, many investors become more averse to holding risks. They want to sell. But we can't all sell—a fact routinely ignored in much financial advice and commentary. Instead,

prices must fall and prospective returns rise until some investors are willing to buy. Unsurprisingly, upward spikes in the dividend yield [in the past] came in bad economic times.[5]

## More Is Better

Even under the best of circumstances, one variable can only do so much. There are limits to the depth and duration of foresight that a single financial or economic factor can impart. The markets are too complex for reducing the pricing mechanism to one number that continually spits out accurate forecasts. The dividend yield, for instance, is surely a better predictor when the market is at extremes. It follows, then, that most of the intervening periods between extremes are likely to be less productive if not irrelevant for discounting the future using dividend yield alone.

At the same time, if each variable harbors a small but unique bit of economic intelligence, common sense suggests that routinely looking at numerous factors may deliver broader, deeper intelligence about expected returns beyond the clues provided in any one metric. In fact, researchers are beginning to find evidence that this is a useful way to look at the data.

Rapach et al. (2009) undertake an expansive review of financial variables and offer encouraging results for predicting the equity risk premium. They demonstrate that combining fifteen metrics, including dividend yield, price-to-earnings ratio, the long-term Treasury yield, etc., provides "convincing evidence of the out-of-sample predictive ability … over a number of periods."[6]

Research on evaluating combinations of variables is still a relatively new field, but a promising one. Having spent the last several decades identifying the various factors that enhance the forecasting of risk premia, financial economists are only just beginning to reconsider the possibilities by looking at the data in a broader, integrated context. Rapach et al., in fact, build on some of the early efforts in this line of inquiry and offer a survey of the literature. One of the recurring themes is that forecasting the equity premium with "combination methods" demonstrates a strong connection to the economic cycle. A growing body of research has been telling a similar story over the years. The more compelling forecasting opportunities, in other words, are grounded in economic logic, which in turn supports the efficient market hypothesis and an updated view of modern portfolio theory. The reasoning proceeds as follows, according to Rapach et al. (2009):

1. In times of economic contraction, risk aversion rises. In order to attract buyers, equities must be priced to offer a higher risk premium.
2. Dividend yield and other variables used in out-of-sample tests tend to offer the most value as predictors at extreme periods in the economic cycle, particularly during recessions. This finding is compatible with previous research that indicates that investors demand higher risk premiums during periods of economic stress.
3. The fifteen variables used in combination to forecast the equity risk premium also deliver strong out-of-sample predictions of the business cycle, defined by inflation-adjusted changes in gross domestic product, profits, and net cash flow. Linking predictability to the economic cycle strengthens the case for arguing that the fifteen variables are enduring factors for estimating stock returns, as outlined by Cochrane (2008a).
4. Individual predictors suffer periods of instability and so the forecasting value fades, perhaps completely at times. These periods of instability are linked with trends in the economic cycle. Fortunately, the forecasting power of the fifteen individual factors fluctuates with some degree of independence from one another, which explains why using the full complement of predictors offers a superior model for estimating the equity risk premium compared with analyzing just one variable in isolation.

The notion that returns in the capital and commodity markets are intimately tied up with the economic cycle is an old idea, but an intuitive one that's increasingly supported by financial economic research. Even short-term price momentum,[7] a long-running thorn in the side of the efficient markets theory, now appears to be explained by macroeconomic-linked variables: the dividend yield, default spread, three-month Treasury bill yield, and shape of the yield curve, according to Chordia and Shivakumar (2002). In other words, profits generated by momentum strategies appear to be payoffs for time-varying risk, a framework that's consistent with rational pricing models.

If return predictability is sensitive to macroeconomic variables, then the view of a rational pricing system that sets market prices and influences returns seems not only plausible but inevitable. It should shock no one that markets attempt to discount the future on a real-time basis amid a constant inflow of new information and shifting perceptions of risk by investors. Is the market price always correct? Of course not, nor should we expect it to be. Discounting the future is hazardous business, and mistakes are inevitable. But saying that the market sometimes gets it wrong doesn't automatically negate the idea that markets are generally efficient or that partial return predictability precludes efficiency.

Market prices are equilibrium prices: they reflect the point at which buyers and sellers agree to trade. That doesn't make prices omniscient, although history and theory suggest that as a general rule market prices are likely to be pretty good attempts at discounting the future mix of expected return and risk. If it were otherwise, minting positive alpha would be far more common on a recurring, risk-adjusted basis.

At the same time, there's no reason why equilibrium prices shouldn't convey some information about future returns. Indeed, the degree of predictability is subject to change. When there's a higher confidence in a predictor's message, the general economic risk is usually higher. Meanwhile, the predictability aspect offered by dividend yield, yield curve, and so on seems to be less reliable in times of economic plenty. It would only be surprising and inefficient if it were otherwise. Investors are more willing to speculate during economic expansions. During periods of economic turmoil, by contrast, the demand for visibility is at a premium, guarded behavior is common, and the market tends to respond by offering a higher level of predictability, albeit one that's still well short of absolute.

Pesaran and Timmermann (1995), for example, show that economic factors have predictive qualities for estimating U.S. equity returns and the power of those factors changes. Their study suggests that "predictability of stock returns may indeed be particularly pronounced in periods of economic 'regime switches' where the markets are relatively unsettled and investors are particularly uncertain of which forecasting model to use for trading."[8] In the comparative calm of the 1960s, for instance, stock return predictability was relatively low, Pesaran and Timmermann report. That was followed by the volatile 1970s, when predictability increased. The basic message: economic variables, including interest rates, inflation, and the money supply, offer clues about expected stock returns, and the predictive value of these clues fluctuates over time with market volatility.

It's doubtful if markets could function if the prospective return was constant while macroeconomic conditions swing to and fro. Imagine that in late 2008, as the economic outlook soured, there was no commensurate rise in expected equity return. Now *that* would be inefficient and astonishing. If the prospective risk premium is steady, there would be little reason to buy stocks in the throes of the worst recession since the Great Depression. But someone was buying stocks in late 2008, despite the dark clouds threatening the economy and by extension the financial markets.

The question is *why* were some people buying at a time of unusually high anxiety and fear? Did they anticipate higher-than-normal returns? Probably, which suggests that the market operates in a generally rational fashion by repricing risk as informed by current news. As a result, expected risk premia vary and in a partly predictable way.

If it's economically logical for expected returns to vary, it's also reasonable to anticipate that the system drops some hints about future returns. But these clues aren't blatantly obvious in any one variable at all times. It takes effort and skill to tease out economically robust forecasts. In turn, that suggests that two, three, or more factors are better at making estimates under conditions of uncertainty than is any one. The collective judgment of all the factors is the market price, which has proven itself competitive as a general rule.

The power of group analysis is hardly limited to financial markets. In James Surowiecki's book *The Wisdom of Crowds*, the collective intelligence that sometimes flows from groups is chronicled through history and across professions and social settings. The opening example offers a simple but clear illustration of the phenomenon in action. Strolling through an agricultural fair in England in 1906, an aging Francis Galton, a polymath and cousin of Charles Darwin, witnessed a contest where small bets were made on the weight of an ox. The wagers that came closest to the animal's true weight would be awarded prizes. Some 800 people tried their luck, representing a mix of farmers and butchers, as well as people who would have little inside knowledge of oxen. After the contest was over, Galton analyzed the results and found that the crowd's average guess (1,197 pounds) was nearly the actual weight of the ox (1,198 pounds). "In other words, the crowd's judgment was essentially perfect," as Suroweicki explains.[9]

Was it simply a freak case of collective brainpower? No, argues Surowiecki, who offers varied examples from history in favor of the idea that "under the right circumstances, groups are remarkably intelligent, and are often smarter than the smartest people in them. Groups do not need to be dominated by exceptionally intelligent people in order to be smart. Even if most of the people within a group are not especially well-informed or rational, it can still reach a collectively wise decision."[10]

Critics are fond of pointing out instances that appear to contradict the idea of market wisdom. But in the context of investing, if we don't fully understand how the market prices securities, how can we fully dismiss efficiency as a possible answer? Could the claim of inefficiency simply be a fig leaf to cover up our ignorance about how the market's pricing mechanism works?

It's helpful to consider how former mysteries sometimes become less mysterious in financial economics as research unfolds. There was a time, for instance, when the capital asset pricing model appeared hopelessly broken. The market beta of CAPM didn't seem to explain risk and return very well, at least when looking at historical results. But in the wake of numerous studies over the past thirty years, including the research that produced the Fama-French 3-factor model, we now have a deeper understanding of how markets work. Dismissing the CAPM, as a result, looks premature.

The CAPM, it turns out, isn't "wrong" so much as it is a blunt tool for making a generalized statement of market activity. The logic of the model remains strong, although trying to explain securities behavior exclusively with market beta may be asking too much, at least if we're considering historical returns.[11] But extending CAPM's framework by adding other betas offers a richer and more accurate description of how the market prices securities. In a multi-factor world, the basic insight of CAPM works better. Asset pricing that incorporates CAPM *and* small-cap-value beta, for example, provides a more satisfying description of equity market behavior. We still don't have a complete explanation, nor are we likely to arrive at such a state of financial nirvana. But we're continually getting closer to the truth, even if the final destination remains elusive and the various tools employed offer less-than-perfect solutions.

That suggests that what some say is evidence of the market's inefficiency may simply be a lack of a deeper understanding of the rational pricing system. One reason for thinking so is that generating excess returns over beta for extended periods, using a relevant benchmark, remains difficult. If CAPM offered no insight into how markets behave, it's unlikely that index funds based on market capitalization (which owe an intellectual debt to the model) would continue to remain competitive with active management.

Meantime, it's unconvincing to point out that certain fund managers outperform their benchmark and therefore the market's inefficient. In an efficient market, you'd expect something on the order of half of all participants to deliver above-average returns. Of course, that's offset by the likelihood that half of investors will trail the market. In fact, something approaching that result prevails in the actual track records of mutual funds over time. Unfortunately, predicting the above-average winners in advance is difficult, which is why opting for the market is so compelling over the long haul.

Critics also claim that large market moves are evidence of market inefficiency. But this charge is meaningless without a theoretical response that offers an economically sound alternative description of pricing behavior. Specifically, we need an explanation for why prices shouldn't change beyond a certain degree. Some say, for instance, that the volatility of stock prices relative to dividends is the smoking gun. But as noted earlier, Cochrane (2008b) advises that this argument isn't entirely persuasive.[12]

An efficient market hardly precludes price changes, big or small. In fact, market efficiency anticipates if not demands price fluctuations, perhaps large fluctuations at times, depending on the news and the resulting adjustment in investor risk aversion. Asserting that investors are irrational based on the degree of price change, in other words, falls short of a convincing response.

But let's assume that investors are irrational. Why should proponents of market inefficiency expect satisfaction if such a framework dictates pricing behavior? Inefficiency implies that prices are "wrong." If markets are unreasonable in setting prices, by what means might investors anticipate earning a profit from the system? Perhaps the expectation is that an irrational price will become less irrational at some point. If so, should we call such a state a rational price? And does that mean that investors who think the markets are irrational are assuming that rational pricing will return at times?

Even if you think of yourself as a rational investor in a world of irrational pricing, you'll still need at least one other rationally minded investor to take the securities off your hands at some point if you're intent on cashing in on your analysis. But why would you expect such a person to exist in an inefficient market?

## A Grand Unified Theory?

The fact that an updated version of modern portfolio theory now echoes the basic points made by Graham and Dodd (1934) strengthens the case for thinking that financial economics continues to inch closer to a fundamental truism about market behavior and investment strategy. There are many contentious notions in the investment universe, but few are more radical than claiming that the value strategies of Ben Graham and his disciples look increasingly compatible with a twenty-first-century reading of modern portfolio theory (MPT).

On the surface, it sounds absurd. MPT, after all, is the suite of financial theories that spawned index funds and the view that market prices are the best estimate of intrinsic value as a general rule over the long haul. Applied in MPT's original theoretical chassis, these notions are antithetical to Graham and Dodd, who assert that enlightened investors should question Mr. Market's estimates.

MPT and value investing, it would seem, are natural adversaries. Yet the two appear increasingly connected as well, thanks to the evolution of MPT. There are still differences, but a finer reading of the literature now suggests that there are also common links.

Nonetheless, the popular perception of MPT remains stuck in the 1960s and 1970s, when the efficient market hypothesis (EMH) and indexing first arrived on the financial scene. But decades of research have refined our understanding of how markets work and so the leading-edge interpretation of MPT has evolved. As the financial literature has moved closer to a Graham-inspired view of the world, the possibility arises that something akin to a grand unifying theory of investing may be possible in the future.

Meanwhile, an updated view of MPT, like Graham and Dodd, tells us that price matters. Mindlessly owning the market and ignoring valuation no longer looks as compelling as it did in, say, 1975. *When* you buy and sell is as critical as *what* you buy and sell. No wonder, then, that the idea of blending some of the value-inspired thinking of Graham and Dodd for managing a portfolio of multiple betas no longer sounds counterintuitive; instead, it's now the basis for real-world money management.[13]

That's all well and good, but why should investors care? Because if the classic strategies of active and passive investing are more closely related in favor of using valuation techniques, the union lends more authority to a value-informed view of investing strategies generally. In that case, investors can be that much more confident that the evolution reflects a vital message about how markets operate.

Card-carrying members of the Graham school of investing can rightfully say, "We told you so." But while academics are late to the party, the fact that they've arrived only adds more weight to what Graham taught: ignore valuation at your peril. True for individual securities, true for asset classes. Unlikely or not, a twenty-first-century reading of MPT now echoes Graham's basic advice to consider prospective return based on discounting risk.

Graham and Dodd, of course, explained the power of valuation as a function of looking for market mistakes. But that's no longer a satisfying analysis. What looks like a market "mistake" in pricing securities may simply be a reflection of time-varying risk premia. Yet even that may not suffice as a full explanation. A "mistake" in the eyes of one investor might also be explained by a difference of time horizon or risk tolerance among market participants. None of this makes Graham and Dodd's basic counsel any less potent. Yet it's clear that investors have different expectations, preferences, etc. compared to the market. Until and if we adjust for those differences, it's possible that what appears to be inefficient pricing for, say, a five-year time horizon for an investor with $y$ risk aversion is actually rational pricing for a three- or seven-year view for an investor with an $x$ aversion to risk.

More broadly, one might wonder if the market prices securities for a single investment horizon and risk aversion. Even after fifty years of financial economics, we've only started to scratch the surface of deciphering market behavior and reverse engineering the rules for investment strategy on such matters. But we have picked up a few clues along the way, and the limited knowledge we've earned continues to suggest that claims of rational pricing's death are greatly exaggerated.

No one argues that the markets are always perfectly efficient at all times or that markets are infallible, or that the efficient market hypothesis is the definitive, all-encompassing explanation for how assets are priced. Markets make mistakes, as you'd expect from a system that draws judgment on the collective decisions of mere mortals. But figuring out when and where those mistakes occur, in advance, with consistency through time, isn't easy. Yes, the so-called anomalies that seem to signal market error are numerous. But they, too, are prone to misinformation about future prices, and over time these indications of general investor overreaction and underreaction may be evenly split, just as you'd expect in an efficient market. In other words, pricing anomalies in the aggregate may average out as the market price. You can accept Mr. Market's estimate, or you can venture down the more precarious path of picking and choosing anomalies that seem to offer better prospects.

In any case, rejecting extremism on one end of the efficiency spectrum requires the same on the other. If we accept that the market is less than purely efficient at all times, isn't it reasonable to also assume that the market is not completely inefficient over the long haul? Of course, that opens up an intellectual can of worms since a little efficiency goes a long way. If rational pricing prevails part of the time, investors should think twice before ignoring market efficiency as a general rule.

Fifty years of financial research tell us to start with the idea that the market portfolio—as broadly defined as we can reasonably make it—is everyone's benchmark. That generally translates into a globally diversified basket of stocks, bonds, real estate (REITs), and commodities. How should we weight these asset classes and their major subgroups? We can start by considering the asset allocation informed by the respective market values. This is the portfolio that everyone can own without impacting prices. Over time, this ends up being the portfolio that the average investor holds. That's why it's a robust benchmark.

Should we change the market's asset mix for our own portfolio? Should we adjust the weights of the major asset classes? Should we leave out one or more asset classes entirely? Perhaps, although only for compelling reasons, namely: your risk tolerance and investment horizon are different than the market's. In addition, you have specific risks that arise from your personal circumstances, such as your job, and that implies holding something different from the market's asset allocation. But there are less compelling reasons for altering the market portfolio, such as thinking that you're smarter than everyone else.

Once you've designed an asset allocation, you may also want to manage it dynamically and shift the strategic mix from time to time. You should do so for personal reasons, such as aging, which affects your risk outlook and financial needs. Finance theory also tells us to consider market predictability as a source of dynamic asset allocation. But we need to proceed cautiously. Do you have sufficient confidence in your forecasts? Even then, how much extra risk that flows from the hazards of predicting are you willing to assume? And even if you're right, are your forecasts likely to overcome any associated taxes and trading costs?

Ultimately, predictions must be grounded in economic logic. In turn, that inspires a fundamental question: is your expectation of excess return easily arbitraged away if too many investors chase the idea? Most apparent sources of excess return above and beyond what's offered by the market are vulnerable if they become popular strategies. Other promising trades simply fade after adjusting for risk or real-world frictions, such as taxes and trading costs. And, as always, your analysis may be fundamentally wrong to begin with.

The market portfolio's expected risk premium, by comparison, is quite a bit more durable, at least relative to any one asset class or security. The market's risk premium changes of course, and in the short run it's been known to evaporate entirely for a time. Even a casual study of the past tells us so in clear and unambiguous terms. One ten-year run can dispense dramatically different results from another. But it's also clear that the average investor owns the market portfolio through time, and she receives its premium in the long run. That's why it's everyone's benchmark.

The indispensable and recurring lesson in financial economics over the past fifty years is that we're all risk managers and the basis of sound risk management begins with identifying a prudent benchmark. The details of what to do next are forever contentious, but at least we know how to begin. That may not sound like much, but in fact it represents enormous progress in the theory of investing.

The money game, after all, has a different standard of advancement compared with professions beyond finance. Engineering, medicine, and most other vocations are satisfied only with clear and measurable progress. Investing, by contrast, is considered a great success if we do no worse than our predecessors. But even that lowly yardstick isn't always possible, much less guaranteed.

Understanding why that's so, and why we should be skeptical that we'll break free of this fate any time soon, is at the heart of what separates money management from virtually all other disciplines. It also explains why the market portfolio—the true market portfolio—is likely to be such a potent strategy over time, and why we should second-guess it cautiously.

We've learned a lot over the last fifty years, but not nearly as much as we sometimes assume. In fact, in the grand scheme of deciphering markets and drawing sensible conclusions for investment strategy, our inquiries have only just begun. Invest accordingly.

## Chapter Notes

1. See Ellis (1998).
2. Ellis (1998), pp. 3–4.
3. For a survey on the literature of dynamic portfolio choice theory through the early twenty-first century, see Campbell and Viceira (2002).
4. Cochrane (2008b), p. 1571.
5. Cochrane (2008c).
6. Rapach et al. (2009), p. 33.
7. See Jegadeesh and Titman (1993).
8. Pesaran and Timmermann (1995), p. 1212.
9. Surowiecki (2004), p. xiii.
10. Ibid., pp. xiii–xiv.
11. The evidence documenting CAPM's flaws is primarily based on analysis of ex post returns, i.e., historical results, and for an obvious reason: ex ante returns, or expected returns, are directly unobservable. That leaves

the question of whether CAPM works better with ex ante returns? Yes, according to Levy (1997), who uses simulated ex ante parameters for testing CAPM. He concludes that CAPM "is alive and doing better than previous empirical studies have revealed" (p. 119). That's unsurprising since CAPM is focused on identifying the *expected* relationship between risk and return, which implies that testing the model in an ex post context can mislead.

12. See Cochrane (2008b), p. 1571.

13. Fusing components of indexing with value investing concepts is an intriguing idea with an expanding menu of real-world applications. One example is the so-called fundamental indexing approach outlined by Robert Arnott and his colleagues at Research Affiliates, a consultancy that designs benchmarks for this niche of ETFs and index mutual funds (see Arnott et al. [2008] for an overview of the methodology). Meanwhile, Bernstein (2007) reviews how modern portfolio theory has influenced investing strategy generally in the money management business, including some active management shops.

# Bibliography

Achuthan, Lakshman and Anirvan Banerji, 2004. *Beating the Business Cycle: How to Predict and Profit from Turning Points in the Economy*, New York: Currency Doubleday.

Ackert, Lucy F. and Brian F. Smith, 1993. "Stock Price Volatility, Ordinary Dividends, and Other Cash Flows to Shareholders," *Journal of Finance*, Vol. 48, No. 4, pp. 1147–1160.

Alexander, Sidney S., 1961. "Price Movements in Speculative Markets: Trends or Random Walks," *Industrial Management Review*, Vol. 2, No. 2, pp. 7–26.

Alford, Andrew W. and James R. Boatsman, 1995. "Predicting Long-Term Stock Return Volatility: Implications for Accounting and Valuation of Equity Derivatives," *Accounting Review*, Vol. 70, No. 4, pp. 599–618.

Alliance Bernstein Investments, 2005. "Understanding Investment Behavior: A Brief Look at the Investment Decision-Making Process," research monograph: therightmix.alliancebernstein.com.

Ambrosio, Frank J., 2007. "An Evaluation of Risk Metrics," Vanguard research monograph: institutional.vanguard.com/iip/pdf/ICRERM.pdf.

Andersson, Magnus, Elizaveta Krylova, and Sami Vahamaa, 2008. "Why Does the Correlation Between Stock and Bond Returns Vary Over Time?" *Applied Financial Economics*, Vol. 18, No. 2, pp. 139–151.

Arnott, Robert D., 1995. "Investment Strategy," in *The Portable MBA in Investment*, Peter L. Bernstein, ed., New York: Wiley.

____, 2009. "Bonds: Why Bother? Investors May Have Some Misconceptions About Fixed Income," *Journal of Indexes*, Vol. 12, No. 3, pp. 10-17.

Arnott, Robert D., Andrew L. Berkin, and Jia Ye, 2000. "How Well Have Investors Been Served in the 1980s and 1990s?" *Journal of Portfolio Management*, Vol. 26, No. 4, pp. 84–91.

Arnott, Robert D., Jason C. Hsu, and John M. West, 2008. *The Fundamental Index: A Better Way to Invest*, Hoboken, New Jersey: Wiley.

Arnott, Robert D. and Robert M. Lovell Jr., 1992. "Rebalancing: Why? When? How Often?" First Quadrant research monograph, No. 3.

Arnott, Robert D. and James N. von Germeten, 1983. "Systematic Asset Allocation," *Financial Analysts Journal*, Vol. 39, No. 6, pp. 31–38.

Asness, Clifford, 2006. "The Value of Fundamental Indexing," *Institutional Investor*, October 19.

Bachelier, Louis, 1900. "Théorie de la Spéculation," *Annales Scientifiques de l'École Normale Superieure*, Vol. 3, No. 17, pp. 21–86, in

*Random Character of Stock Market Prices*, Paul Cootner, ed., Cambridge, Massachusetts: MIT Press, 1969, 1964.

Banz, R. W., 1981. "The Relationship Between Return and Market Value of Common Stocks," *Journal of Financial Economics*, Vol. 9, No. 1, pp. 3–18.

Barber, Brad M. and John D. Lyon, 1997. "Firm Size, Book-to-Market Ratio, and Security Returns: A Holdout Sample of Financial Firms," *Journal of Finance*, Vol. 52, No. 2, pp. 875–883.

Barberis, Nicholas, 2000. "Investing for the Long Run When Returns Are Predictable," *Journal of Finance*, Vol. 55, No. 1, pp. 225–264.

Barro, Robert J., 1974. "Are Government Bonds Net Wealth?" *Journal of Political Economy*, Vol. 82, No. 6, pp. 1095–1117.

Baruch, Bernard M., 1957. *Baruch: My Own Story*, New York: Holt, Rinehart and Winston.

Basu, Sanjoy, 1977. "Investment Performance of Common Stocks in Relation to Their Price-Earnings Ratios: A Test of the Efficient Market Hypothesis," *Journal of Finance*, Vol. 32, No. 3, pp. 663–682.

Bekkers, Niels, Ronald Q. Doeswijk, and Trevin W. Lam, 2009. "Strategic Asset Allocation: Determining the Optimal Portfolio with Ten Asset Classes," research monograph, Institute for Research and Investment Services (Rabobank and Robeco), The Netherlands.

Bernoulli, Daniel, 1738. "Exposition of a New Theory on the Measurement of Risk" (translated from Latin into English by Louise Sommer), *Econometrica*, Vol. 22, No. 1 (1954), pp. 23–36.

Bernstein, Peter L., 1992. *Capital Ideas: The Improbable Origins of Modern Wall Street*, New York: Wiley.

____, 1996. *Against The Gods: The Remarkable Story of Risk*, Hoboken, New Jersey: Wiley.

____, 2007. *Capital Ideas Evolving*, Hoboken, New Jersey: Wiley.

Bernstein, William J., 1996. "The Rebalancing Bonus: Theory and Practice," research monograph: www.efficientfrontier.com/ef/996/rebal.htm.

____, 2002. *The Four Pillars of Investing: Lessons for Building a Winning Portfolio*, New York: McGraw-Hill.

Bernstein, William J. and David Wilkinson, 1997. "Diversification, Rebalancing, and the Geometric Mean Frontier," research monograph: www.effisols.com/basics/rebal.pdf.

Bhandari, Laxmi Chand, 1988. "Debt/Equity Ratio and Expected Stock Returns: Empirical Evidence," *Journal of Finance*, Vol. 43, No. 2, pp. 507–528.

Black, Fischer, 1972. "Capital Market Equilibrium with Restricted Borrowing," *Journal of Business*, Vol. 45, No. 3, pp. 444–455.

_____, 1993. "Beta and Return," *Journal of Portfolio Management*, Vol. 20, No. 1, pp. 8–18.

Black, Fischer, Michael C. Jensen, and Myron Scholes, 1972. "The Capital Asset Pricing Model: Some Empirical Tests," in *Studies in the Theory of Capital Markets*, Michael Jensen, ed., New York: Praeger, 1972.

Bogle, John, 2000. *Common Sense on Mutual Funds: New Imperatives for the Intelligent Investor*, New York: Wiley.

Bollerslev, Tim, 1986. "Generalized Autoregressive Conditional Heteroskedasticity," *Journal of Econometrics*, Vol. 31, No. 3, pp. 307–327.

Booth, David G. and Eugene F. Fama, 1992. "Diversification Returns and Asset Contributions," *Financial Analysts Journal*, Vol. 48, No. 3, pp. 26–32.

Brennan, Michael J., Eduardo S. Schwartz, and Ronald Lagnado, 1997. "Strategic Asset Allocation," *Journal of Economic Dynamics and Control*, Vol. 21, No. 8, pp. 1377–1403.

Brinson, Gary P., 1995. "Global Management and Asset Allocation," in *The Portable MBA in Investment*, Peter L. Bernstein, ed., New York: Wiley.

Brinson, Gary P., L. Randolph Hood, and Gilbert L. Beebower, 1986. "Determinants of Portfolio Performance," *Financial Analysts Journal*, Vol. 42, No. 4, pp. 39–44.

Brinson, Gary P., Brian D. Singer, and Gilbert L. Beebower, 1991. "Determinants of Portfolio Performance II: An Update," *Financial Analysts Journal*, Vol. 47, No. 3, pp. 40–48.

Brocato, Joe and Steve Steed, 1998. "Optimal Asset Allocation over the Business Cycle," *Financial Review*, Vol. 33, No. 3, pp. 129–148.

Brooks, John, 1999, 1973. *The Go-Go Years: The Drama and Crashing Finale of Wall Street's Bullish 60s*, New York: Wiley.

Buetow, Gerard W., Jr., Ronald Sellers, Donald Trotter, Elaine Hunt, and Willie A. Whipple Jr., 2002. "The Benefits of Rebalancing," *Journal of Portfolio Management*, Vo. 28, No. 2, pp. 23–32.

Burton, Jonathan, 1998. "Revisiting the Capital Asset Pricing Model," *Dow Jones Asset Manager*, May/June.

Campbell, John Y., 1987. "Stock Returns and the Term Structure," *Journal of Financial Economics*, Vol. 18, No. 2, pp. 373–400.

Campbell, John Y. and John H. Cochrane, 1999. "By Force of Habit: A Consumption-Based Explanation of Aggregate Stock Market Behavior," *Journal of Political Economy*, Vol. 107, No. 2, pp. 205–251.

Campbell, John Y. and Robert J. Shiller, 1998. "Valuation Ratios and the Long-Run Stock Market Outlook," *Journal of Portfolio Management*, Vol. 24, No. 2, pp. 11–26.

Campbell, John Y. and Luis M. Viceira, 2002. *Strategic Asset Allocation: Portfolio Choice for Long-Term Investors*, New York: Oxford.

_____, 2005. "The Term Structure of the Risk-Return Trade-Off," *Financial Analysts Journal*, Vol. 61, No. 1, pp. 34–44.

Campbell, John Y. and Tuomo Vuolteenaho, 2004. "Bad Beta, Good Beta," *American Economic Review*, Vol. 94, No. 5, pp. 1249–1275.

Campbell, Sean D. and Francis X. Diebold, 2009. "Stock Returns and Expected Business Conditions: Half a Century of Direct Evidence," *Journal of Business and Economic Statistics*, Vol. 27, No. 2, pp. 266–278.

Canner, Niko, N. Gregory Mankiw, and David N. Weil, 1997. "An Asset Allocation Puzzle," *American Economic Review*, Vol. 87, No. 1, pp. 181–191.

Carhart, Mark M., 1997. "On Persistence in Mutual Fund Performance," *Journal of Finance*, Vol. 52, No. 1, pp. 57–82.

Chan, K. C. and Nai-Fu Chen, 1991. "Structural and Return Characteristics of Small and Large Firms," *Journal of Finance*, Vol. 46, No. 4, pp. 1467–1484.

Chan, Louis K. C., Narasimhan Jegadeesh, and Josef Lakonishok, 1995. "Evaluating the Performance of Value Versus Glamour Stocks: The Impact of Selection Bias," *Journal of Financial Economics*, Vol. 38, No. 3, pp. 269–296.

Chordia, Tarun and Lakshmanan Shivakumar, 2002. "Momentum, Business Cycle, and Time-Varying Expected Returns," *Journal of Finance*, Vol. 57, No. 2, pp. 985–1019.

Chow, George, Eric Jacquier, Mark Kritzman and Kenneth Lowry, 1999. "Optimal Portfolios in Good Times and Bad," *Financial Analysts Journal*, Vol. 55, No. 3, pp. 65–73.

Clark, Truman A., 1999. "Efficient Portfolio Rebalancing," Dimensional Fund Advisors research monograph.

_____, 2001a. "Rebalancing, When, How & Why–Part 1," Dimensional Fund Advisors research monograph.

_____, 2001b. "Rebalancing, When, How & Why–Part 2," Dimensional Fund Advisors research monograph.

_____, 2001c. "Rebalancing, When, How & Why–Part 3," Dimensional Fund Advisors research monograph.

Clarke, Roger G., Harindra de Silva, and Robert Murdock, 2005. "A Factor Approach to Asset Allocation," *Journal of Portfolio Management*, Vol. 32, No. 1, pp. 10–21.

Clews, Henry, 1915. *Fifty Years in Wall Street*, New York: Irving.

Clothier, Eric T., 1990. "Strategies for Exploiting the Market Risk Premium Phenomenon," *Quantifying the Market Risk Premium Phenomenon for Investment Decision Making*, Charlottesville, Virginia: Institute of Chartered Financial Analysts, pp. 44–49.

Coaker, William J., II, 2007. "Emphasizing Low-Correlated Assets: The Volatility of Correlation," *Journal of Financial Planning*, Vol. 20, No. 9, pp. 52–70.

Cochrane, John H., 1991. "Production-Based Asset Pricing and the Link Between Returns and Economic Fluctuations," *Journal of Finance*, Vol. 46, No. 1, pp. 209–231.

_____, 1997. "Where is the Market Going? Uncertain Facts and Novel Theories," *Economic Perspectives* (Federal Reserve Bank of Chicago), Vol. 21, No. 6, pp. 3–37.

_____, 1999a. "New Facts in Finance," *Economic Perspectives* (Federal Reserve Bank of Chicago), Vol. 23, No. 3, pp. 36–58.

_____, 1999b. "Portfolio Advice for a Multifactor World," *Economic Perspectives* (Federal Reserve Bank of Chicago), Vol. 23, No. 3, pp. 59–78.

_____, 2008a. "Financial Markets and the Real Economy," in *Handbook of the Equity Risk Premium*, Rajnish Mehra, ed., Amsterdam, The Netherlands: Elsevier.

_____, 2008b. "The Dog That Did Not Bark: A Defense of Return Predictability," *Review of Financial Studies*, Vol. 21, No. 4., pp. 1533–1575.

_____, 2008c. "Is Now the Time to Buy Stocks?" *Wall Street Journal*, November 12.

Constantinides, George, 1986. "Capital Market Equilibrium with Transactions Costs," *Journal of Political Economy*, Vo. 94, No. 4, pp. 842–862.

Courtault, Jean-Michel, Yuri Kabanov, Bernard Bru, Pierre Crépel, Isabelle Lebon, and Arnaud Le Marchand, 2000. "Louis Bachelier on the Centenary of *Théorie de la Spéculation*," *Mathematical Finance*, Vol. 10, No. 3, pp. 341–353.

Cowles, Alfred, III, 1933. "Can Stock Market Forecasters Forecast?" *Econometrica*, Vol. 1, No. 3, pp. 309–324.

_____, 1944. "Stock Market Forecasting," *Econometrica*, Vol. 12, No. 3/4, pp. 206–214.

Dahlquist, Magnus and Campbell R. Harvey, 2001. "Global Tactical Asset Allocation," *Journal of Global Capital Markets*, Spring, pp. 1–9.

Dammon, Robert M., Chester S. Spatt, and Harold H. Zhang, 2003. "Capital Gains Taxes and Portfolio Rebalancing," TIAA-CREF Institute research monograph, No. 75: www.tiaa-crefinstitute.org/articles/75.html.

Darst, David H., 2008. *The Art of Asset Allocation: Principles and Investment Strategies for Any Market*, New York: McGraw-Hill.

Daryanani, Gobind, 2008. "Opportunistic Rebalancing: A New Paradigm for Wealth Managers," *Journal of Financial Planning*, Vol. 21, No. 1, pp. 48–61.

David, F. N., 1998, 1962. *Games, Gods and Gambling: A History of Probability and Statistical Ideas*, Mineola, New York: Dover.

de Goeij, Peter and Wessel Marquering, 2004. "Modeling the Conditional Covariance Between Stock and Bond Returns: A Multivariate GARCH Approach," *Journal of Financial Econometrics*, Vol. 2, No.4, pp. 531–564.

Dumas, Bernard, and Elisa Luciano, 1991. "An Exact Solution to a Dynamic Portfolio Choice Problem Under Transactions Costs," *Journal of Finance*, Vol. 46, No. 2, pp. 577–595.

Ellis, Charles D., 1998. *Winning the Loser's Game: Timeless Strategies for Successful Investing*, New York: McGraw-Hill.

Engle, Robert F., 1982. "Autoregressive Conditional Heteroskedasticity with Estimates of the Variance of United Kingdom Inflation," *Econometrica*, Vol. 50, No. 4, pp. 987–1007.

____, 1993. "Statistical Models for Financial Volatility," *Financial Analysts Journal*, Vol. 49, No. 1, pp. 72–78.

Erb, Claude B. and Campbell R. Harvey, 2006. "The Strategic and Tactical Value of Commodity Futures," *Financial Analysts Journal*, Vol. 62, No. 2, pp. 69–97.

Erb, Claude B., Campbell R. Harvey, and Tadas E. Viskanta, 1994. "Forecasting International Equity Correlations," *Financial Analysts Journal*, Vol. 50, No. 6, pp. 32–45.

Estrella, Arturo and Gikas A. Hardouvelis, 1991. "The Term Structure as a Predictor of Real Economic Activity," *Journal of Finance*, Vol. 46, No. 2, pp. 555–576.

Faber, Mebane T., 2007. "A Quantitative Approach to Tactical Asset Allocation," *Journal of Wealth Management*, Vol. 9, No. 4, pp. 69–79.

Faber, Mebane T. and Eric W. Richardson, 2009. *The Ivy League Portfolio: How to Invest Like the Top Endowments and Avoid Bear Markets*, Hoboken, New Jersey: Wiley.

Fama, Eugene F., 1965a. "The Behavior of Stock Market Prices," *Journal of Business*, Vol. 38, No. 1, pp. 34–105.

____, 1965b. "Random Walks in Stock Market Prices," *Financial Analysts Journal*, Vol. 21, No. 5, pp. 55–59.

____, 1970. "Efficient Capital Markets: A Review of Theory and Empirical Work," *Journal of Finance*, Vol. 25, No. 2, pp. 383–417.

____, 1990. "Stock Returns, Expected Returns, and Real Activity," *Journal of Finance*, Vol. 45, No. 4, pp. 1089–1108.

____, 1991. "Efficient Capital Markets: II," *Journal of Finance*, Vol. 46, No. 5, pp. 1575–1617.

____, 1996. "Multifactor Portfolio Efficiency and Multifactor Asset Pricing," *Journal of Financial and Quantitative Analysis*, Vol. 31, No. 4, pp. 441–465.

____, 1998. "Market Efficiency, Long-Term Returns, and Behavioral Finance," *Journal of Financial Economics*, Vol. 49, No. 3, pp. 283–306.

Fama, Eugene F. and Kenneth R. French, 1988. "Permanent and Temporary Components of Stock Prices," *Journal of Political Economy*, Vol. 96, No. 2, pp. 246–273.

\_\_\_\_, 1989. "Business Conditions and Expected Returns on Stocks and Bonds," *Journal of Financial Economics*, Vol. 25, No. 1, pp. 23–49.

\_\_\_\_, 1992. "The Cross-Section of Expected Stock Returns," *Journal of Finance*, Vol. 47, No. 2, pp. 427–465.

\_\_\_\_, 1993. "Common Risk Factors in the Returns on Stocks and Bonds," *Journal of Financial Economics*, Vol. 33, No. 1, pp. 3–56.

\_\_\_\_, 1995. "Size and Book-to-Market Factors in Earnings and Returns," *Journal of Finance*, Vol. 50, No. 1, pp. 131–155.

\_\_\_\_, 1996. "Multifactor Explanations of Asset Pricing Anomalies," *Journal of Finance*, Vol. 51, No. 1, pp. 55–84.

\_\_\_\_, 1998. "Value Versus Growth: The International Evidence," *Journal of Finance*, Vol. 53, No. 6, pp. 1975–1999.

\_\_\_\_, 2004. "The Capital Asset Pricing Model: Theory and Evidence," *Journal of Economic Perspectives*, Vol. 18, No. 3, pp. 25–46.

Fama, Eugene F. and James D. MacBeth, 1973. "Risk, Return and Equilibrium: Empirical Tests," *Journal of Political Economy*, Vol. 81, No. 3, pp. 607–636.

Fama, Eugene F. and G. William Schwert (1977), "Asset Returns and Inflation," *Journal of Financial Economics*, Vol. 5, No. 2, pp. 115–146.

Faugere, Christophe and Julian Van Erlach, 2009. "A Required Yield Theory of Stock Market Valuation and Treasury Yield Determination," *Financial Markets, Institutions & Instruments*, Vol. 18, No. 1, pp. 27–88.

Ferguson, Robert, 1986. "How to Beat the S&P 500 (Without Losing Sleep)," *Financial Analysts Journal*, Vol. 42, No. 2, pp. 37–46.

Ferri, Richard A., 2006. *All About Asset Allocation: The Easy Way to Get Started*, New York: McGraw-Hill.

Ferson, Wayne E. and Campbell R. Harvey, 1991. "The Variation of Economic Risk Premiums," *Journal of Political Economy*, Vol. 99, No. 2, pp. 385–415.

Figlewski, Stephen, 1997. "Forecasting Volatility," *Financial Markets, Institutions and Instruments*, Vol. 6, No. 1, pp. 1–88.

Fisher, Irving, 1930. *The Theory of Interest: As Determined by Impatience to Spend Income and Opportunity to Invest It*, New York: Macmillan.

Fisher, Lawrence and James H. Lorie, 1964. "Rates of Return on Investments in Common Stocks," *Journal of Business*, Vol. 37, No. 1, pp. 1–21.

Fleming, Jeff, Chris Kirby, and Barbara Ostdiek, 2001. "The Economic Value of Volatility Timing," *Journal of Finance*, Vol. 56, No. 1, pp. 329–352.

Fouse, William L., 1987. "The Evolution of Asset Allocation: Theory and Practice," in *Asset Allocation for Institutional Portfolios*, Charlottesville, Virginia: Institute of Chartered Financial Analysts, pp. 11–17.

French, Kenneth R. and James M. Poterba, 1991. "Investor Diversification and International Equity Markets," *American Economic Review*, Vol. 81, No. 2, pp. 222–226.

French, Kenneth R., G. William Schwert, and Robert F. Stambaugh, 1987. "Expected Stock Returns and Volatility," *Journal of Financial Economics*, Vol. 19, No. 1, pp. 3–29.

Friesen, Geoffrey C. and Travis R. A. Sapp, 2007. "Mutual Fund Flows and Investor Returns: An Empirical Examination of Fund Investor Timing Ability," *Journal of Banking & Finance*, Vol. 31 No. 9, pp. 2796–2816.

Fung, William and David A. Hsieh, 1997. "Empirical Characteristics of Dynamic Trading Strategies: The Case of Hedge Funds," *The Review of Financial Studies*, Vol. 10, No. 2, pp. 275–302.

Gibson, Roger C., 1996. *Asset Allocation: Balancing Financial Risk*, Chicago: Irwin.

Goetzmann, William N. and Philippe Jorion, 1993. "Testing the Predictive Power of Dividend Yields," *Journal of Finance*, Vol. 48, No. 2, pp. 663–679.

Goetzmann, William N., Lingfeng Li, and K. Geert Rouwenhorst, 2005. "Long-Term Global Market Correlations," *Journal of Business*, Vol. 78, No. 1, pp. 1–38.

Goldman Sachs, 2003. "Global Tactical Asset Allocation," research monograph (Primer).

Gordon, Myron J., 1959. "Dividends, Earnings and Stock Prices," *Review of Economics and Statistics*, Vol. 41, No. 2, pp. 99–105.

_____, 1962. *The Investment, Financing, and Valuation of the Corporation*, Homewood, Illinois: Irwin.

Gorton, Gary and K. Geert Rouwenhorst, 2006. "Facts and Fantasies About Commodity Futures," *Financial Analysts Journal*, Vol. 62, No. 2, pp. 47–68.

Grable, John, 2008. "RiskCAT: A Framework for Identifying Maximum Risk Thresholds in Personal Portfolios," *Journal of Financial Planning*, Vol. 21, No. 10, pp. 52–62.

Graham, Benjamin, 1996. *Benjamin Graham: The Memoirs of the Dean of Wall Street*, New York: McGraw-Hill.

Graham, Benjamin and David L. Dodd, 1934. *Security Analysis*, New York: McGraw-Hill.

Grossman, Sanford J. and Joseph E. Stiglitz, 1980. "On the Impossibility of Informationally Efficient Markets," *The American Economic Review*, Vol. 70, No. 3, pp. 393–408.

Gruber, Martin J., 1996. "Another Puzzle: The Growth in Actively Managed Mutual Funds," *Journal of Finance*, Vol. 51, No. 3, pp. 783–810.

Hall, Robert E., 2001. "Struggling to Understand the Stock Market," *American Economic Review Papers and Proceedings*, Vol. 91, No. 2, pp. 1–11.

Hallahan, Terrence A., Robert W. Faff, and Michael D. McKenzie, 2004. "An Empirical Investigation of Personal Financial Risk Tolerance," *Financial Services Review*, Vol. 13, No. 1, pp. 57–78.

Hamilton, James D. and Gang Lin, 1996. "Stock Market Volatility and the Business Cycle," *Journal of Applied Econometrics*, Vol. 11, No. 5, pp. 573–593.

Harvey, Campbell R., 1988. "The Real Term Structure and Consumption Growth," *Journal of Financial Economics*, Vol. 22, No. 2, pp. 305–333.

Heathcotte, Bryan and Vincent P. Apilado, 1974. "The Predictive Content of Some Leading Economic Indicators for Future Stock Prices," *Journal of Financial and Quantitative Analysis*, Vol. 9, No. 2, pp. 247–258.

Herper, Matthew, 2002. "Mandelbrot: A Math Maverick Takes Stock," Forbes.com, April 2 (www.forbes.com/2002/04/02/0402mandelbrot.html).

Hill, Joanne M., 2006. "Alpha as a Net Zero-Sum Game," *Journal of Portfolio Management*, Vol. 32, No. 4, pp. 24–32.

Hilsenrath, Jon E., 2004. "As Two Economists Debate Markets, The Tide Shifts," *Wall Street Journal*, October 18.

Hood, L. Randolph, 2005. "Determinants of Portfolio Performance—20 Years Later," *Financial Analysts Journal*, Vol. 61, No. 5, pp. 6–8.

Horvitz, Jeffrey E., 2002. "The Implications of Rebalancing the Investment Portfolio for the Taxable Investor," *Journal of Wealth Management*, Vol. 5, No. 2, pp. 49–53.

Huang, He, Georg Keienburg and Duane R. Stock, 2007. "The Economic Value of Predicting Correlation for Asset Allocation," working paper: www.fma.org/Texas/Papers/econ_value_11.29_fma.pdf.

Ibbotson, Roger G. and Peng Chen, 2003. "Long Run Stock Returns: Participating in the Real Economy," *Financial Analysts Journal*, Vol. 59, No. 1, pp. 88–98.

Ibbotson, Roger G. and Paul D. Kaplan, 2000. "Does Asset Allocation Explain 40, 90 or 100 Percent of Performance?" *Financial Analysts Journal*, Vol. 56, No. 1, pp. 26–33.

*Ibbotson SBBI 2009 Classic Yearbook*, 2009, Chicago: Morningstar.

Idzorek, Thomas M., 2006. "Strategic Asset Allocation and Commodities," research monograph, Ibbotson Associates.

Idzorek, Thomas, Michael Barad, and Steve Meier, 2006. "Commercial Real Estate: The Role of Global Listed Real Estate Equities in a Strategic Asset Allocation," research monograph, Ibbotson Associates.

Israelsen, Craig L., 2001. "Rebalancing Acts," *Financial Planning*, June.

Jacquier, Eric and Alan J. Marcus, 2001. "Asset Allocation Models and Market Volatility," *Financial Analysts Journal*, Vol. 57, No. 2, pp. 16–30.

Jagannathan, Ravi and Zhenyu Wang, 1996. "The Conditional CAPM and the Cross-Section of Expected Returns," *Journal of Finance*, Vol. 51, No. 1, pp. 3–53.

Jahnke, William W., 2003. "Bad Practices," *Journal of Financial Planning*, Vol. 16, No. 9, pp. 26–29.

_____, 2004. "Death to the Policy Portfolio," in *The Investment Think Tank: Theory, Strategy, and Practice for Advisers*, Harold Evensky and Deena B. Katz, eds., Princeton, New Jersey: Bloomberg Press.

Jegadeesh, Narasimhan, 1990. "Evidence of Predictable Behavior of Security Returns," *Journal of Finance*, Vol. 45, No. 3, pp. 881–898.

Jegadeesh, Narasimhan and Sheridan Titman, 1993. "Returns to Buying Winners and Selling Losers: Implications for Stock Market Efficiency," *Journal of Finance*, Vol. 48, No. 1, pp. 65–91.

Jensen, Gerald R. and Jeffrey M. Mercer, 2003. "New Evidence on Optimal Asset Allocation," *Financial Review*, Vol. 38, No. 3, pp. 435–454.

Jensen, Michael C., 1968. "The Performance of Mutual Funds in the Period 1945–1964," *Journal of Finance*, Vol. 23, No. 2, pp. 389–416.

Jung, Jeeman and Robert J. Shiller, 2005. "Samuelson's Dictum and the Stock Market," *Economic Inquiry*, Vol. 43, No. 2, pp. 221–228.

Kaplanis, Evi C., 1988. "Stability and Forecasting of the Comovement Measures of International Stock Market Return," *Journal of International Money and Finance*, Vol. 7, No. 1, pp. 63–76.

Karnosky, Denis S., 1993. "Global Investment in a CAPM Framework," *The CAPM Controversy: Policy and Strategy Implications for Investment Management*, Charlottesville, Virginia: Association for Investment Management and Research.

Keim, Donald B. and Robert F. Stambaugh, 1986. "Predicting Returns in the Stock and Bond Markets," *Journal of Financial Economics*, Vol. 17, No. 2, pp. 357–390.

Kendall, M. G., 1953. "The Analysis of Economic Time-Series, Part I: Prices," *Journal of the Royal Statistical Society. Series A (General)*, Vol. 116, No. 1, pp. 11–34.

Kleidon, Alan W., 1986. "Variance Bounds Tests and Stock Price Valuation Models," *Journal of Political Economy*, Vol. 94, No. 5, pp. 953–1001.

Kothari, S. P. and Jay Shanken, 1997. "Book-to-Market, Dividend Yield, and Expected Market Returns: A Time Series Analysis," *Journal of Financial Economics*, Vol. 44, No. 2, pp. 169–203.

Latane, Henry A. and Donald L. Tuttle, 1970. *Security Analysis and Portfolio Management*, New York: Ronald Press.

Leavens, D. H., 1945. "Diversification of Investments," *Trusts and Estates*, May, pp. 469–473, in *The Theory and Practice of Investment Management*, 1972, p. 28, Frank J. Fabozzi and Harry M. Markowitz, eds., Hoboken, New Jersey: Wiley.

Lee, Stephen and Simon Stevenson, 2005. "The Case for REITs in the Mixed-Asset Portfolio in the Short and Long Run," *Journal of Real Estate Portfolio Management*, Vol. 11, No. 1, pp. 55–80.

Leland, Hayne E., 1985. "Option Pricing and Replication with Transaction Costs," *Journal of Finance*, Vol. 40, No. 5, pp. 1283–1301.

____, 1996. "Optimal Rebalancing in the Presence of Transaction Costs," working paper No. RPF-261, University of California, Berkeley, Haas School of Business: www.haas.berkeley.edu/groups/finance/WP/rpf261.pdf.

LeRoy, Stephen F., 2004. "Rational Exuberance," *Journal of Economic Literature*, Vol. 42, No. 3, pp. 783–804.

LeRoy, Stephen F. and Richard D. Porter, 1981. "The Present-Value Relation: Tests Based on Implied Variance Bounds," *Econometrica*, Vol. 49, No. 3, pp. 555–574.

Lettau, Martin and Sydney Ludvigson, 2001a. "Consumption, Aggregate Wealth, and Expected Stock Returns," *Journal of Finance*, Vol. 56, No. 3, pp. 815–849.

____, 2001b, "Resurrecting the (C)CAPM: A Cross-Sectional Test When Risk Premia Are Time-Varying," *Journal of Political Economy*, Vol. 109, No. 6, pp. 1238–1287.

Levy, Haim, 1997. "Risk and Return: An Experimental Analysis," *International Economic Review*, Vol. 38, No. 1, pp. 119–149.

Liew, Jimmy and Maria Vassalou, 2000. "Can Book-to-Market, Size and Momentum Be Risk Factors That Predict Economic Growth?" *Journal of Financial Economics*, Vol. 57, No. 2, pp. 221–245.

Lintner, John, 1965. "The Valuation of Risk Assets and the Selection of Risky Investments in Stock Portfolios and Capital Budgets," *Review of Economics and Statistics*, Vol. 47, No. 1, pp. 13–37.

Litterman, Robert, 2003. *Modern Investment Management: An Equilibrium Approach*, Hoboken, New Jersey: Wiley.

Litterman, Robert and Fischer Black, 1991. "Global Asset Allocation with Equities, Bonds, and Currencies," Goldman Sachs research monograph (Fixed Income Research), October.

Litzenberger, Robert H. and Krishna Ramaswamy, 1979, "The Effect of Personal Taxes and Dividends on Capital Asset Prices: Theory and Empirical Evidence," *Journal of Financial Economics* Vol. 7, No. 2, pp. 163–195.

Lo, Andrew W. and A. Craig MacKinlay, 1999. *A Non-Random Walk Down Wall Street*, Princeton, New Jersey: Princeton University Press.

Longin, Francois and Bruno Solnik. 1995. "Is the Correlation in International Equity Returns Constant: 1960–1990?" *Journal of International Money and Finance*, Vol. 14, No. 1, pp. 3–26.

Loomis, Carol, 2001. "Warren Buffett on the Stock Market," *Fortune*, December 10.

Mackay, Charles, 2003, 1841. *Extraordinary Popular Delusions and the Madness of Crowds*, Petersfield, England: Harriman House.

MacKinnon, Gregory and Ashraf Al Zaman, 2009. "Real Estate for the Long Term: The Effect of Return Predictability on Long-Horizon Allocations," *Real Estate Economics*, Vol. 37, No. 1, pp. 117–153.

Maddison, Angus, 2009. "Statistics on World Population, GDP and Per Capita GDP, 1–2006 A.D.," www.ggdc.net/maddison.

Malkiel, Burton, 1997, 1973. *A Random Walk Down Wall Street*, New York: Norton.

_____, 2003. "The Efficient Market Hypothesis and Its Critics," *Journal of Economic Perspectives*, Vol. 17, No. 1, pp. 59–82.

Mandelbrot, Benoit, 1963. "The Variation of Certain Speculative Prices," *Journal of Business*, Vol. 36, No. 4, pp. 394–419.

Mandelbrot, Benoit and Richard L. Hudson, 2004. *The (Mis)Behavior of Markets: A Fractal View of Risk, Ruin, and Reward*, New York: Basic Books.

Markowitz, Harry M., 1952. "Portfolio Selection," *Journal of Finance*, Vol. 7, No. 1, pp. 77–91.

_____, 1959. *Portfolio Selection: Efficient Diversification of Investments*, New York: Wiley.

_____, 1991. "Foundations of Portfolio Theory," *Journal of Finance*, Vol. 46., No. 2, pp. 469–477.

_____, 1999. "The Early History of Portfolio Theory: 1600–1960," *Financial Analysts Journal*, Vol. 55, No. 4, pp. 5–16.

Marquering, Wessel and Marno Verbeek, 2004. "The Economic Value of Predicting Stock Index Returns and Volatility," *Journal of Financial and Quantitative Analysis*, Vol. 39, No. 2, pp. 407–429.

Marsh, Terry A. and Robert C. Merton, 1986. "Dividend Variability and Variance Bounds Tests for the Rationality of Stock Market Prices," *American Economic Review*, Vol. 76, No. 3, pp. 483–498.

Masters, Seth J., 2002. "Rules for Rebalancing," *Financial Planning*, December.

Mauboussin, Michael J., 2005a. "Capital Ideas Revisited: The Prime Directive, Sharks, and the Wisdom of Crowds," research report (March 30), Legg Mason Capital Management.

_____, 2005b. "Capital Ideas Revisited–Part 2," research report (May 20), Legg Mason Capital Management.

Mayers, David, 1976. "Nonmarketable Assets, Market Segmentation, and the Level of Asset Prices," *Journal of Financial and Quantitative Analysis*, Vol. 11, No. 1, pp. 1–12.

Merton, Robert C., 1969. "Lifetime Portfolio Selection Under Uncertainty: The Continuous-Time Case," *Review of Economics and Statistics*, Vol. 51, No. 3, pp. 247–257.

_____, 1971, "Optimum Consumption and Portfolio Rules in a Continuous-Time Model," *Journal of Economic Theory*, Vol. 3, No. 4, pp. 373–413.

_____, 1973. "An Intertemporal Capital Asset Pricing Model," *Econometrica*, Vol. 41, No. 5, pp. 867–887.

Minsky, Hyman P., 1992. "The Financial Instability Hypothesis," working paper #74, Jerome Levy Economics Institute of Bard College.

Mitchell, Mark L. and Jeffry M. Netter, 1989. "Triggering the 1987 Stock Market Crash: Antitakeover Provisions in the Proposed House Ways and Means Tax Bill?" *Journal of Financial Economics*, Vol. 24, No. 1, pp. 37–68.

Mitchell, Wesley C. and Arthur Burns, 1938. "Statistical Indicators of Cyclical Revivals," National Bureau of Economic Research, Bulletin 69, May 28.

Modigliani, Franco and Merton H. Miller, 1958. "The Cost of Capital, Corporation Finance and the Theory of Investment," *American Economic Review*, Vol. 48, No. 3, pp. 261–297.

Moskowitz, Tobias J., 2003. "An Analysis of Covariance Risk and Pricing Anomalies," *Review of Financial Studies*, Vol. 16, No. 2, pp. 417–457.

Mossin, Jan, 1966. "Equilibrium in a Capital Asset Market," *Econometrica*, Vol. 34, No. 4, pp. 768–783.

Nguyen, Que, 2004. "The Case for Global Tactical Asset Allocation," Morgan Stanley research monograph (Issues of Interest), Morgan Stanley.

Nicholson, S. F. 1960. "Price-Earnings Ratios," *Financial Analysts Journal*, Vol. 16, No. 4, pp. 43–45.

Osborne, M. F. M., 1959. "Brownian Motion in the Stock Market," *Operations Research*, Vol. 7, No. 2, pp. 145–173.

Perold, Andre F., 2007. "Fundamentally Flawed Indexing," *Financial Analysts Journal*, Vol. 63, No. 6, pp. 31–37.

Perold, Andre F. and William F. Sharpe, 1988. "Dynamic Strategies for Asset Allocation," *Financial Analysts Journal*, Vol. 44, No. 1, pp. 16–27.

Pesaran, M. Hashem and Allan Timmermann, 1995. "Predictability of Stock Returns: Robustness and Economic Significance," *Journal of Finance*, Vol. 50, No. 4, pp. 1201–1228.

Peters, Edgar E., 1996. *Chaos and Order in the Capital Markets: A New View of Cycles, Prices, and Market Volatility*, New York: Wiley.

Phalon, Richard, 2001. *Forbes Greatest Investing Stories*, New York: Wiley.

Poon, Ser-Huang and Clive Granger, 2005. "Practical Issues in Forecasting Volatility," *Financial Analysts Journal*, Vol. 61, No. 1, pp. 45–56.

Poterba, James and Lawrence H. Summers, 1988. "Mean Reversion in Stock Prices: Evidence and Implications," *Journal of Financial Economics*, Vol. 22, No.1, pp. 27–59.

Previts, Gary John and Barbara Dubis Merino, 1979. *A History of Accounting in America: An Historical Interpretation of the Cultural Significance of Accounting*, New York: Wiley.

Rapach, David E., Jack K. Strauss, and Guofu Zhou, 2009. "Out-of-Sample Equity Premium Prediction: Combination Forecasts and Links to the Real Economy," forthcoming in *Review of Financial Studies*.

Reichenstein, William and Dovalee Dorsett, 1995. *Time Diversification Revisited*, Charlottesville, Virginia: The Research Foundation of the Institute of Chartered Financial Analysts.

Riepe, Mark W. and Bill Swerbenski, 2006. "Rebalancing for Tax-Deferred Accounts: Just Do It–Don't Worry How" *Journal of Financial Planning*, Vol. 19, No. 4, pp. 40–44.

_____, 2007. "Rebalancing for Taxable Accounts," *Journal of Financial Planning*, Vol. 20, No. 4, pp. 40–44.

Roll, Richard, 1977. "A Critique of the Asset Pricing Theory's Tests," *Journal of Financial Economics*, Vol. 4, No. 2, pp. 129–176.

Rosenberg, Joshua V. and Samuel Maurer, 2008. "Signal or Noise? Implications of the Term Premium for Recession Forecasting," *Economic Policy Review* (Federal Reserve Bank of New York), Vol. 14, No. 1, pp. 1–11.

Rosenberg, Barr, Kenneth Reid, and Ronald Lanstein, 1985. "Persuasive Evidence of Market Inefficiency," *Journal of Portfolio Management*, Vol. 11, No. 3, pp. 9–17.

Ross, Stephen, 1976. "The Arbitrage Theory of Capital Asset Pricing," *Journal of Economic Theory*, Vol. 13, No. 3, pp. 341–360.

Roszkowski, Michael J. and John Grable, 2005. "Estimating Risk Tolerance: The Degree of Accuracy and the Paramorphic Representations of the Estimate," *Financial Counseling and Planning*, Vol. 16, No. 2, pp. 29–47.

Rouwenhorst, K. Geert, 2004. "The Origins of Mutual Funds," working paper no. 04-48, Yale School of Management, International Center for Finance.

Roy, Arthur D., 1952. "Safety First and the Holding of Assets," *Econometrica*, Vol. 20, No. 3, pp. 431–449.

Rozeff, Michael S., 1984. "Dividend Yields Are Equity Risk Premiums," *Journal of Portfolio Management*, Vol. 11, No. 1, pp. 68–75.

Rubinstein, Mark, 2002. "Markowitz's 'Portfolio Selection': A Fifty-Year Retrospective," *Journal of Finance*, Vol. 57, No. 3, pp. 1041–1045.

_____, 2006. "Bruno de Finetti and Mean-Variance Portfolio Selection," *Journal of Investment Management*, Vol. 4, No. 3, pp. 1–2. For related articles, see: Markowitz, Harry M., 2006. "De Finetti Scoops Markowitz," *Journal of Investment Management*, Vol. 4, No. 3, pp. 3–18; and Barone, Luca, 2008. "Bruno de Finetti and the Case of the Critical Line's Last Segment," *Insurance: Mathematics and Finance*, Vol. 42, No. 1, pp. 359–377.

Samuelson, Paul A, 1965. "Proof That Properly Anticipated Prices Fluctuate Randomly," *Industrial Management Review*, Vol. 6, No. 2, pp. 41–49.

_____, 1969. "Lifetime Portfolio Selection by Dynamic Stochastic Programming," *Review of Economics and Statistics*, Vol. 51, No. 3, pp. 239–246.

Schumpeter, Joseph A., 1942. *Capitalism, Socialism and Democracy*, New York: Harper & Row.

Schwert, G. William, 1990. "Stock Returns and Real Activity: A Century of Evidence," *Journal of Finance*, Vol. 45, No. 4, pp. 1237–1257.

_____, 2001. "Anomalies and Market Efficiency," in *Handbook of the Economics of Finance*, 2003, George George M. Constantinides, M. Harris, Rene M. Stulz, eds., Amsterdam: North Holland.

Sharpe, William F., 1964. "Capital Asset Prices: A Theory of Market Equilibrium Under Conditions of Risk," *Journal of Finance*, Vol. 19, No. 3, pp. 425–442.

_____, 1966. "Mutual Fund Performance," *Journal of Business*, Vol. 39, No. 1, pp. 119–138.

_____, 1987. "Integrated Asset Allocation," *Financial Analysts Journal*, Vol. 43, No. 5, pp. 25–32.

_____, 1988. "Determining a Fund's Effective Asset Mix," *Investment Management Review*, Vol. 2, No. 6, pp. 59–69.

_____, 1990. "Investor Wealth Measures and Expected Return," *Quantifying the Market Risk Premium Phenomenon for Investment Decision Making*, Charlottesville, Virginia: Institute of Chartered Financial Analysts, pp. 22–37.

_____, 1991. "The Arithmetic of Active Management," *Financial Analysts' Journal*, Vol. 47, No. 1, pp. 7–9.

_____, 1992. "Asset Allocation: Management Style and Performance Measurement," *Journal of Portfolio Management*, Vol. 18, No. 2, pp. 7–19.

_____, 1994. "The Sharpe Ratio," *Journal of Portfolio Management*, Vol. 21, No. 1, pp. 49–58.

Shawky, Hany and Yajun Peng, 1995. "Expected Stock Returns, Real Business Activity and Consumption Smoothing," *International Review of Financial Analysis*, Vol. 4, No. 2, pp. 143–154.

Shefrin, Hersh, 2002. *Beyond Greed and Fear: Understanding Behavioral Finance and the Psychology of Investing*, New York: Oxford University Press.

Shiller, Robert J., 1981. "Do Stock Prices Move Too Much to Be Justified by Subsequent Changes in Dividends?" *American Economic Review*, Vol. 71, No. 3, pp. 421–436.

_____, 1990. "Historical Evidence," *Quantifying the Market Risk Premium Phenomenon for Investment Decision Making*, Charlottesville, Virginia: Institute of Chartered Financial Analysts, pp. 5–12.

_____, 2000. *Irrational Exuberance*, Princeton, New Jersey: Princeton University Press.

Shleifer, Andrei, 2000. *Inefficient Markets: An Introduction to Behavioral Finance*. New York: Oxford University Press.

Siegel, Jeremy J., 1994. *Stocks for the Long Run: A Guide to Selecting Markets for Long-Term Growth*. Burr Ridge, Illinois: Irwin.

Siegel, Laurence B., Kenneth F. Kroner, and Scott W. Clifford, 2001. "The Greatest Return Stories Ever Told," *Journal of Investing*, Vol. 10, No. 2, pp. 1–12.

Smith, David M. and William II. Desormeau, Jr., 2006. "Optimal Rebalancing Frequency for Bond/Stock Portfolios," *Journal of Financial Planning*, Vol. 19, No. 11, pp. 44–53.

Sobel, Robert, 1965. *The Big Board: A History of the New York Stock Market*, New York: Free Press.

Soros, George, 2003. *The Alchemy of Finance*, Hoboken, New Jersey: Wiley.

_____, 2008. *The New Paradigm for Financial Markets: The Credit Crash of 2008 and What It Means*, New York: Public Affairs.

Stanyer, Peter, 2006. *Guide to Investment Strategy: How to Understand Markets, Risk, Rewards and Behaviour*, Princeton, New York: Bloomberg Press.

Statman, Meir, 1999. "Behavioral Finance: Past Battles and Future Engagements," *Financial Analysts Journal*, Vol. 55, No. 6, pp. 18–27.

Summers, Lawrence H., 1986. "Does the Stock Market Rationally Reflect Fundamental Values?" *Journal of Finance*, Vol. 41, No. 3, pp. 591–601.

Sung, Jamie and Sherman Hanna, 1996. "Factors Related to Risk Tolerance," *Financial Counsel and Planning*, Vol. 7, pp. 11–19.

Surowiecki, James, 2004. *The Wisdom of Crowds: Why the Many Are Smarter Than the Few and How Collective Wisdom Shapes Business, Economies, Societies, and Nations*, New York: Doubleday.

Sylla, Richard and George David Smith, 1995. "Information and Capital Market Regulation in Anglo-American Finance," in *Anglo-American Financial Systems: Institutions and Markets in the Twentieth Century*, 1995, Michael D. Bordo and Richard Sylla, eds., Irwin: Burr Ridge, Illinois.

Taleb, Nassim Nicholas, 2005. *Fooled by Randomness: The Hidden Role of Chance in the Markets and Life*, New York: Random House.

Tapiero, Charles S., 1998. *Risk and Financial Management: Mathematical and Computational Methods*, Chichester, England: Wiley.

Tesar, Linda L. and Ingrid M. Werner, 1995. "Home Bias and High Turnover," *Journal of International Money and Finance*, Vol. 14, No. 4, pp. 467–492.

Thaler, Richard H., 1992. *The Winner's Curse: Paradoxes and Anomalies of Economic Life*, Princeton: Princeton University Press.

Tobin, James, 1958. "Liquidity Preference as Behavior Towards Risk," *Review of Economic Studies*, Vol. 25, No. 2, pp. 65–86.

Tokat, Yesim, 2006. "Portfolio Rebalancing in Theory and Practice," Vanguard research monograph, No. 31: institutional.vanguard.com/iip/pdf/ICRRebalancing.pdf.

Treynor, Jack L., 1962. "Toward a Theory of Market Value of Risky Assets," unpublished manuscript.

Tsai, Cindy Sin-Yi. 2001. "Rebalancing Diversified Portfolios of Various Risk Profiles," *Journal of Financial Planning*, Vol. 14, No. 10, pp. 104–110.

Vassalou, Maria, 2003. "News Related to Future GDP Growth as a Risk Factor in Equity Returns," *Journal of Financial Economics*, Vol. 68, No. 1, pp. 47–73.

Vinocur, Barry, 1995. "Setting the Record Straight on Style Analysis," *Dow Jones Fee Advisor*, November/December.

von Neumann, John and Oskar Morgenstern, 1944. *Theory of Games and Economic Behavior*, Princeton, New Jersey: Princeton University Press.

Wainscott, Craig B., 1990. "The Stock-Bond Correlation and Its Implications for Asset Allocation," *Financial Analysts Journal*, Vol. 46, No. 4, pp. 55–60, 79.

Weigel, Eric J., 1991. "The Performance of Tactical Asset Allocation," *Financial Analysts Journal*, Vol. 47, No. 5, pp. 63–70.

Welch, Ivo and Amit Goyal, 2008. "A Comprehensive Look at the Empirical Performance of Equity Premium Prediction," *Review of Financial Studies*, Vol. 21, No. 4, pp. 1455–1508.

Williams, John Burr, 1956, 1938. *The Theory of Investment Value*, Amsterdam: North Holland.

Wolf, Michael, 2000. "Stock Returns and Dividend Yields Revisited: A New Way to Look at an Old Problem," *Journal of Business & Economic Statistics*, Vol. 18, No. 1, pp. 18–30.

Working, Holbrook, 1934. "A Random-Difference Series for Use in the Analysis of Time Series," *Journal of the American Statistical Association*, Vol. 29, No. 185, pp. 11–24.

Yogo, Motohiro, 2006. "A Consumption-Based Explanation of Expected Stock Returns," *Journal of Finance*, Vol. 61, No. 2, pp. 539–580.

Yook, Ken C, and Robert Everett. 2003. "Assessing Risk Tolerance: Questioning the Questionnaire Method," *Journal of Financial Planning*, Vol. 16, No. 8, pp. 48–55.

# Index

# About the Author

**James Picerno** is editor of *The Beta Investment Report* (BetaInvestment.com), a monthly newsletter focused on asset allocation using index funds and ETFs. He also edits CapitalSpectator.com, a popular financial and economics blog. For more than twenty years, he's been writing about portfolio strategies, economics, and finance at Bloomberg, Dow Jones, and other media groups and is now an independent analyst and writer. For comments and questions about the book, e-mail the author at daa_book@yahoo.com.

# About Bloomberg

**Bloomberg L.P.**, founded in 1981, is a global information services, news, and media company. Headquartered in New York, the company has sales and news operations worldwide.

Serving customers on six continents, Bloomberg, through its wholly-owned subsidiary Bloomberg Finance L.P., holds a unique position within the financial services industry by providing an unparalleled range of features in a single package known as the Bloomberg Professional® service. By addressing the demand for investment performance and efficiency through an exceptional combination of information, analytic, electronic trading, and straight-through-processing tools, Bloomberg has built a worldwide customer base of corporations, issuers, financial intermediaries, and institutional investors.

Bloomberg News, founded in 1990, provides stories and columns on business, general news, politics, and sports to leading newspapers and magazines throughout the world. Bloomberg Television, a 24-hour business and financial news network, is produced and distributed globally in seven languages. Bloomberg Radio is an international radio network anchored by flagship station Bloomberg 1130 (WBBR-AM) in New York.

In addition to the Bloomberg Press line of books, Bloomberg publishes *Bloomberg Markets* magazine. To learn more about Bloomberg, call a sales representative at:

| | |
|---|---|
| London: | +44-20-7330-7500 |
| New York: | +1-212-318-2000 |
| Tokyo: | +81-3-3201-8900 |